WOMEN UNSILENCED

OUR REFUSAL TO LET TORTURER-TRAFFICKERS WIN

Jeanne Sarson & Linda MacDonald

 FriesenPress

Suite 300 - 990 Fort St
Victoria, BC, V8V 3K2
Canada

www.friesenpress.com

ISBN
978-1-5255-9323-9 (Hardcover)
978-1-5255-9322-2 (Paperback)
978-1-5255-9324-6 (eBook)

1. SOCIAL SCIENCE, VIOLENCE IN SOCIETY
2. POLITICAL SCIENCE, HUMAN RIGHTS
3. BIOGRAPHY, AUTOBIOGRAPHY, WOMEN

Distributed to the trade by The Ingram Book Company

CONTENTS

To the women who entrusted us to listen to
their stories, we know this book would never have been
written had you remained silent. Your voices provide insight that reach
out to help make the world safer for all women and children. As Carrie
shares in herstory, "As children there was no one to tell...who would have
listened to us...who was willing to listen...who was prepared to listen?"
We and all who read *Women Unsilenced* are listening.

FOREWORD

Reader, you have already demonstrated moral courage by choosing to read this groundbreaking book, *Women Unsilenced Our Refusal To Let Torturer-Traffickers Win*, by Jeanne Sarson and Linda MacDonald. Now, please choose to be open to the knowledge the authors have brought into the light. After reading the first chapter, I was reminded of the alert one sees above certain news clips and films: « Viewer discretion advised » erected for our « protection », to « warn » us of information we may not want to receive because we may find it disturbing. After the warning, we have a choice to make. In that moment, we choose what we let into our minds and our hearts and, if we choose to access the knowledge, however troubling, we then must decide if we are going to take any action on that knowledge. This is what we must do with this book: find the moral courage to pay attention to what Jeanne and Linda have recorded and researched; then draw upon that courage to face the implications that what is in this book is not fiction – nor is it information from which we can justly turn away.

I first met Jeanne and Linda at a UN meeting over 15 years ago, where I observed the impact they were having on their listeners. Their powerful narrative threw me back to hearing testimony from a patient in an inquiry I had chaired in 1991 on the sexual abuse of patients by medical doctors. I listened with shock – and to be honest with you – some disbelief – as my colleagues and I on the independent task force (commissioned by the

College of Physicians and Surgeons of Ontario) were told of ritualistic sexual abuse by a group in the basement of a church hall in a small town, near to where our hearing was being held that evening. The patient was clear: their doctor was an active participant in the group assault; indeed he was instrumental in getting the patient into that basement. When the hearing adjourned, I sought my task force colleague, Dr. Harvey Armstrong, an acclaimed psychiatrist who had many patients who came to him because he was known as a skilled and compassionate therapist for people who had experienced a wide range of abuse and violations in their lives. I was deeply shaken by the patient's testimony and even more shaken when Dr. Armstrong put that night's testimony into context. What we had heard was longstanding, widespread and woven into entrenched networks of « torturer-traffickers » often cloaked in social positions of credibility and authority in their communities – as detailed by Jeanne and Linda at that UN session, and now in their much more comprehensive book. I also need to tell you that the testimony I heard thirty years ago was certainly not the only one brought to my attention in the past decades.

I have been tempted to shelter behind « Viewer discretion advised »; I didn't want to believe this degree and frequency of organized evil operates with impunity, for the most part, in my country, or that the *Criminal Code of Canada* has been largely ineffective. But I know it is imperative to believe in the dignity and voices of humans, mostly women and girls, who have endured non-State torture (NST), who have been silenced by inadequacies – and sometimes complicity – in our systems of law, health and education. I know what Jeanne and Linda risked – professionally and personally – to care so deeply and bravely, to deliver hope and healing as allies with the women we meet in this book. Through 28 plus years of creating space for women and girls who have endured NST, Jeanne and Linda continue to call upon UN treaties and our Canadian Charter of Rights and Freedoms to fight for them and their human rights.

So, what can we, the readers, do?

We have already taken the first crucial step: exercising our discretion in reading this book. Discretion has been defined as: individual choice or judgment; the power of free decision or latitude of choice within certain legal bounds; the quality of having or showing discernment or good judgment; the ability to make responsible decisions. Let us now use our power of discretion to choose a paradigm shift for examining this specific form of violence against women and girls – non-State torture – as a grievous human rights violation that our laws must be changed to address effectively.

Senator Marilou McPhedran
Parliament of Canada

February 2021

PROLOGUE

In 1993, when hit with the reality that torture is perpetrated within families, we were determined to speak out; otherwise, our silence would have meant our willingness to side with such torturers. It is unconscionable an infant is born into a torturing family system. Also unacceptable is that women's telling continues to be questioned or disbelieved. Over the past 28 years, we have witnessed women struggle to escape such families and groups, and to heal. We write not only to assist them in breaking the silence, but to create—to demand—a space in civil society's collective consciousness to accept that family-based torture happens and must be stopped.

Also, in 1993, there was no specific social knowledge to help women heal from family-based torture crimes, so we sought input from as many other resources as possible. We interviewed whoever was open to speaking to us. This included Bliss Cole, a POW survivor, and Philip Riteman, a survivor of five Nazi death camps and an outspoken educator. Both are no longer with us. From Bliss, we learned how physically painful starvation was. This helped us understand Hope, a Nova Scotia woman whose story is included in our chapters. She told of being so hungry when she was a child that she drew pictures of food on scraps of paper, and then ate the paper. Philip asked us to his home to "break bread." At his kitchen table he told stories, he said, he had never uttered before. He taught us how important it was to be able to listen to unvoiced atrocities.

To Louise Frei Rebelle we are most appreciative for her unwavering belief in us to write *Women Unsilenced,* valuing we wanted to share our own personal stories. She has offered much expertise by assisting us with her skilled editing of our manuscript, and freely shared her wisdom as a publishing advisor. We also express our deep gratitude to Eleanor Cowan for her great care in the final throes of editing and proofreading our manuscript. And to Darl Wood and all others for their time, patience, and skill in reading our manuscript to offer suggestions that indeed 'polished' our writing.

This book's title, *Women Unsilenced,* is adapted from terms Meredith Mantooth captured in her 2012 thesis, *Reconstructing Disrupted Lives: The Canadian Exhibition of Children's Art From Refugee Camps.* It feels exceptionally fitting because the women whose voices are expressed in the chapters of this book have had their lives destructively disrupted. Often the prime way they can begin to be unsilenced is through sharing their drawings or art, which they have contributed to this book. We are deeply appreciative of their trust.

Feminist women's stories of challenging patriarchy helped us break our sense of isolation and aloneness, as we battled within the narrow band and desolate margin in society designed for feminist social activists. Breaking through patriarchal resistance is akin to repeatedly hitting walls of a titanium fortress—walls embedded with corruption, lies, deceitfulness, and cover-ups by those abusing positional power who contribute to the social and legal impunity enjoyed by family-based torturers. We hope this book makes them much more visible.

Over the years, during some of our darkest hours, writings by international organizations that focus on State torture helped. The work of Amnesty International and others,[1] functioned as our lifelines. Their

---

1 Brownmiller, S. (1975). *Against our will Men, women and rape.* Bantam Books; Herman, J. L. (1992). *Trauma and recovery. The aftermath of violence—From domestic abuse to*

articles about the intentional actions of human evil perpetrated by State torturers, police, or military, and the knowledge torture recovery could be possible, strengthened our ability to care. Women trusted us to be with them in their horrendous suffering of torture, terror, and horror memories, as they struggled to heal. This was a vital relationship healing connection.

Women Unsilenced is a testimonial that exposes women's realities. Readers are introduced to the value of truth-telling, as difficult as this may be. We make no apologies for our and the women's herstorical truth-telling that reveals and describes the meaning and impact of the non-State torture and human trafficking victimizations they survived (Sarson & MacDonald, 2019a). To do otherwise would mean to remain silent, and to collaborate with the patriarchal system that refuses to criminalize torture by non-State actors as a distinct human right violation, suffered by women and girls in the domestic or private sphere. Our silence would mean we were siding with the torturers and their prime directive to the women and girls to never tell on them. It would be wrong to agree with the ancient system that has pathologized women and girls as disordered or mentally ill whenever they tried to tell their truths about being victimized. Never speaking the truth to reality will forever block the prevention of non-State torture crimes—we persist in speaking the truth.

Therefore, it has been a privileged journey of unsilencing with the women in this book and all the women their voices represent.

---

political terror. Basic Books; Lifton, R. J. (1986). *The Nazi doctors medical killing and the psychology of genocide.* Basic Books; McGuire, C., & Norton, C. (1988). *Perfect victim.* Arbor House; Sampson, W. (2005). *Confessions of an innocent man Torture and survival in a Saudi Prison.* McClelland & Stewart Ltd.; Shatan, C. (1997). Living in a split time zone: Trauma and therapy of Vietnam combat survivors. *Mind & Human Interaction, 8*(4), 204–222; Staub, E. (1993). *The roots of evil: The origins of genocide and other group violence.* Cambridge University Press; Ussher, J. (1991). *Women's madness Misogyny or mental illness?* University of Massachusetts Press.

CHAPTER I
11:11 P.M.—THE PHONE RINGS

Crossing the room I, Jeanne, wondered why I felt compelled to answer my business phone given how late it was. Glancing at the clock, it read 11:11 p.m.; I picked up the receiver, saying, "Hello?" in a questioning tone.

A woman replied. "I wasn't expecting anyone to answer. It's so late, almost midnight. This is the last time I'm reaching out."

I replied, "I don't understand what you mean. Can you please tell me more?"

"I'm going to die on the 29th."

"What do you mean?" I asked.

"It's all planned…my death…for the 29th…before I have to go back to work."

"So, you're reaching out hoping someone can help you? Hear you?" I asked.

"I don't know why I called. Maybe I was thinking if I reached out one last time at such a late hour no one would answer, which would mean there's no one out there who can help me. With no help it…it…it would mean it's the right thing to do…to die. I don't know what to say because I didn't expect anyone to answer the phone."

"You wanted someone to hear you? To care? I care."

"Why would you care? You don't know me," said the woman.

"That's true, but I don't have to know someone to care about them. I hear that you're suffering, that you're reaching out. What can I do to help?"

"Why aren't you asking me my name...my telephone number...or where I live? Or where I work? That's what everyone else has done when I've called for help...when I call helplines. All they want to do is send the police to my place. They weren't interested in me...in listening to me. I'd hang up on them. So, why aren't you asking me those questions?"

"Because," I said, "if you wanted me to know that information, you would tell me. I don't need that information to care, to care about you, to hear you are suffering. What I need to know is how I can help you."

This woman's desperate and suffering voice catapulted me into a state of electrified attentiveness. My mind swung into high gear as I raced to make a connection with her. My emotions settled into a place of deafening stillness so as not to interfere with my ability to respond to this life-threatening plea for help.

We duelled—the woman and I—a duel for connection versus disconnection. As I struggled to make genuine connection with the woman on the phone, she resisted making connection with me. She fought me, trying to find ways to justify staying disconnected from my genuine caring. Remaining disconnected from the thought anyone might care, that I cared, would be all the proof she needed. Proof she was worthless; proof that would justify continuing with the plan for her death in four days' time.

Four days' time—I could not think that far into the future. I was only functioning in this event which felt unattached to time. Time felt as if it—and I in it—had been frozen, had ceased, yet the clock told me our duel of connection-disconnection had lasted for over an hour. Our struggle ended with the woman agreeing to call me the next evening. Her overwhelming cry for help was agonizing. I was exhausted. Apprehension set in. Had she and I really won the first round of making a relationship connection?

CHAPTER 2
OUR JOURNEY BEGINS

We, Linda and Jeanne, met in 1990, while working together as public health nurses in the small town of Truro, Colchester County, Nova Scotia, Canada. Truro's population is approximately 13,000. Many small rural communities fill Colchester County, making for a total population of around 50,000.

Our public health nursing work took us throughout the county into its schools and homes, connecting with babies, children, youth, and adults of all ages. As public health nurses we were not surprised when children and women disclosed experiences of past and present emotional, physical, and sexualized violence. The World Health Organization's (WHO) research states that one in three of the world's women have suffered physical or sexualized assaults perpetrated by an intimate partner (WHO, 2017). We knew that harm caused by the many forms of violence within intimate relationships creates major public health concerns.

Our professional interest involved combating violence within relationships. This was also motivated by our own childhood experiences of being born into families with violent, alcoholic fathers. Our caring led us, in January 1993, to open a one-night-a-week, fee-for-service private practice, while maintaining our public health day jobs. We called our practice "Flight into Freedom."

"FLIGHT INTO FREEDOM"

We chose the name "Flight into Freedom" to deliver the message that it is possible to recover from the hurts suffered by violence perpetrated within relationships. Our nursing practice was feminist, educational, and human-rights-based. Fundamental was imparting the knowledge that relational violence was a human rights violation, meaning the person has been criminally victimized and was not disordered, "crazy," or mentally ill. We understood when women survived violent victimizations as children and/or as adults, coping and survival responses developed. These responses created difficulties in their lives once leaving or escaping the violent relationship. Identifying, naming, and developing awareness to address troublesome coping and survival responses was the focus of our caring work.

We worked together with those who sought our support, creating a "mini group." We assured women not to be concerned about whether or not we could cope with their disclosures. When such a worry occurs, a woman might not disclose what she needs to, if she thinks the details of her victimization might be too much for a single caring person to hear. Harmful realities not spoken can delay healing. The mini-group framework supported women's full disclosures in their efforts to heal. Working together also meant we Self-cared by emotionally debriefing with each other.[2] It also gave us the time to problem-solve and design caring interventions.

Group work can increase healing effectiveness. Telling only one person of the harms suffered can feel like keeping secrets; telling two people helps shatter this oppressive silence. Group work helps prepare women to tell many if, for example, they decide to participate in activism movements.

---

2 We spell "Self" with a capital throughout our book, aware that having a relationship with one's Self is similar to owning a name. This concept was vital for the women we intensely supported who had been dehumanized to the point of not perceiving they were even human.

Our mini group also facilitated educational and healing activities. We role-played situations and illustrated role-modeling to increase women's learning about non-violent relationships.

Our practice offered home visits. We were familiar with this professional experience because our nursing careers in public health meant working with people in their homes. Assessing safety prior to agreeing to a home visit was a practice protocol, as was sharing that we had a legal responsibility to report children at risk of harm to child protection services.

A feminist-based approach meant including discussions about how patriarchy socially positions men and boys as dominant and women and girls as subordinate. This ignores we are of the same species and as "all human beings are...equal in dignity and rights" as written in Article 1 of the United Nations (UN) *Universal Declaration of Human Rights*. These discussions also meant sharing herstorical knowledge, so women could develop concepts that reframed and eliminated their perceptions of Self-blaming that they were somehow responsible for the violence they suffered.[3]

As nurses, we valued the power of caring as holistically multi-layered and involving (Bobak et al., 1989):

- transformative caring, which means offering support to a woman to learn to consider new ways of understanding and seeing her world, and to be open to possibilities and hope;

- reintegrative caring, which is supporting a woman to gain her ability to re-establish a meaningful life when her challenges seem insurmountable;

- advocacy caring, which is interpreting a woman's situation and identifying the overwhelming obstacles she faces, then taking the

---

3   We use the term herstorically because women's lives have been different than men's historical lives. It is way past time that this truth is named and appropriately respected.

actions required to support her in overcoming the situational crisis confronting her;

- healing caring, which means developing a helping relationship with the woman to respectfully advance an understanding with her that encourages her to identify, build on, then draw on her strengths to heal;

- participatory caring, which is staying present with a woman in painful, difficult situations, encouraging her to draw on her available strengths; and

- problem-solving caring, which is about identifying issues and working with the woman to seek effective solutions, including evaluating her achievements.

These nursing skills were the foundations of our caring practice. Healing caring was always present; at other times our caring was a mixture that involved several or all of these multi-layered caring skills. All of our nursing skills were needed when supporting women who were victimized by torturer-traffickers.

We closed "Flight into Freedom" in 2000. We became specifically focused on addressing violence against women and girls that amounted to non-State torture. Our social advocacy and activism took over. We decided to challenge the professional, national, and global invisibilization that denied women's telling that torture was a specific form of violence perpetrated against women and girls within family-based relationships. We decided to expose the organized crimes of these torturer-traffickers.

HERSTORICAL KNOWLEDGE

The UN *Declaration on the Elimination of Violence against Women* in 1993 describes violence as physical, sexualized, or psychological harm perpetrated against women in their public or private lives. It further states that women are not to be subjected to torture (UN General Assembly, 1993). This means the *Declaration* acknowledges the violence women suffer in their public or private lives can amount to torture. Likewise, the UN Committee Against Torture states that women can be subjected to acts of torture in their private lives, and if subjected to human trafficking they may suffer torture (2008).

Even before the 1993 *Declaration*, and the 2008 Committee's statement, the 1948 *Universal Declaration of Human Rights* was very clear. It stated all human beings are equal, meaning women and men are equal human beings. In other words, women and men are of the same human species— different but the same human species. It stated that all human beings have the right not to be subjected to torture victimization, meaning that women have the right to be equally protected from torture. The *Universal Declaration* also said all human beings—meaning women and girls and men and boys—are entitled without discrimination to equal protection of the law. This is what was globally written of women and girls as human beings with full human rights equality.

In reality, historically, the human right to be protected from torture has been globally applied to the protection of warring men—to protect, for example, warring men from being tortured by other warring men (Coomaraswamy, 1996; Méndez, 2018). In 1932, torture victimization, especially sexualized torture perpetrated against women and girls in war, was historically reframed as sexual services provided to warring men. For example, the dehumanizing ordeal of over 200,000 non-Japanese girls and young women who were transported to what were named "comfort stations" and were subjected to continuous raping or sexualized slavery by the military men (Copelon, 2000). Herstorically, sexualized violence perpetrated against women and girls in the public and private spheres remained largely dismissed and invisible globally at the UN level, until the 1990s.

The extensive torture and rape of women in private life began being voiced in 1993, at the Vienna World Conference on Human Rights (Bunch, 2018; Pietilä, 2002). Women attending the conference spoke "of how being female…makes many women vulnerable to routine forms of torture, terrorism, slavery, and abuse that have gone unchecked for too long" and that such violence is perpetrated within family relationships mainly by husbands, boyfriends, or fathers (Bunch & Reilly, 1999, p.18). And the sexualized human trafficking of women and girls is often referred to as a form of slavery (Government of Canada, 2012).

This book details how being female made the women, as adults and as girls, vulnerable to many forms of torture, including sexualized human trafficking, perpetrated by fathers, mothers, other family members, their parents' friends and neighbours, and like-minded others, such as the buyers whose pleasure was also to torture.

This book embraces the details of women's lives, herstorically and of present day. Our chapters are filled with details gathered in woman-to-woman meetings, in emails, and in telephone and Skype conversations. Responding to our participatory research questionnaires, women told us what they considered were acts of "classic" torture.[4] Women describe the torture they survived, whether it was perpetrated within family relationships, when trafficked as children or as women, and exploited into prostitution, or suffered during pornographic victimizations.

Participating in our kitchen-table research project, women shared their herstorical victimization stories, often seated at their kitchen tables.

---

4   "Classic" torture is a term frequently used to describe forms of torture such as electric shocking or waterboarding inflicted, for example, by police, military, or individuals who are representatives or employees of a country.

Finding it too difficult to both tell and write their stories, they allowed us to document their journals with and for them. Book chapters are filled with their storytelling taken from these herstorical journals.

Twenty-eight years of professional notes inform our chapters. When we say *we,* this refers to both Linda and Jeanne. Other sections are clearly identified as our first-person stories. Unsilencing women's stories means we are also part of all women's stories, meeting women in this book with equality, woman to woman, including the woman on the 11:11 p.m. phone call.

SAVING SARA

The day after the woman's 11:11 p.m. telephone call, there was a dire need for us to decide what or how to respond if the woman called back.

Linda's Reflections, 25 August, 1993

I remember the look in Jeanne's eyes as she told me about her telephone conversation and the woman's desperation to kill her-Self. Her eyes were deep and dark. She looked very concerned and distracted as we discussed whether we could help the woman. I knew intuitively if we decided to help we would be taking on a very serious task; I remember saying to my-Self, "I have a responsibility to try to help this woman." I took a deep breath and made my commitment. I agreed to help her in the best way I knew how.

Jeanne's Reflections

Around 11:00 p.m. on August 25, my business telephone rang for the second time.

I heard her voice. Over time, we would come to understand the significance of these late-night connections. As had happened the previous night, our relationship resumed as a duel of relational connection versus relational disconnection. Only now, the woman had heightened emotional terror. She was more desperate because she was one day closer to the 29th of August—one day closer to deciding she had to die. And she was angry.

She questioned:

"Why should I take a chance on you…on your offer to help me? Why should I believe you care? How do I know I can trust you? If I don't die on the 29th, how will I ever endure my pain and suffering…my terror? I'll be back to work next week and it will be too late then…too late to die…the 29th will have gone by. I'm not sure if I will have the courage to go through with the plan at another time. If I don't have the courage, what will I do then? I'm so very, very terrified!"

These were taxing questions which I struggled to answer. I was desperately hoping I was making a relational connection with her, so she would feel and know that Linda and I cared about her.

Suddenly, she sighed and uttered, "My name is Sara."[5]

"Sara?"

"Yes, Sara."

I can't remember exactly how I felt when Sara shared her name, maybe relief and extreme tension. Trying to meet Sara in her space of being was like the world, the room, ceased to exist. The tension in my body was like a laser beam focused on connecting with her. There was only she and I—this is the feeling that returns as I share this memory. Perhaps I felt some relief that we were making a relational connection with each other, but also more tension because knowing her name added a layer of intimacy to our relationship. The woman was now a person with a name—Sara. Before I heard her name, her voice was the only image I had.

I explained to Sara that Linda and I worked as a team and that we would meet her to discuss whether we could offer her support. Sara agreed. A date, time, and place for a meeting were set.

_____

5   Sara is not her real name. It is one chosen by her to protect her identity.

CHAPTER 3

MEETING SARA

————————

Seated on a wooden bench, we wondered: Would Sara appear? We had agreed to meet outdoors in a public place. Sara wanted to be close to her purple two-door car, able to flee if necessary. This is why we were seated on the green bench almost hidden by an out-of-control juniper bush growing in a large square planter box on Dominion Street.

Waiting. We watched as an unknown woman, guarded and suspicious-looking, approached us. She asked: "Are you Jeanne and Linda?"

"Yes. Are you Sara?"

Nodding, she looked up and down the street. She appeared to examine it for potential dangers only she suspected might be present. Apparently perceiving there were none, Sara sat on the edge of the bench. We talked.

Eventually, Sara agreed to come with us to our rented office room, which was behind us. It was in an older wooden house that hid its age under coats of deep blue paint. Beams of sunlight streaming through the window greeted us. We invited Sara to sit and she chose to perch on the soft couch, ignoring the two large armchairs also occupying the room. Choosing these chairs, we sat in a mini-group arrangement with Sara. She immediately began telling us of her terror and confusion, saying there was "no hope for people like me." She feared trusting us and feared having to live. The date of her plan or "*need*" to die had passed.

We quickly learned Sara was a professional woman in her late 20s. She had a university degree at the master's level. She was single, and described living alone in an apartment. It would be quite some time before we fully understood she was living two realities, that of a professional woman and that of a woman who was still being tortured and trafficked. Much like a woman who lives with a violent male partner, she goes to work, does her job, but when she goes home she becomes a woman victimized —battered emotionally, physically, and sexually. Both women are living violent and forcedly silenced realities, frequently invisible to others.

Suddenly, like a lightning flash, Sara bolted off the couch and squeezed her-Self into a ball on the floor in a corner of the room, hugging her knees to her chest. Sara's eyes overflowed with a look of terror. She whimpered, "They're coming to get me. They're going to get me. Please…please help me!"

"Who's coming to get you?" Desperation coated our voices as we struggled to understand what was happening.

"Get them away from me. See them. They're getting closer, please stop them, please."

Sara's plea sent us into an emergency response mode. Intuitiveness clicked in. We guessed she was flashbacking. Flashbacking is like time-travel. Basically, Sara appeared to have flashed back in time, into a memory that placed her in danger. We did not know the threat Sara perceived; however, we immediately realized her plea for help meant she must have perceived a need to escape. We needed to reach Sara in her back-in-time-place to help her come back into the present—back into the room—back into her-Self.

Sara needed to be rescued. Visualization was our only tool.

"We're coming to get you Sara. We're driving a big black car, speeding between you and them. We'll open the back passenger door. Jump in.

Cover your-Self with a blanket. What colour would you like the blanket to be?"

"Purple."

"Sara, you'll be safe."

Rescued, Sara was confused as to what had just happened. Her confusion cleared as we helped her locate her-Self in the office room. We asked her to move her feet on the floor.

"Tell us the colour of the walls. Do you see the sun rays shining into the room?" we said, all the time calling her by name, repeating, "Sara, you'll be okay."

Because we did not react with fear to her flashbacking experience, Sara did settle. We explained that we understood her sudden behaviour to be a flashbacking response.

Before leaving this first-time meeting, Sara was safely stabilized. We informed her we were not a 24-hour service, nor on-call for suicide support. When we explained that we would try to find her the appropriate support, she emphatically stated she was not going to seek institutionalized care. We planned another meeting with the intent to try to find appropriate support for her.

Would Sara be back? If so, what were we going to do?

CRASH-LANDING INTO A CRIMINAL CO-CULTURE

Sara returned. Prior to Sara's second meeting, we contacted different provincial services and out-of-province agencies. Unable to find support for Sara, we made the intense decision not to abandon her.

Unbeknown to us, this decision not to abandon Sara would transform our lives and worldview forever. Coming into connection with Sara catapulted us into a Canadian and global reality we can only describe as crash-landing into an unknown culture with violent, manipulative relational practices. This crash-landing was shocking. It introduced us to an organized family-based criminal culture. We would learn Sara had been tortured and trafficked all her life.

Over the many years since 1993, we have learned from other women's stories; they, too, had families similar to Sara's. They are women from many countries besides Canada. They are women from the US, the UK, Western Europe, Australia, and New Zealand. Listening to so many women's disclosures presented a context in which like-minded, torturer-trafficking families or groups exist globally. They are not necessarily connected to each other, but certainly have the sexualized torturing of girls and women at the core of their violent pleasures.

Eventually, we named such families and groups as having their own *criminal co-culture* (Sarson & MacDonald, 2016b). They were not identifiably different than everyday families. They were next-door family neighbours. They were individuals who worked, played, and volunteered in mainstream society. They were often individuals—mainly men but also some women—with positional power, professional jobs, and businesses. They were also farmers and fishers. In other words, they were from many walks of life. They were torturer-traffickers. They were families and individuals who took pleasure in torturing and trafficking their daughters to organized like-minded individuals and groups. For some women, this began when they were babies. Or the perpetrators tortured and trafficked a spouse to buyers whose pleasure was also torturing.

Torture perpetrated by such private individuals, families, or groups is identified as *non-State torture*. We have focused our practice for the past 28 years on emphasizing the non-State torture victimization of women and girls. These private individuals, families, or organized groups who perpetrate torture are known as *non-State torturers*. This term, non-State torturers, distinguishes them from State torturers, for example, police, military, or employees of a government who commit acts of torture, often called "classic" torture.

Developing this co-cultural perspective has meant gaining insights into the family-based torturer-traffickers' modus operandi (MO). It was the only way to understand what the torturer-traffickers had subjected Sara to, and for us to comprehend her victimization and traumatization responses. Our challenge then became designing effective ways of caring about her and about other women. This is the journey we unsilence in our book.

We write this book to share, in a general step-by-step manner, the key interventions we had to create, such as the models we designed to make sense of Sara's chaos. Little did we know how vital journal writing, role-playing, and the impacts of promoting free play would be in helping Sara. Our provision of full-life educational experiences in nature, in our out-of-office healing sessions would be essential for Sara to find meaning in her life. The grave complexities of the acts of torture Sara revealed drove our efforts to make sense of the unravelling of Sara's life. This meant late night hours of brainstorming to the point our brains ached. In this book, we share many of our interventions in raw form—meaning sharing what happened as it happened during specific meetings with Sara. Our hope is to offer tools and support to others. Perhaps by sharing our way of knowing we will provide caring options for others to consider.

When Sara entered our lives in 1993, there was no literature that we could find about how to care for a woman who had suffered non-State torture since childhood. Sara had almost three decades of being tortured. Being non-State tortured was not even named or considered a distinct form of violence inflicted on women or girls in the domestic private sphere. Therefore, we could not find non-State torture-informed support for Sara. We were indeed in uncharted nursing, political, and global territory. We made the decision not to abandon her. We told Sara we had no experience in providing such care. The most we offered was to do our best—to do no harm.

We cannot tell our story independent of Sara. However, in this book we are not alone. Other women have joined us and Sara. They share their voices and images on the pages of this book. Other women's voiced knowledge is present in our research projects. We are all women unsilenced!

CHAPTER 4
OUR WORLDVIEW TRANSFORMED FOREVER

OUR SECOND MEETING WITH SARA

Sara arrived on August 30, describing her-Self as "*bad.*" Although she could not explain her-Self, Sara was, in fact, wondering why her familiar method of dissociative coping was not keeping at bay her memories and physical flashback responses. Sara was confused and terrified by her decision to live instead of die, as planned on the 29th of August, as she had stated on her first 11:11 p.m. telephone call. She was afraid to trust that there might be caring and hope for someone, she said, "*like me.*"

While experiencing another flashback, Sara saw "him" coming to get her. Responding as we previously had when Sara flashbacked the first time we met, we devised another escape. Sara knew visualization was the intervention. We had explained this to her following her flashbacking episode in the first meeting. Sara valued learning about this rescue tool. She felt she had visualization skills. Escape she must. We said:

> Sara, you are going to push him away. We are going to help you. We are going to count to five and with each count we will all work together to push him back, until he is pushed over the cliff. Do you feel us pushing with you? Great! Now: One…push…two…push…three…push…four…push… five…push…he's gone!

The flashback lasted about five minutes. This visualization meant success to Sara. She smiled. Her smile gave a droplet of hope that her healing might be possible.

The only suicide intervention Sara could manage was her one-day-at-a-time agreement not to die by suicide. Agreeing to return the following week, we left with a feeling of dread. Little did we know we would be walking into developing, uncharted methods of collecting knowledge and healing—ways that drove our caring about Sara underground.

What had Sara suffered? What confronted us?

SEPTEMBER MEETINGS, 1993

September 6th

Sara was overflowing with anger, wanting to strike out. This necessitated developing safety rules of no hitting, throwing objects, or other harmful behaviours. Alternatively, Sara was free to verbally share or write out her emotional anger.

To promote Sara's sense of equality in our relationship, we asked Sara to identify what she expected from us. She listed: (1) we were not to say to her "trust me," (2) no quick movements, (3) no swearing, raising of voices, or angry outbursts, (4) no staring or laughing at her when she cried, (5) no dancing around her, (6) to honestly answer her questions, and (7) to assist her in developing a healthy relationship.

Why Sara asked, for example, that we not dance around her confused us. In time we would understand this and her other strange-to-us points. But not yet. At this time the intervention was about staying present with Sara, who said she didn't like our manner, "too much talk theory and not much doing…what about abuse stuff."

Sara was in acute distress and suffering massively. We needed to focus on building her relationship with her-Self by promoting stabilization and her ability to successfully escape from her flashbacks. We were not to jump into "abuse stuff," this would be unsafe. Respectfully responding to Sara's comment that we were "not doing much," we wrote goals together for the next meeting. Sara requested we explain our work and focus on her goal to develop a healthy relationship with her-Self.

September 14th

Respecting Sara's request that we clarify our practice framework, we explained that we would begin meetings by writing goals and identifying achievements at the end of each healing meeting. We further stated that learning and healing increase by combining talking and listening with *seeing* and *doing*. Writing down goals is about *seeing*. *Doing* means working to achieve the goals, and closing the meeting by evaluating success.

We offered Sara large flipchart paper to promote her learning by writing and seeing. This size of paper provided Sara with greater freedom for her emotional release. Writing also promoted the feeling of being seen and heard. Coloured markers and pencils offered Sara decision-making choices. Free space for movement versus the confines of remaining seated at a table meant sitting on the floor. These interventions helped Sara stabilize her overwhelming stress and fear by supporting her sense of having equal control in the meeting.

Model of Self. Respecting Sara's seventh request that we focus on providing her with support to develop a healthy relationship, was easy. This was

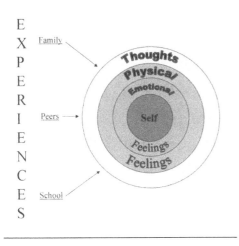

Fig. 1: Model of Self

our caring framework. We knew it was critical to assist Sara to develop her awareness that she was a person and had a relationship with/to/for Self. Maximizing Sara's need to hope she could heal, we drew on her visualization skills, showing and describing our Model of Self illustrated in figure 1.

Thoughts. This is the outer ring of the model. We explained to Sara this refers to beliefs, values, attitudes, and everyday knowledge about experiences, including with family and peers, and being in school or at work, for example.

Physical Feelings. Next, the "physical feelings" ring refers to physical sensations experienced for instance, when working hard and having sore muscles, or how a headache hurts.

Emotional Feelings. This identifies the next ring on the model. For example, this can be feeling happy when talking with a friend, or experiencing anxiety over a job interview. Expanding further, emotional feelings can also produce physical feelings—anxiety may produce physical chest tightness, whereas happiness makes one want to physically jump with excitement.

We further explained that thoughts and physical and emotional feelings contribute to understanding a relationship *with/to/for Self*. "*With*" Self means understanding how I as a person choose to think, what attitudes to hold, and how to practice being present *with* my beliefs. The "*to*" raises the issue of how I want *to* treat my-Self. Do I want *to* take care of my-Self by respecting my personal boundaries? And the "*for*" relates to when I respect my boundaries, I do so *for* my-Self. *With/to/for Self* assists shaping who I want to be as a person—it helps gain awareness of: Who am I?

To offer insights for Sara to understand physical and emotional feelings, we provided this scenario for her to visualize:

> Sara, imagine a young woman walking across a stage in front
> of a large audience. Crossing the stage, she hits her toe, trips,

and falls. Physically, could you imagine the young woman's toe hurt? "Yes." Emotionally would you, for instance, say the young woman felt embarrassed? "Yes." Then we asked, can you imagine two years going by and the young woman recalled this experience. In doing so, would her toe physically begin to hurt? "No." Would she re-feel the emotional embarrassment? "Probably."

We did not ask Sara to imagine she walked across the stage because we did not know if Sara could connect with her-Self in this way. But the educational points the scenario offered were that the young woman had thoughts and she experienced both physical and emotional feelings. And when she recalled her experience years later, the physical pain of her sore toe was gone. When the young woman remembered her emotional feeling of embarrassment, it probably came back because emotions can stick to a person like glue. Emotional feelings produce physical sensations. For embarrassment, this might mean body muscle tension. The young woman's face might become flushed again. We explained further that if a child has continuously been put down, called useless, good for nothing, stupid, ugly, and worthless, such name-calling sticks emotionally. It can dramatically shape how a child would feel and think about her-Self or him-Self, whereas a child supported with encouraging and respectful personhood messages would have a much different relationship with/to/for Self. Emotional feelings, therefore, do influence our relationship with/to/for Self.

Sara became very quiet. Then she said, "*Is it possible that I'm hidden under the pain of suffering?*"

September 20th

At this meeting Sara drew the "black box" image shown in figure 2. Such free drawing would prove to be an essential healing tool for Sara. There was no explanation of its meaning except saying she had the "black box" in her head. We share Sara's drawing as raw information that Sara was not capable of clarifying further. She just needed the freedom to let it out.

We share the drawing to illustrate that, for us, our intervention was not to place any meaning on the drawing until Sara could explain its meaning. And finally, we share the drawing to show and respect how a woman who has suffered decades of torture and trafficking might present. We do this so a woman would not be misunderstood, or wrongfully labelled as disordered, "crazy," or mentally ill. Understanding the meaning of Sara's black box drawing developed over time and became critical to our future interventions in assisting her to heal and escape from "the family." We learned that this term, "the family," referred to her biological family and their criminal connections to like-minded others and groups.

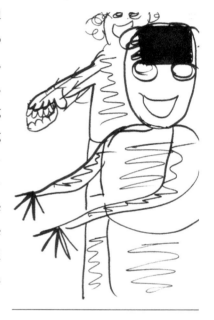

Fig. 2: "Black box" conditioning

Staying true to her goal of spending meeting time to develop a healthy relationship, Sara began writing. She wrote on the paper that she was told:

> No one will believe you. That they will lock you up and throw away the key! That you would have to spend all your life in a hospital. No one would love you. You would destroy the family. You are a terrible person. You will die.

Then she said, "I was afraid of the men, I was in a trance, I got abused again as usual." She said that her father was "doing bad things" to her during her bath. "Put things in places that hurt." And, "the babysitter and her boyfriend were sometimes present during her bath." Sara wrote that her "father was using her for his friends" and her aunt was "making her sleep with her son and making them do things while she watched." And that "dogs were used."

Revelations poured out of Sara, although we were not asking. The revelations were a form of release. These were not issues to be discussed. Sara realized we saw her writing. We read these aloud if she asked, and heard what she told us.

Sara was revealing a mixture of past childhood victimizations, as well as disclosing that she was presently being victimized. Along with these revelations, Sara was conversely asking us not to care about her. The tug-of-war of connection and disconnection was hyper-active. At this meeting we began writing positive and encouraging letters for Sara to take home to read. An example letter was,

> Dear Sara,
>
> Thoughts that were coming to me are the courage and strength you have to take the risk to put your feelings down on paper and to be able to have them read aloud. It was a privilege for me to share this time with you and to participate by reading your words. Linda

Sara grew to want our letters. This was an intervention she looked forward to. Our messages were a paradox, a positive challenge to Sara's internalized Self-destructive thoughts and feelings. Was Sara to keep believing she was "bad," or risk thinking and believing our positive reinforcing messages and the recovery work she was doing?

September 27th

Sara wrote:

I am very sad today. Also very anxious. I wasn't going to come today *or* anymore. My dad has been mean to me. A lot of people in my family have been mean to me…I don't like Sara. I know I'm supposed to be positive, or I'm not helping myself but ~~God dam it~~ I hurt a ~~hell of~~ a lot…I'm sad & angry!!!!!!

Sara crossed out "God dam it" and "hell of," but could not explain why. Much later we learned she was afraid of swearing. Sara's statement was accompanied by

Fig. 3: Sara's raw emotional writing

angrily writing of her hate as shown in figure 3. She could not explain who her anger and hate were directed at or what "monster" referred to.

At every meeting, relational goals that were reasonable and achievable for Sara, and for us, were equally negotiated. Working to achieve Sara's successes meant Sara risked wondering, as she had said at the September 14 meeting, "Is it possible that I'm hidden under the pain of suffering?" These are our recordings of Sara's achievements. She was:

- expressing her emotions—anger, sadness, and anxiety
- writing and drawing more of her feelings and thoughts
- wanting to tell about the "abuse stuff"
- stating her future goal was to cry

We wrote success letters to Sara that celebrated her achievements. To promote a sense of positive Self-connection, we asked Sara to take them home to try and read them during the week.

A Short Home Visit. When we passed through Sara's community, Sara asked us to drop in for a short visit. We did so, as home visits were a normal nursing practice for us. This home visit provided unexpected insights.

We rang the buzzer to Sara's apartment. Climbing the stairs, we knocked on her door. Sara opened it. We couldn't see her. Sara was standing hidden behind the open door. Witnessing this response offered us a glaring insight into her present vulnerability for ongoing victimization. Her response needed immediate attention because we became aware this was her pattern of dissociating. Whenever "the family" and other perpetrators—men and women—rang the buzzer to her apartment, then knocked on her door, Sara, we learned, automatically let them in. She had absolutely no concept she did not have to answer the buzzer or open her door to let perpetrators into the apartment. Our realization of her present-day vulnerability dramatically hit us. Safety interventions were immediately needed.

Sara needed to understand she did not have to respond to the buzzer or to answer the door. She began by covering the apartment buzzer with a sign reminding her not to answer. She also made signs reminding her not to answer the door or the telephone when she realized perpetrators were calling. These interventions took much effort for Sara to initiate. But practice she did. Additionally, we suggested both a peep-hole and especially a chain-lock mechanism be installed on her door because Sara did not know who had keys to her apartment. We realized we would need to help Sara develop awareness of her physical dissociative responses so she could train her-Self not to dissociate when she heard the apartment buzzer or a knock on her door.

All these interventions would prove vital to Sara's escaping "the family." We would learn that it would take Sara seven years to end being chronically and mentally dominated, controlled, tortured, and physically and sexually re-victimized.

So much to do!

OCTOBER—WHAT WAS HAPPENING IN SARA'S LIFE?

October 4th

We were at a beach near the town of Truro, which is located on Cobequid Bay. Sara wanted to write "Why?" in the sand and throw rocks into the beach mud as a releasing intervention for her anger. She wanted to feel the freedom to run along the beach. In doing so, Sara had taken the risk to trust us to provide this safe outdoors healing intervention. This began our experiences in nature in our out-of-office healing meetings.

October 11th

Sara came saying, "There's too much junk, filth. I feel so extremely dirty. I want to cry, not on cue. I need to talk about it to cry aloud! Oh I hurt so much!"

Sara could not explain what she meant about not crying on cue. When she was driven to write how she felt about her-Self, her writing often looked like figure 4. After writing, Sara would get angry and scribble over what she wrote. We share this image to show how she was expressing her-Self.

Fig. 4: Sara's writing often looked like this

Writing and drawing became Sara's normal responses in her efforts to release and ease her physical-emotional tension. This tension, she said, made her feel like she would explode if she did not "get it out." Her feeling of getting "*it*" out helped ease the minute-by-minute risk she might die by suicide. She needed safety, understanding, and acceptance. This free and raw writing was providing her with a physical sense of release. Getting it out was all she could manage.

For us, it felt like Sara was on a roller coaster that seemed ready to fly off its tracks. Knowing we were present to witness, to hear, and to see what she wanted to express was validating her Self-worth. We were struggling to try to keep her on the tracks, out of Self-harming, and out of dying by suicide.

October 18th

Sara disclosed she was seeing another counsellor—one her physician suggested. She said she told the physician this counsellor's sessions were "*bad.*" Not having been asked to explain what bad meant, Sara said the physician encouraged her to keep trying and it would get better. At this meeting, Sara began telling us about these sessions. Sara described she felt "abused by" the counsellor but had "to care for" the counsellor, expressing that she was "being treated like at home." The crises in Sara's life just expanded.

We made it absolutely clear to Sara she was not required to see us. It was painfully difficult to look at Sara, realizing she did not yet comprehend harmful and abusive relationships. She did not understand her right to end such relationships.

So much stress! Sara was suicidal but as she was an adult, we could not rescue her. We now had more concerns. What truly was Sara's reality? What were all the victimizations Sara was suffering? Were there no others in her life who were safe and respectfully cared about her?

We were beginning to wonder if Sara was surrounded by perpetrators. She absolutely did not comprehend why she was so suicidal. She did not comprehend the harms inflicted by violent attacks and abuses of power. And we struggled to grasp what was happening to her and how to offer hope and healing. We knew healing was painful enough; was it possible for Sara when she was apparently being chronically victimized by so many people? We had committed our support to care about Sara. Given her desperation, we decided not to stop unless Sara her-Self ended her connection with us.

We were living a horrific reality, as was Sara, unbeknownst to her.

October 21st

Unable to find informed support for Sara in our province, we wrote to out-of-province services. On this day we received a letter from one group. It said how frequently victimized individuals are not believed. They enclosed literature, and were open to further contact. In our phone conversation with them, we explained our caring interventions and what we understood about Sara's overwhelming victimizations—past and present. They told us we obviously knew what we were doing to have the successes we were, and to continue.

Sara's telling was like a dripping water faucet that could not be shut off. It was as if she could not contain the memories dripping out of her, and these were collecting in a clogged sink. Sara could not comprehend what her memories truly meant. It was clear she did not understand why she was suffering, even though she was writing and telling about a lifetime of sexualized, physical, psychological, family-based, and group-based torture and trafficking victimizations. We were trying to care while living in a nightmare.

October 28th

This was a home visit that lasted from 7:30 p.m. until 12:30 a.m. More stress.

We were beginning to professionally operate undercover, meaning it was unsafe to disclose to the health care system the amount of time required for Sara's healing. In 1993, it was considered inappropriate practice to spend this much time with a person, especially in their home, so we went professionally silent. At the same time, we knew this was the critical caring Sara desperately needed if she was to heal and escape the torture victimizations she was describing. There was no safe non-pathologizing caring in the health care system for women who were trying to tell, to be believed, and to heal from non-State torture crimes. This was 1993; the world did not acknowledge such dehumanizing brutality as non-State torture, as a form of violence being inflicted on girls and women within family relationships.

Sara feared she would Self-harm if she could not keep "getting it out." Although Sara still did not comprehend what "it" was, she just knew she needed to get "it" out. "*Get it out. Get it out. GET IT OUT!*" These were desperately spoken phrases Sara repeated for years. And in 2020, she knew that "it" meant all the crimes perpetrated against her. She said, "I know they didn't want me to die because I was their commodity."

During this home visit Sara drew this victimization Halloween "skeleton" image in figure 5. Sara said this ordeal took place in the basement of her home at age 11. Sara detailed this past ordeal involved her mother and father, married friends of her parents, two other men, and Sara's parents' pet dog.

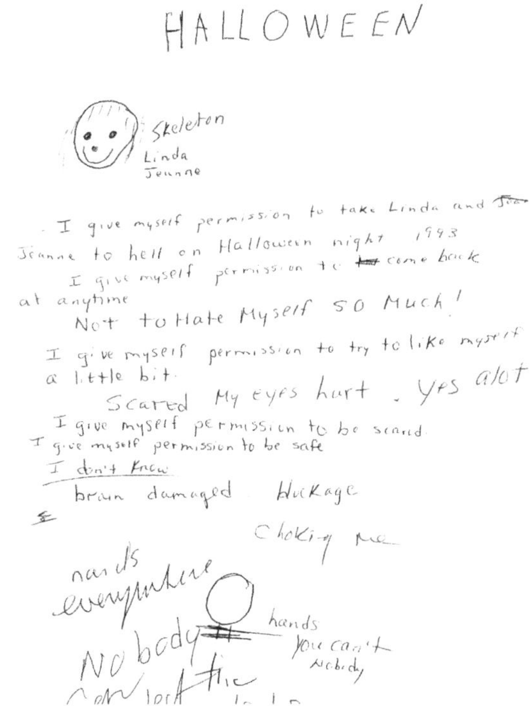

Sara said they used candles, encircled her as she lay on a blanket and beat her with straps. As

Fig. 5: Halloween

she spoke, Sara began re-experiencing the body pain memories of the beating and the group-rape in all orifices of her body. She described the pain in her stomach and breasts. We did not know what Sara meant when she wrote about taking us to hell. And Sara could give no clear explanation. As we stated before, Sara was delivering raw drawings to us as a survival intervention for "getting it out." We respected that Sara did not have the capability to explain and integrate the meanings of her raw drawings; she was too overwhelmed.

However, the positive of Sara's drawing was it included expressions of her efforts to try to develop Self-care and Self-worth.

Although not seen on this journaling sheet, Sara expressed both anger and fear. Fear because she was telling despite her conditioning never to tell; anger at the organized group she described as having their "hands everywhere" over her, which is unclearly written. Yet Sara did not understand her pain was a consequence of being chronically victimized by her family and their like-minded friends. Violent and torturing relationships were the only kind of relational connections Sara knew, which is why Sara could not comprehend that these relationships were causing her suffering. Observing Sara's suffering was painful.

After getting "it" out—of letting go of this Halloween ordeal—Sara said she "felt better, was very tired, and worried about telling." We helped Sara settle, and she asked us to read her a story out loud. We did. The story was from a children's book.

Even though we knew, based on our nursing observations, that we were meeting Sara's healing requirements, we also considered our caring would not be accepted by the health care system. We were practicing underground because the Canadian and Nova Scotian health care system had no place for caring, believing, and understanding non-State torture informed care was other than labelling Sara as mentally ill or disordered.

In *From Novice to Expert* Patricia Benner (1984), explains that expert nurses with vast professional experience have "an intuitive grasp of each situation" without wasting time considering unfruitful solutions. We were relying on our professional intuitiveness and our skills. We knew reading aloud could be cognitively beneficial for Sara. Reading positive storytelling books was in opposition to her internalized emotional and cognitive destructive messages, which demeaned her as a person, such as she had written in figure 4. And when we had no books, Sara frequently asked us to make up a story, which we did. Over time we would learn how important these interventions were in contradicting the "die messages" Sara had been forced to repeat aloud as a child. At this point we simply believed reading these stories aloud was important for Sara's potential to heal.

Before leaving the home meeting with Sara, we established with her what she could do if she awoke and felt unsafe. Sara liked to squeeze her-Self onto the floor of her closet; we asked she take bedding with her. We did this in an effort to encourage Sara to Self-care. This act of not lying uncovered and cold on the closet floor opposed rather than reinforced one of the dehumanizing, misogynistic tactics inflicted by the torturer-traffickers, who had forced her to lie naked and cold on a closet floor.

The home visit lasted five hours, plus two hours of driving. As we drove home we processed our *caring*. We were trying to understand fully what Sara had survived and what we could do. After a few hours of sleep, we were up the next morning for our day jobs.

We felt out on the edge of a cliff. In fact, in our notes, we wrote that Sara was being tortured but we had to wait until Sara revealed this to us. Ethically, we remained committed to our decision not to abandon her. Professionally, we knew if Sara had the potential of surviving she required extensive *caring time.*

It was not until 1997 that we found literature stating that persons who have suffered human brutality, cruelty, torture, and dehumanization needed prolonged hours of committed caring to recover. In Chaim F. Shatan's 1997 article entitled "Living in a Split Time Zone: Trauma and Therapy of Vietnam Combat Survivors," he wrote that working with combat survivors was gut-wrenching work and that "sessions often lasted four to seven hours rather than the two hours planned." This was exactly how we began practicing with Sara shortly after she sought our support. Prolonged hours of staying present with Sara and her massive suffering would remain the reality for many years—*a caring reality unknown in 1993.* Added to this is the need to acknowledge, as Carroll Weinberg notes, that the torturers of women can leave them not only feeling destroyed but also ashamed of being female (1997).

October 31st, 9 p.m.

Sara left this telephone message, "Jeanne, I'm in trouble." Sara's voice sounded frightened and far away. We were unable to contact her by phone.

NOVEMBER—ATROCITIES SARA RE-REMEMBERS

November 1st

Upon arrival, Sara stated she didn't know if she could continue coming, then, without catching her breath, explained she had gone to her parents' home for Halloween. Continuing, she wrote *there was a whole bunch of them* and *I was bleeding today around 4 p.m.* She described being sore with physical wounds on the entire left side of her body, with punctures to her left breast which, she said, were bleeding and infected.

Sara then fell asleep for about 20 minutes, not an unusual response for Sara, knowing we were there for protection. We supported Sara's need to sleep because a person's brain needs sleep time to integrate very stressful new knowledge. Based on our nursing experiences, we know that sleep is important for healing. Our perspective was that Sara's telling seemed to have somewhat broken through her wall of distancing and dissociating the victimizations she suffered when connecting with "the family." Sara, for the first time, was developing fleeting realizations of the meaning of her descriptions of relational violence.

When Sara awoke our immediate sense of urgency was to encourage her to participate in a *thought and belief boundary clarification* intervention. Thought and boundary clarification means that when Sara was telling us about her Halloween victimization, her language was replicating that of the perpetrators of "wanting to die and be a sacrifice" for "the family." To clarify and differentiate her thought and perceptual boundaries from that of the perpetrators, Sara needed to answer these questions: Whose messages was she repeating? Whose beliefs was she verbalizing? Were her thoughts and beliefs different than those of "the family"?

To help Sara gain Self-clarification by trying to answer these questions, we drew two columns on a sheet of paper illustrated in figure 6. One column said Sara's words; the second column was labelled "others' words"

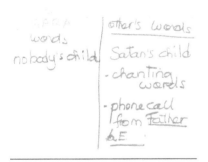

Fig. 6: Thoughts and beliefs

which referred to her father and a man we will refer to as "Lee." Sara told us he was a torturer. Sara had broken her silence—Sara had spoken of torture.

This intervention required Sara to decide what her beliefs were and try to verbalize them. Sara responded by saying she was *"nobody's child."* Under the "others' words" was *"satan's child."* She also identified their behaviours as "chanting words." The purpose of this thought and belief boundary clarification was to immediately capture a teachable moment, to encourage Sara to develop her relationship *with/to/for her-Self*. For instance, Sara identified being *"nobody's child"* as a thought that belonged *to* her; she clarified this thought *for* her-Self, and this was building her relationship *with* her-Self. Sara was not aware of this development, but we certainly were. And we were aware how essential this differentiation of Self from the torturer-traffickers was for Sara's healing.

November 12th

We were meeting in Sara's apartment because she needed to process the Halloween night victimizations in a place safe for her. She started by explaining her right leg hurt because "they bent it backwards." As Sara began explaining the violent acts that caused her injuries, this telling began ever so slowly to eliminate Sara's disconnecting or dissociating from the reality of her life. It began her healing by slowly integrating she was being physically hurt with the need of how to try to protect her-Self from chronic revictimizations.

Processing Halloween night, Sara described how her mother and father had driven her to the private cabin in the woods where others were waiting. Risking exposing her emotional embarrassment, Sara said her parent's friends, Lee and his wife, sat in the back seat of the car with her, "touching her in private places…getting her ready." Sara described being dressed in black and she was "satan's child—the chosen one." Sara did not and could not explain the significance of these phrases. Moving on, she depicted people in robes, chanting around a bonfire with animals—referring to bestiality. Speaking in a monotone voice, Sara recalled as many details of her ordeal as she said she needed to.

The Rescuing Intervention. When Sara indicated she had finished describing her Halloween ordeal, our intervention was to initiate a "rescue." We were learning Sara had been victimized since infancy. It appeared she had never had safe relationships in most aspects of her relational life. Growing up, Sara had been totally alone, powerless, trapped by family-based torturer-traffickers, in a state of violent, relational, unrecognized captivity. Sara was now in her late 20s, still feeling powerless and trapped—no longer in the cabin in the woods but trapped in all the feelings that came with the victimization memories she suffered in the cabin in the woods.

Formulating an imaginary rescue is about reframing feelings of being trapped with no escape. Rescuing is about creating a psychological image of escaping the violent ordeal. Creating a rescue intervention involved visualization such as imagining she had female warrior friends who arrived and, by dousing the bonfire, turned the torturers sightless, so Sara and her female warrior friends could escape and flee into a castle of caring, safety, and security. Framing a rescue, Sara and other women tell us, helps reframe the ending of their re-remembered victimization ordeals. When processing the torture memory, instead of being left with all the captivity emotions, a rescue reframes the ending from captivity into escaping.

Rescuing was effective in helping Sara reframe, leave, or escape these violent flashbacking ordeals. Rescuing helped transform Sara's feelings of being abandoned, alone, powerless, and in a state of violent captivity. Rescuing became a genuine and effective intervention in our care for Sara. Following the framing of a psychologically healing rescue, Sara repeated as if talking to her-Self, "*Someone came to help me. No one has ever come before. Someone came to help me. No one has ever come before.*" Framing a rescue from the Halloween victimization was healing for Sara; it broke her sense of aloneness and captivity. This was, we think, why she automatically kept repeating these sentences.

Experiencing a flashback of being transported into a violent memory is akin to time-travelling. It takes a woman away from the here and now and places her back into her victimization ordeal, at the age she was, feeling the torture, feeling all alone and abandoned without the possibility of escaping. Based on our experiences, when supporting a woman through such a flashback, it is essential to ask the woman if she has shared all the details of her flashback memory that she needs to. We have found if a woman leaves a memory by not processing all that she re-remembers, the rescue is not as effective. She can feel as if she is still stuck in the torturers' victimizations.

The other element of rescuing is shaping it to fit for the woman. Or, when rescued, she may have a specific image of a safe landing place. A woman might find sailing off to a treehouse filled with soft pillows and blankets is a safe landing place. For another woman it might mean landing on a floating lily pad wrapped in warm flower petals; these visualizations can become ongoing comforting meditation.

Consideration can also be given to imagining the torturers being held responsible for their violent actions, such as being glued to the wall of the room in which they perpetrated their crime. Imaging the perpetrators' inability to break free and remaining behind in a captive state can promote a visualization of reclaiming power and achieving justice. For some women, incorporating the achievement of justice images can satisfy their need to express torture-humour justice. Expressing torture-humour justice is a piece of healing that may not be achieved in any other way. When these conditions are met, when a woman feels she can let go of her emotions of having been held in captivity, alone, and victimized, reframing an escape can help her move forward with her healing.

Visualizing their escape has proven to be a powerful healing intervention for women similarly victimized. Elizabeth Gordon described how a visualized escape reframed her physical and emotional captivity memories and was essential to her healing (Sarson et al., 2019). She wrote:

> I believe rescues are a social, moral, and ethical responsibility both for the person so harmed who is reliving the torture and for persons who are supporting. Each rescue is an exit opportunity toward freedom. A rescue helps me learn I am important enough to be cared about. It is always a surprise to me to receive gentle care.

November 13th, 9 a.m.

Sara telephoned saying, "Feel like I haven't come all back after yesterday. Feel like I didn't do as good yesterday as the last time we did [release] work. Held back." Sara was given support that lasted one hour.

November 30th

We were working with Sara's backlash response, triggered as a consequence of her telling about "the family." This was the "black box" effect. Sara was now describing that when she tries to tell, the "black box" comes into the front of her forehead and interferes with her telling, so she does not remember; however, she was re-remembering by writing and "getting it out." Re-remembering was triggering. This was going against "the family's" rule of "never to tell." Sara was healing. However, because she was telling, November ended with Sara's journaling filled with Self-destructive messages, such as:

> In my head I hear kill, kill, kill yourself! Hurry! The hurt will then stop! In my head I hear drive over that cliff, drive into the water—get it over with now. Hurry. Time is running out. Don't be a coward! Get the knife, get the pills, get the booze, slice deep cut your chest…cut your wrist cut your vagina, bleed to death fast! Cut deep! Deeper. Don't be a coward! Do something right for once for good!

When we asked Sara why she was hearing the perpetrators' voices and destructive instructions she responded with, "I'm not sure…maybe because I have lived my life doing what others wanted me to with the hope they might love me or come to care for me even a little."

Sara then journaled: *Those two women challenge me and make me so tired!* She was referring to us. Challenging Sara eventually became known as the "C word" intervention. She would learn our challenging occurred because we *cared*. Sara needed to rebuild her relationship with/to/for her-Self. This would only happen with challenges to her thoughts and beliefs. We challenged Sara to decide whose words she was listening to—the torturers or hers. In time, much time, Sara would laugh, saying, "Here comes the C word again."

DECEMBER—HANGING ON!

December 7th

Sara began with, "I wasn't going to come tonight. Had a knot in my stomach."

Three journaling interventions had been planned. These were done on flipchart sheets.

First was identifying Sara's thoughts about why she wouldn't make it out alive. Sara's response included:

- being hopeless
- remembering more bad stuff
- we were pretending to care
- we were not strong enough
- she was not strong enough
- she was tired of living because memories can drive her crazy
- too many perpetrators
- a wish to kill her-Self
- it was the time to die

The "time to die" had an invisible meaning—it would become clear but not for some time.

Second was listing the major themes about what she had done to try and make it—to stay alive. Sara listed:

- believing people listen

- believing she is not nuts

- trying to react safely

- trying not to listen to the perpetrators' voices

- reaching out to tell

- leaning on our hopefulness

- asking and receiving caring hugs

- acquiring the skill for safe and effective visualizations

- not yet giving up

The third journaling theme made Sara angry. We challenged her by asking what she had to let go of in order to make it out alive. Sara said we were asking her to (a) believe in what we were doing to care about her, and (b) check out the ways she was resisting developing a healing partnership relationship with us. Sara then identified she needed to let go of responsibility for the thoughts and feelings of others. Sara was referring to her November 30th statement, "*I have lived my life doing what others wanted me to with the hope they might love me or come to care for me even a little.*"

Sara decided she would return. Sometimes Sara left banging the office door because she was angry with us for not backing down about our "C" caring challenges.

December 13th

Sara wanted to bang her head on the wall to redirect her anger. It would be a few years before we learned from her that when she was a toddler her father told her to bang her head on the wall, saying to Sara, "This will make you pretty." The "pretty" referred to the colour of the bruises that appeared and were dismissed by others as accidents. In time, we understood that promoting head-banging was a tactic her father used to redirect and refocus Sara's awareness away from the sexualized and physical torture-pain, to the pain created by head-banging.

Head-banging was conditioned Self-harming. When Sara banged her head on the wall as a toddler, this refocused the pain away from her vaginal and anal regions to a headache pain. Sara needed to understand this was learned behaviour. Her urge to violently head-bang was dangerous to her health. Calling on Sara's visualization abilities, we, along with Sara, created a Self-comforting visualization that helped her cease head-banging. But there would be episodes where dangerous head-banging reoccurred before eventually this response completely resolved.

This torture tactic of refocusing pain away from the pain suffered when tortured was not unique to Sara. Other women have also described similar tactics, such as when a grandmother quietly held the woman when she was a child, repeatedly telling her to focus on a doll. We learned that women—mothers and grandmothers—who knew what had happened to the women when they were children—engaged in this tactic of refocusing a child's attention away from the severe torture-pain. From our experience, this is a form of reinforcing distancing or even dissociative conditioning.

December 24th

Jeanne's Reflection

I and my husband had been invited out for the evening. The phone rang. It was Sara. We did not go out. I can still see my husband's disappointment. In these early days the struggles to support Sara totally impacted my life, that of my husband, and our sons. It was and would be for years, life-supporting work to help Sara stay alive and safe. My family contributed much in their own ways.

CHAPTER 5
TORTURED AND THE TORTURERS' MO

Looking back at 1994, we had patches of naivety. We were unknowingly heading into challenges that could have been relationally catastrophic. We knew about the abuses and assaults perpetrated within family relationships; we were well acquainted with the hurt feelings and demanding work of healing from such harms. This knowledge and the resilience to overcome harms prepared us to connect with Sara. However, what we did not know was that connecting with Sara meant our view of the relational world would be life-altering. Our affinity with Sara created powerful physical reactions in us, such as brain-pain, nausea, body aches, and deep inner bone-marrow chills as we stayed present with her throughout her disclosures of surviving acts of human evil. This is what torture is—it is the destruction of a human being—it is *the actions* of a torturer that dehumanize and attempt to destroy another human being—it is a bone-chilling reality.

How could it be that acts of human evil embedded within family relationships have remained socially invisibilized? How was it, and how is it, that the perpetrators of acts of human evil were and are capable of manipulating their social invisibility? Were they or are they invisible, or was it, is it, that societal bystanding occurs? Why, when women and girls are tortured, are they disbelieved and "simply" labelled disordered?

Sara's victimizations contrasted with our childhood experiences of being born into family violence. We wondered if these family-based non-State torturers and traffickers and the destructive impact on their children were totally socially invisible? Examining our own family violence memories, thinking about invisibility versus visibility, and about the manipulative behaviours of our fathers and or our mothers, would we discover similarities to Sara's description of believing people in the community knew, suspected, or denied all was not right?

OUR CHILDHOODS—VISIBILITY OR INVISIBILITY?

Jeanne's Childhood Reflections

The childhood violence in my home was very visible. Ted, my father, owned his own business. I assume he functioned fine at work. Once home, it took no time for the violence to begin. Day after day, night after night, the neighbourhood could hear my father's ranting rage. They could see him chasing Evelina, my mother, down the neighbourhood street as if to swoop down on his prey—which she was.

On the nights he let his guard down, my mother, my brother Raymond, and I fled the house to hide in the woods, staying there until my father fell into a drunken stupor. Then we risked entering the house and getting into bed. I remember lying in bed thinking and feeling how wrong it was my mother had to get into bed with the man that battered her. This must have a confusing and harmful impact on a child witnessing violent domestic relationships, seeing that a woman—their mother—has to sleep with the man who battered her.

Sally, a neighbour, lived in the house next to ours, but on a hill. She could look down into a window of our house. She watched. When she thought my mother was being dangerously beaten she called the police. As soon as the police drove into the driveway, my father would flip into being the nicest man they ever met. When the police left my father continued his rage and misogynistic rant. The point is my father's violence was very visible to the community. I used to wonder why the police did nothing. This social neglect hurt, sometimes as much as the family violence.

I learned from these experiences. As a pre-schooler I grew to understand my father was extremely manipulative. I have clear memories of being three and a half years old and knowing this. Not in a language sense, but in an emotional, intellectual, intuitive sense. I can recall the following event very clearly. It happened during one of the many times my mother fled Halifax where we lived to stay with her mother in Hectanooga, Nova Scotia, where my mother grew up. Halifax was over a three hour drive away.

One day my father appeared. He had come to Hectanooga to convince my mother to go back with him. Arriving by car, he parked in the driveway of my mother's brother's house up on a hill not far from my grandmother's house. I have a distinct memory of walking up that hill with my mother; she was carrying my brother Raymond, who was about six months old. When I saw my father, he was holding a big doll. When the doll's hand was held it could take steps. I remember so clearly looking at him and thinking that bringing a doll was not going to stop me from telling my mother not to go back, that I did not want to go back. At that moment in time I came to understand, in an emotional, intellectual, intuitive sense, my father was attempting to manipulate or bribe me. Of course, I could not have verbalized this at that time, but as I grew older I could explain what I had learned at that eventful moment in time.

It is insightful to reflect on memory. I have no recall of how my mother managed to flee and get us to Hectanooga. The only way to arrive there was by car or by train—and she had no car. To arrive by train meant a three or four hour walk to reach my grandmother's home because my grandmother lived deep in the countryside where there were no telephones or electricity, and oxen were still in use for farming. I have absolutely no memory of these aspects of this fleeing experience. However, I have a clear memory—even a visual memory—of seeing my-Self walking up that hill with my mother who was carrying my baby brother, of seeing my father standing by his car in my uncle's driveway with the doll. This experience of seeing my-Self in visual memory provided valuable experiential insights about Sara's victimization recalls. Obviously, the childhood violence I was enduring was very visible, but my uncle, a bystander, explained it away as a "family matter."

Linda's Childhood Reflections

My parents worked hard at keeping a perfect family social face. My father never missed a day of work. He hid his violence from outside society. I dragged friends home trying to get them to see my father as he was, not how he pretended to be on the street. As a child I told my teachers and other adults about his violence. Eventually I gave up trying to get society to care that my father was violent. I was probably not as surprised as Jeanne that Sara's family of perpetrators got away with their cruelty, given that my father seemed to effectively manipulate his outside relationships into thinking he was a "great guy." This is how they talked about him after he died. He even had a model airplane field named after him because that was his social hobby. In this sense the violence of my childhood was invisible.

As I look back at my childhood, two of the key lessons I learned about violence were that my father's violence was wrong and my mother's response of hiding and not dealing with his behaviour was wrong. After my second sibling was born I felt desperately alone. My father was becoming progressively more violent with the birth of this third child and my mother became increasingly obsessed with my father. It was as if I did not exist. As a capable child I became over-responsible for my family, continually trying to get my father to stop his drinking and violent acts. My mother treated me more as an adult even though I was just a little girl of four.

One day, feeling so distressed and desperately alone, I can remember a bright whitish light suddenly around me. Such angst of aloneness propelled me into the awareness that adults, including my parents, are not always loving or right, and can be destructive and deceptive. This gave me a strong sense of knowing that people were not always who they pretend to be. This prepared me for all the deception I would encounter while helping Sara. I was, nonetheless, shocked when Jeanne and I started talking publicly about evil human actions and were ignored. I should not have been surprised because even after I showed or told people about my father's violent side, they still did not believe me.

Our Conclusion

Patriarchal social attitudes contributed to both accepting and invisibilizing our childhoods filled with family-based violence. This occurred by renaming the violence as a "family matter," or by disbelieving or ignoring the reality. Patriarchal social attitudinal conditioning did the same to Sara.

1994: RED AND IT HURTS RE-ENACTMENT

We were still trying to understand Sara's life-threatening misery and perpetual crises. Visualizations appeared to relieve the overwhelming pain and suffering that came with flashbacks which she often could not yet comprehend or explain.

February 7th

Sara arrived to our meeting expressing great fear. Wanting to sit on the floor next to the door in case she wanted to run, Sara asked us to sit on each side of her—we did.

Seated on the floor, Sara began disclosing she had had intermittent vaginal bleeding for three weeks, plus abdominal pain. Trembling, she said she was emotionally filled with:

Confusion

Hopelessness

Fear—drowning in fear

Anger

Disbelief, and

Sadness

Sara then explained she was having a rhythmic cycle of abdominal pain that felt like waves that came every two minutes, saying, "There is a monster inside of me." Struggling through her fear, Sara described the monster as a coil stuck in her vagina.

From day one, our practice was to work respectfully with the physical and emotional responses Sara described when in a flashback or re-enactment. Our response to this flashbacking re-enactment that was about to come was to rely on Sara's visualization strengths. On the count of three, we asked Sara to take a deep breath in and then blow out. With each breath she blew out, we asked her to visualize the coil moving through her vagina one inch at a time. When ready, Sara was to visualize the coil appearing outside of her vagina—outside of her-Self—onto the flipchart page on which her re-enactment experience was being written, called "red and it hurts."

Our journaling of Sara's "*monster inside of me*" re-enactment, identified as "red and it hurts" is described as follows:

Red and it Hurts

Hurts big time Jeanne

Down in my back

Hurts low over my bone [pubis]

Sharp and sometimes stabbing hurt

I'm scared

All curled up tight

Two coils – one on each side

Getting lower and lower

Don't want to let it out

Pains come in waves every two minutes

More frequently to one minute

The coils too big to come out

Making them smaller and smaller

Easier to come out

They're sharp

They're going together – not soft

Getting soft – coming as one

Softer now as one

But big

Stuck in vagina

Three pushes – three inches

Till pushed on paper

At Sara's request, her re-enactment was written in red on the flipchart paper. Being present with Sara to release this re-enactment ordeal took one hour. Following this we sat in the room throughout her one and a half hours of recovery sleep, essential for her body and her brain to heal. When Sara woke she had no more pain, saying her body felt relaxed and open. She talked awhile, not of her release work, but generally about how she felt. Eventually she was safe to drive home. In total, this was almost a four-hour session.

It would be many months before we would fully comprehend this re-enactment. Before we came to understand its meaning, Sara needed to make sense for her-Self, and then explain its meaning to us. We were following Sara's need to release her misery related to this re-enactment. We were following her desperate need to *"get it out."*

Four-hour sessions would continue. We adapted our meeting times with Sara, so she would be the last person we would see during our "Flight into Freedom" practice. We did this because we never knew the amount of time needed to provide Sara with caring support. Four to seven-hour sessions were common for persons who had survived atrocities. As mentioned in Chapter 4, evidence for this came in 1997 when reading Shatan's article about Vietnam combat veterans. This was so validating. It felt to us that Sara was a victim of a war she did not comprehend. Nor did we; not fully as yet. It seemed to us Sara lived, as Shatan's article described, in a split time zone. Often, we did not know whether Sara was reliving atrocities of her deep past or reliving present ordeals.

In the same journal as Shatan's article was one by Frank Ochberg (1997). **He validated our praxis that the impact human cruelty has on a person is about victimization, and a person so violated needs to tell their victimization ordeals more than they need to tell their consequential traumatization responses.** This has been our *caring framework* offered to Sara. She needed to tell her victimization ordeals or "get it out" and absolutely needed the extended time Shatan said was essential to heal from atrocities.

By the time we read both Shatan's and Ochberg's articles, our practice of supporting Sara included these frameworks of extended hours and Sara's need to tell of her torture victimizations to "get it out." We knew this was needed if Sara was to heal. In these early years it did not matter if Sara did not understand her ordeals; what mattered was staying present with her flashbacking and re-enactments so she could "get it out." Although Sara did not understand what "it" meant, getting "it" out relieved her suffering. We also worked to assist and maintain Sara's psychological safety because we knew we could not address the full meaning of the victimizations she "got out" any faster than she was capable of handling such integration. In the meantime, Sara must have intuitively trusted us as she kept seeking our support. And we did as Sara had asked of us back on September 6, 1993, which was to never say to her "trust us." She would need to decide for her-Self if we were trustworthy.

We realized Sara was struggling with all her might to stay alive; at the same time, she also maintained a tight grip on dying by suicide. This was her escape route out of misery. There was no safe place in society for the *caring* Sara needed, so we remained professionally silent about our caring interventions with Sara. This was extremely professionally isolating. At the same time, we struggled to keep our families functional and manage our paid employment.

MARCH—IT FELT LIKE A RELATIONAL WAR ZONE

Sara came into the March 10 meeting saying, "I got raped by another female. I hate all the noise, the vacuum, woman on the phone. She did some terrible acts. I'll not soon forget I'm sure. Suicide!"

Sara was still being accessed and victimized by so many in horrific ways, including, she said, raped by a vacuum cleaner hose. This was what she meant when she said "I hate all the noise, the vacuum."

As victimization stories kept falling out of Sara onto flipchart sheets, her reality jumped out at us, as shown in figure 7. This was the moment she identified in writing she had been tortured.

The reality of Sara's massive victimizations became intensely clearer. A careful reading of this March 10 flipchart sheet explained Sara's suffering. Although Sara had mentioned torture during previous meetings, she had never before identified torture victimization so concretely. Now she was writing she had survived being tortured in the woods. Her flipchart sheet

Fig. 7: Sara's March 10 flipchart journaling sheet

presented us with her herstorical record of the violent harms she had and was enduring. The non-State torture, Sara said, began from the time of her earliest memories. Reading Sara's flipchart sheet, we learned about her internalized perceptions. Torture-rapes she perceived as *"sex," "bad games,"* or *"bad things happened."*

Sara's writing revealed that her parents were involved in her victimizations. It revealed she was violated by professionals such as the doctor her parents forced her to see. He would not always be alone in his office. Sometimes others were present and joined in the harming of Sara. This exposed the doctor's previously planned intentional organized group victimization of Sara.

Her writing also disclosed an organized group of professionals as perpetrators who first terrorized her before inflicting their acts of violence. The group, Sara wrote, included *"big people, adults! Ministers, gov't worker, cops, pilots."* Sara's writing described suffering organized victimization in *"basement orgies like other people have parties or Tupperware etc.,"* and of being *"taken way back in woods & tortured and raped continuously."*

Further violent organization was evidenced when Sara identified "*Dad's buddies*" were involved.

Frank Ochberg's article stated that people victimized by acts of human cruelty and evil need to get their victimizations out. This was exactly what Sara was doing. The flipchart sheet was a victimization storytelling of her lifetime of surviving acts of human cruelty—acts of human evil. Ochberg also said a person who has been harmed by acts of human evil is full of Self-harming responses. This we already knew about Sara. Studying Sara's flipchart story sheet identified her Self-harming thoughts as:

> I am disgusting!!
> I'm just dirt toy.
> Me—sicko.
> Should be killed.
> I wish with all my heart I would Die soon!
> Unlovable, unworthy, dirt, etc.

Sara went on to say, "Nobody wanted me for their kid. I really did try to be perfect; no one ever attempted to help me even if they suspected… No one helped not even when they thought something might be going on."

During the early months of 1994, Sara's writings were tug-of-war messages of wanting to die yet struggling to live. She scribbled at one point, *Death I would welcome with open arms, take me away please.* Her intensity of wanting to die increased as she began to understand the meaning of her victimizations. But also, Sara gradually unfolded that she had been taught—"*trained*" she said—to kill her-Self if she ever told on "the family." Therefore, being trained to kill her-Self or wanting death was never ending.

Trying to help Sara stay alive meant we were up against this act of human evil, her Self-destructive "training" that conditioned her to want to—had to— ordered to—must do—kill her-Self. Every time she revealed the victimizations she survived, this Self-destructive training kicked in. Some days helping Sara felt like we were functioning in a relationally catastrophic war zone.

NAMING THE TORTURE

Sara wrote that she had survived being tortured. But what is or how is torture defined? We knew we could not simply say that torture in domestic or family relationships occurred; we knew the risk of being discredited was real. We believed Sara. But society did not.

By researching the literature on State torturers, we discovered that acts of torture perpetrated by State officials such as police or military personnel were frequently described as "classic" torture. This literature, as well as UN reports, described the same acts of torture Sara described. Regardless of who the torturers were, State or non-State, our research clarified that similar acts of dehumanizing brutality were committed, albeit in different places, in jails versus private homes, for example, using whatever tools torturers had at their disposal. Sara, and the women with similar herstories, tell of knowing and feeling the torturers gained pleasure from their acts, frequently describing the torturers' smiles and laughter as evil.

Respectfully, we listened to Sara describe the violence in the family system as involving days of being abused and tortured, and at times being trafficked to organized groups. Group-torturers incorporated ritualized drama patterns into their brutal gathering. Thus, we first named the victimization Sara described as ritual abuse-torture. Sara, as well as other women, shared that when they were children they were told these organized torture-group gatherings were called "parties." However, in 2000, after we had spent two years supporting Lynn, we would need to rethink the appropriate naming for torture that was perpetrated within family relationships (Sarson & MacDonald, 2009a, 2019d).

Introducing Lynn

Lynn detailed how she had been manipulated and groomed to be victim-ized by her future husband. Lynn described that six months after their marriage she was held captive by him and his three male friends, who tortured and trafficked her into prostitution.

Lynn was an adult when she was tortured; Sara was tortured from her earliest of memories. However, the torture acts Lynn suffered were similar to those Sara survived, except organized ritualized group dramas or "parties" were not a MO of Lynn's husband and his three male friends or the "buyers" who paid to torture Lynn. Lynn explained that her husband did have a torture ritual of anally raping her with a wine bottle, never with his penis.

Not fully understanding or having knowledgeable language to explain their victimizations exacerbated both Sara's and Lynn's sense of powerless-ness. Gaining clear language to explain their non-State torture victimiza-tions was essential to helping dismantle the torturers' MO of psychological manipulations. This is freedom work.

Because Lynn suffered spousal torture and Sara suffered ritual abuse-torture, we renamed the torture inflicted against them, and other women who contacted us, as non-political torture. That is, we recognized spousal torture and ritual abuse-torture as forms of non-political torture. Eventually we would learn this naming was not accurate.

Standing firm that the torture victimization of woman and girls of all ages must not be made invisible by patriarchal misogyny—hatred of women—we attended the United Nations Commission on the Status of Women (CSW) in New York City in 2004. Seeking the wisdom of expe-rienced human rights activists, we were quickly informed that private individuals or groups who inflicted torture were referred to as "non-State actors" (Amnesty International, 2000). We adapted. Non-political torture transformed into "non-State actor torture" then simply to naming our knowledge as non-State torture. With this evolution, both ritual abuse-torture and spousal torture became forms of non-State torture.

PATRIARCHAL DISCRIMINATION: STATE AND NON-STATE ACTS OF TORTURE

Shortly after realizing Sara had been tortured, we learned Canada and other countries only criminalized acts of torture perpetrated by State actors. As discussed in Chapter 2, historically, the human right to be protected from torture was globally considered the human right of warring men and male prisoners of war. Herstorically, because all forms of violence, including torture, perpetrated against women and girls in wartime were not seen as a human rights violation (Gaer, 2012), this made it easy to invisibilize the non-State torture of women and girls that occurred in their private or domestic lives.

Patriarchal Divide Model

We created the patriarchal divide model to illustrate that acts of torture inflicted by State torturers or non-State torturers are similar, shown in figure 8 (Sarson & MacDonald, 2009b, 2018b). The patriarchal divide model illustrates to women and girls the existence of patriarchal human rights discrimination, as shown in figure 8. It also provides researched credibility to women and girls that the victimization they survived is indeed validated as acts of torture. It says to them they have the human right to speak their truth of torture victimization—they have the human right to be unsilenced.

Being listened to and telling their herstories are steps in the healing process. Sara and Lynn, for example, needed to understand the victimizations they suffered in a way that would move them to reject being labelled crazy and worthless. This is the impact of naming. We had finally found the correct terminology. When private persons or groups commit acts of torture, they are non-State actors. The torture they perpetrate is non-State torture. This evolution of naming non-State torture took us 11 years.

Patriarchal Divide Model

STATE TORTURE	PATRIARCHAL DIVIDE	NON-STATE TORTURE
• Electric shocking • Beaten, burned, cut, whipped • Immobilization tortures, tied, hung, caged • Water tortures • Suffocation/strangulation/choking • Sexualized tortures: Rapes, repetitive, gun/knives/hand/object and gang rapes • Forced drugging • Nutritional deprivation • Psychological tortures: Humiliation, degradation, dehumanization, terrorization, horrification, animalization • Forced nakedness • Sleep deprivation • Witnessing torture of others • Powerlessness & captivity	P A T R I A R C H A L D I V I D E	• Electric shocking • Beaten, burned, cut, whipped • Immobilization tortures, tied, hung, caged • Water tortures • Suffocation/strangulation/choking • Sexualized tortures: Rapes, repetitive, gun/knives/hand/object and gang rapes • Forced drugging • Nutritional deprivation • Psychological tortures: Humiliation, degradation, dehumanization, terrorization, horrification, animalization • Forced nakedness • Sleep deprivation • Witnessing torture of others • Powerlessness & captivity

Fig. 8: Patriarchal Divide Model

MO EXPOSED!

In September 1993, Sara wrote the message displayed in figure 9. She said her parents constantly terrified her with the power of this message. They drove her by the psychiatric hospital and threatened to have her admitted. She believed their threats with good reason. Globally, all forms of violence against women and girls continue to be dismissed as unfounded, as deserved, as asked for, or, for women so tortured, they risk being treated with doctor-prescribed psychotropic drugs and labelled mentally ill. Internalizing her parents' threats kept Sara terrified of the mental health care system. By 1994 Sara began understanding the purpose of her parents' threatening message she had shared with us in September 1993. At some level, she realized this was their MO to try and keep her terrified, silent, and captive.

By 1994 Sara was beginning to try to decrease the chronic victimizations she was suffering. She told us "the family" and the women perpetrator group were harassing her day and night, and she was trying not to answer her telephone by turning its ringer off at night. These were forms of learning to say "no." We role-modeled with Sara to practice saying "no," but saying "no" would take her a few years of hard work. For example, this meant learning to tell her-Self to say "no" to the perpetrators who rang the buzzer to her apartment. These were learning-to-stay-safe interventions. This work

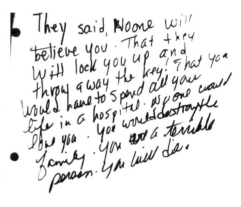

Fig. 9: A threatening message MO

of staying safe and alive meant constant fatigue. The more fatigued Sara was, the more emotionally vulnerable she felt, and the less likely she could manage the work of reducing her Self-harming responses such as over-dosing on prescription drugs or alcohol.

It would take Sara about seven years to be reasonably safe, having developed basic Self-caring skills. But it was a back-and-forth struggle for Sara and us. Over these years, as Sara's awareness grew, so too did her ability to begin to identify who some of the perpetrators were. She needed to learn to walk away if she noticed them, for instance, when she met them grocery shopping. Or, if their MO was to approach Sara and whisper a "trigger word" that initiated a learned dissociative response, Sara's safety necessitated gaining the skill not to dissociate. This was a key intervention to prevent Sara from becoming vulnerable to being re-victimized. The MO of these torturer-traffickers was to also use the telephone to trigger Sara into a learned dissociative response, then directing her to do as they demanded. The ability for Sara to learn to prevent her dissociative response was essential.

In the early years, we would receive desperate telephone calls from Sara, terrified because she just realized she had gone somewhere in the middle of the night but could not remember where. These calls shed insights into why Sara had called our business number at 11:11 that August night in 1993. She was used to receiving late-night calls so it seemed this too was a learned behaviour of making late-at-night calls. Over time we understood that Sara's being out in the middle of the night and not knowing this until she was back in her apartment was related to being triggered into a dissociative state. Once Sara learned not to respond with dissociation, these episodes ended.

Practicing not to dissociate necessitated helping Sara to become aware of the physical sensation produced when her eyes were "going into the back of her head." This term came about because, in our physical observation of Sara, we noted changes in her eyes and asked her: "Sara, where are your eyes?" Sara was able to verbalize she felt a physical sensation of her eyes, feeling as if they were shifting into the back of her head. For us, this dissociative response was observable; for Sara, it was a physical sensation. As soon as she felt this physical sensation, Sara worked diligently to gain control over her dissociative response—and she succeeded. This was life-altering Self-awareness that was vital for Sara's healing.

This healing then led to other successes, whereby gaining psychological space for learning and practicing safe boundaries was made possible. With perseverance, over the next few years, Sara's re-remembering became increasingly holistic, knowingly expressed, and recorded. Sara started to clearly re-remember and describe, for instance, the MO was that her parents "*stuck toys*" in her vagina. Plus, she became capable of explaining why they did what they did—for their pleasure. She became intensely angry at her parents, wanting to let go of them despite knowing the harms they committed, she had conflicting and overwhelming feelings that letting go of them would mean she was "all alone with no family." A psychological and practical breakthrough came when Sara said, "I'll do it. I'll have to accept my parents did these things to me."

There would be months of intense vacillations from being happy to be alive to desperately calling our home numbers. When Sara needed to talk in order to ground her-Self with safe connections, more middle of the night telephone calls occurred. Dozens of telephone calls in one day. If not answered, Sara would keep calling and calling, struggling to stay alive. When feeling life-threateningly desperate Sara sought our connection regardless of where we were. For example, in May of 1994, when we were attending the play *Les Misérables* at Neptune Theatre in Halifax, Sara convinced the theatre employees to seek Jeanne out to answer her in-desperation telephone call.

Chaotic desperation and misery increased when Sara overdosed on prescription drugs and alcohol and Self-cut to cope. More and more we learned the details of the conditioned Self-harming MOs Sara had been subjected to, including carrying a knife and cigarette lighter in her purse,

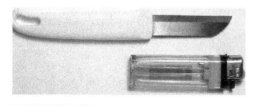

as shown in figure 10. These were her immediate Self-harming tools to use if she started to tell. Sara eventually gave these to us.

Fig. 10: Sara's knife and cigarette lighter for conditioned Self-harming

We noted the cigarette lighter was purple. Sara said

purple was her favourite colour when flashbacking at our first meeting in September of 1993. Perhaps by using the same purple colour for a "goodness rescue," her harmful association with the purple cigarette lighter was countered? More learning about Sara's responses included her leaving a 4 a.m. message on Jeanne's telephone saying she was terrified. She had just woken up and her room was "a mess." Sara said she could not remember how this happened. There would be 10 more telephone calls that night of July 30, 1994.

More learning occurred on July 13, 1994, when Sara wrote, "*I am afraid of you two leaving me. I am very afraid I may someday soon hurt myself real bad—not my choice. I go into weird space—like hypnosis.*" We had become her lifelines. Sara was terrified of losing our connection. Although all the reasons for her heightened fear were not yet clear to us, what was becoming more evident was the meaning of the "black box" drawing of September 1993. We came to understand that the "black box" image represented another MO inflicted by "the family." Sara had been torture-conditioned never to tell, never to remember, and if she did remember and tried to tell, the "black box" response blocked further disclosures. Sara physically felt it and told us when she was having this "black box" blockage that interfered with her ability to develop and share insights into her victimizations. This blockage, for example, occurred when she realized she had been out in the middle of the night but could not remember how or why or what happened. This damaged Sara's safety and survival and challenged our efforts to design healing interventions that would safely care about her.

More learning included supporting Sara to push back at the "black box" MO response; dismantling it was essential. Our interventions included using the "thoughts and beliefs" intervention similar to that illustrated in figure 6 on thoughts and beliefs. Sara had to decide if she believed "the family" could put a black box in her head or whether she believed the torturers had conditioned her to believe this. Sara made the gradual decision that the "black box" was a conditioned belief distortion. Another most effective intervention was for Sara to freely write to "get it out." Writing was different than verbally telling; writing lessened the "black box" response. As Sara healed, the "black box" response dissipated or if she felt this sensation it held no silencing power. Painful but essential insights occurred when Sara wrote:

> I remember my life 1–5…these last 2 days. I can't get it out…I remember when I was a baby what my parents did to me. Stuck toys up my vagina trying to make it bigger for all the sex games. Hotels/motels sick Sara devil's child Sara. I'm getting all filled up…I am an awful Devil's Child.

More learning meant when we entered Sara's "world" we were confronted by a violent co-culture we did not fully understand but desperately needed to. Our challenge over the next few years was to develop a model that clarified the MO of the torturers Sara was exposing. This would help us identify the risks faced and offer some guidance to our caring about Sara. We needed a logical model that explained the chaotic ordeals of torture, terror, horror, and dying by suicide that Sara needed to "*get it out.*" This need led us to design the ritual abuse-torture (RAT) model.

1998: MODEL-MAKING OF RITUAL ABUSE-TORTURE VICTIMIZATIONS

Out came the flipchart sheets and coloured markers, and onto our home office floors we went. It took us several years to transform chaos into a model of clarity. Prior to connecting with Sara, we had never dug into relationships that were based on human evil actions; thus, we had no previous insights about how we would physically respond. However, we became attuned to experiencing the bone-chilling coldness and body aches that often lasted several days following a meeting with Sara as she unravelled, in vivid detail, surviving torture ordeals. The bone-chills and aches spontaneously returned each and every time the torturers' acts of human evil surfaced. These responses also happened to us when we stayed present with other women's similar telling. There was "bone-chilling coldness energy" that came to us when in the presence of human evil memories; sometimes women also mentioned this feeling. Creating a model that accurately defined the torturers' actions of human evil had its own unique responses in each of us.

Jeanne's Responses

During this model-making process, I experienced a mind-bending real sensation of brain-pain. It felt like my brain was stretched outside my skull. The pain was accompanied by migraine-like headaches, flu-like symptoms, and often a runny nose. These responses reflected the thinking power required to problem-solve the chaos Linda and I were working to clarify. These never-ending hours of work unweaving the torturers' actions of human evil were essential so we could effectively care about Sara.

Linda's Responses

I felt like my brain was sometimes a huge blob. I even felt my brain grow and expand over the years. It felt like I was walking in sludge up to my waist with nausea, body ache, and headaches as well.

Creating a Ritual Abuse-Torture (RAT) Model

By 1998, based on Sara's re-remembering and slow but progressive recovery, we had created our ritual abuse-torture model (Sarson & MacDonald, 2008). It was our guide for understanding Sara and other women's similar victimizations. The ritual abuse-torture model is illustrated in figure 11.

MODEL OF RITUAL ABUSE-TORTURE

Graphics: K. Sarson   Sarson & MacDonald©1998

Fig. 11: Model of Ritual Abuse-Torture (RAT)

Ideology. This model identifies the torturers' co-cultural functionality—their ideology, beliefs, goals, and intergenerational connections. Superiority is named in the center of the model as their ideology. This refers to how Sara was told we and all outsiders were stupid. Also included in the ideology was the torturers' MO of their intention and desire to harm.

Inflicting torture is never accidental. Torturing is intentional, purposeful, and for these torturers, pleasurable.

Goals. The next three rings identified three MO goals of maintaining a closed and secretive co-culture by exerting totalitarian power and control over Sara and women and girls so victimized. Their MO of deriving pleasure and entertainment must not be dismissed. The financial benefits gained by "the family" by trafficking Sara are unclear. Sara was trafficked to men with enormous influential positional power, so it is reasonable to assume there were benefits for Sara's parents.

Non-State Torturers' Criminality. The following two rings list forms of violence Sara described surviving. The first ring lists the many forms of abuse that literature commonly identifies. The second ring lists the complex forms of criminality perpetrated within the co-culture by non-State torturers.

The second ring names and lists the torturers' organized MOs of torture and other crimes Sara suffered. Most of these have already begun to be discussed and will be expanded on in all upcoming chapters. The acts of torture will be specifically validated by other Nova Scotian women who participated in our 1998 kitchen-table research project discussed in the next chapter.

Sara said she was abused on some days and tortured on others. However, she was living in a home environment where being tortured was ever-present. She described a "little torture room" in the basement of her parents' home where she was tortured. We question whether any of the acts of violence Sara suffered, that were both perpetrated and organized by her parents, could ever be considered abuse. For example, consider the act of financial abuse. Sara's father took her paycheques with the intent to keep her poor and captive. His MO was maintaining totalitarian power and control over Sara so she could be tortured in the home as well when trafficked to like-minded groups. Torturing was the intention—torturing meant intentional and purposeful destruction of Sara's relationship with/ to/for Self. Sara lived every day under the threat of being tortured; therefore, we raise the question of whether naming what Sara suffered as abuse would ever be just.

For example, when women report being abused in their home and tortured when their father takes them to an organized torturing group, it must be considered that torture is ever-present in their adult-child relationships. These distinct experiential realities surface in the following chapters.

Naming the Model. This ring names the model as ritual abuse-torture. It identifies human evil behaviours and the use of social evilism beliefs and dogma to manipulate and distort Sara's thoughts and perceptions. Since infancy, Sara became the "perfect victim." Upcoming chapters are dedicated to addressing actions of human evil.

We say this is a criminal co-culture because the like-minded families, individuals, groups, or rings function in mainstream society indistinguishable from everyday people, such as doctors, nurses, social workers, dentists, police officers, lawyers, judges, military staff, farmers, and fishers. However, they are not mainstream fathers, mothers, aunts, uncles, grandparents, friends, and neighbours. They are a defined, secretive, and manipulative group of organized criminals. Other women besides Sara explained that perpetrating individuals participated in organized group torture "parties." It did not matter the country of origin, the women all told similar stories. They unsilenced their truths.

Society. The outer three rings include revictimizations. We observed individuals not connected to "the family" could successfully victimize or abuse Sara. For example, in her efforts to make friends, Sara often explained she bought things these individuals asked for, knowing this placed her in debt and crisis. This financial abuse also involved emotional and psychological abuse, causing conditions of neglect. Sara had no money to buy essentials. Sara had a "boyfriend" she let into her apartment whenever he rang her buzzer. He inflicted sexualized violence. He knew she was dissociative, took advantage of her vulnerability and exposed her to verbal abuse and pornographic images. As shown, these two examples involved forms of abuse—financial, neglect, verbal, emotional, psychological, sexualized violence, and exposure to pornography. Sara was vulnerable and others took harmful advantage of her.

The abuse in the power ring refers to how the health care and legal systems fail to recognize non-State torture as a specific crime and ignore the care required for a woman so victimized to recover. These failures are about systemic abuse of power.

Healthy caring is shared in our book and offers the knowledge we have developed since 1993, as an option for others to consider.

CHAPTER 6

KITCHEN-TABLE RESEARCH

─────────

DO WE MAKE SENSE OR NOT?

While supporting Sara as she fought her way through her emotional terror to get her horrifying disclosures out, we often said to her and each other, "This must be the worst memory." We soon gave this up. The worst never ended. Every woman's story of non-State torture victimization is always the worst. The worst will never end until national and global societies actively deal with prevention. To do this, societies must admit and name non-State torture, and make and enforce a law that will hold non-State torturers accountable for the torture crimes they commit.

In our early years of supporting Sara, the social willingness to name Sara's victimization torture was rejected. We believed Sara. Society did not. This was the conflict. Academic literature was hesitant to name torture as a specific form of violence committed against women and the girl child in the domestic or private sphere. We had no such hesitation. However, we knew we were surrounded by risks in the way we were supporting Sara. There was the possibility of discrediting our caring work, or Sara's telling not believed, and subsequently Sara not surviving. We needed to find an academic grounding for our work.

Fritjof Capra's 1988 writing[6] offered a scientific grounding for our developing knowledge, theories, and model-making framework. The historical traditional scientific method, Capra said, did not deal with the values and qualities of human experiences. He concluded that knowledge development was scientific if it satisfied three fundamental criteria: (1) it was based on systematic observations that were consistent albeit limited, (2) that these systematic observations could be transformed into appropriate model-making that presented a consistent network of logical and interconnected concepts based on observed subjective experiences, and (3) that the developing knowledge illustrated patterns of shared experiences. Our knowledge of supporting Sara was developing, filled with subjective observations that we transferred into model-making.

As the years unfolded, Sara's recovery progressed which validated our caring approach. *"Caring is the key"* became Sara's motto. Our expanding knowledge, often shaped into models, helped us undo her life-threatening psychological chaos, understand her victimizations, and respond effectively to her traumatized responses. Could these observations utilizing the ritual abuse-torture model capture the subjective ordeals of others? Had other Nova Scotian women suffered the same ordeals as Sara? Would our emerging knowledge and our model of ritual abuse-torture make sense to them? We needed to learn whether we made sense or not. This would determine whether we met Capra's three fundamental criteria; this would inform our future work.

Capra recognized that the persons doing the scientific process carry their own thoughts, values, and perceptions into their work. Being female and feminist we consider that patriarchy attaches human inequality to

6   Capra's concepts broadened the framework of scientific knowledge to mean that the two elements of systematic observation and model-making were involved in understanding reality by dealing with values and the subjective qualities of human experiences.

women and girls, and promotes misogynistic discrimination that devalues women's herstorical and present-day work. Patriarchy also invisibilizes non-State torture of women and girls, in society and law. These beliefs inform our process. To promote transparency, we share being born into families where spousal violence—male violence against a woman, our fathers' violence against our mothers—has influenced how we practice.

Jeanne's Reflection

Patriarchal oppression and discrimination were real to me. When my mother left my father for the last time, I was about nine. My mother found work that paid around $850 annually. She worked six days a week with Friday and Saturday being very long days. This meant being raised in poverty, living in two rooms, and being a latch-key older child responsible for my younger brother. Besides being paid less for her work, my mother was regularly greeted with sexist put-downs. Like the time two community women, who had never visited before, suddenly appeared. My mother had saved enough money to buy a fridge; the women's reason for visiting was to suggest to my mother she must have prostituted her-Self to afford to buy the fridge. I can still see my mother physically walking them immediately out the door. Women do practice patriarchal misogyny. These experiences learned as a young girl have influenced my work.

Linda's Reflection

What influenced my life was resisting attending the Roman Catholic church or attending a religious-based school, insisting instead on attending public school. I did not agree with the religious school teaching that I was superior to other children because of my religion. As a teenager I tried to escape my lower-middle-class life of living in family violence. I ran to the street trying to find friends to connect with. In my twenties, while attending a folk festival, that night I looked for help to find my tent. I was so drunk and drugged I could hardly see. A long-time male "friend" attempted to rape me after he "helped" me back to my tent. I fought back his misogyny and he stopped. All my experiences of resisting misogyny and patriarchy kept me believing that resistance brings success.

Capra's Influence

We carried Capra's three criteria into our work aware of the influence our experiences had on our perceptions, thoughts, and values. For instance, to immerse our-Self in the subjective, violent ordeals Sara was disclosing was not totally foreign. Just as we were driven to understand and heal from our childhoods of witnessing our fathers' violence, we were likewise compelled to understand and give meaning to the grievous reality Sara was unfolding. However, we needed to attain Capra's three fundamental criteria for our work to be "scientific."

Sara's recovery kept progressing. By 1998, we thought Sara could not be the only woman in Nova Scotia who had survived family-based torture and sexualized human trafficking. Seeking answers to this we quietly shared by word of mouth that we sought contact with Nova Scotian women who considered they had suffered family-based torture. We needed to know if our ritual abuse-torture model made sense to others. Would it describe the MO of other perpetrators and their victimization of women or women when they were children? To check if our developing knowledge made sense meant our work needed to be evaluated by others. Our efforts grew into our kitchen-table herstories research project.

KITCHEN-TABLE HERSTORIES

We respectfully introduce Carrie, Hope, Jessie, Kate, Phoenix's friends, and Jane. They responded to our call seeking connection with women who believed they had suffered torture within relationships. The women invited us to sit with them as they shared the details of their herstories. This began our 1998 kitchen-table research project. Choosing pseudonyms, they consented to our sharing their herstories.

Self-funded, our work progressed slowly. We were often asked, "If you are not making money, why are you doing this?" Answering was and remains simple—we cared. Role-modeling for our children the meaning of taking an ethical stance was important and the right thing to do. We carried our values into our work as supported by Capra's premise.

When meeting the women, we did not tape-record their telling or take notes, we simply listened intensely (Sarson & MacDonald, 2008). Guiding the kitchen-table research interviews was respecting the women's ability to cope with their telling, the duration of each specific interview, and the time required for them to recoup between interviews. The shortest interview lasted several hours. Another lasted half a day; other interviews required numerous days or several weeks. One woman's story unfolded over several years. Twenty-seven hours of telephone conversations took place and many emails were exchanged.

After each meeting, we immediately drove to a quiet, private place to handwrite what we had comprehended when listening to the women's herstories. When the weather was warm, most often we sat in our car before we drove home. This was our practice until the day we both fell asleep while driving. Waking first, Linda woke Jeanne, who was at the wheel. It had been an exhausting afternoon of being present with a woman as she disclosed the horrors she had survived. We knew women needed their rest after disclosing. Obviously so did we, after such intense listening. On this day we underestimated our mental fatigue. From this could-have-been-deadly-incident, we learned to take pillows when travelling to meetings in warm weather. After writing our notes and before driving home, we took short, restful naps in the car.

The next step was typing our comprehension notes of the women's subjective life ordeals. Because they could not write and tell at the same time, our notes were their journals. The arrangement was that we listened to the women and after the meeting we wrote notes of what we remembered and understood. At our next meeting, we shared these notes with the women; they read and corrected them. With every returning visit we took the women their revised journals. The last meeting was for closure. We left the women with a copy of their typed journal if they wanted one. The women were then shown our ritual abuse-torture model. We asked if the model described their victimizations. For two women, the model did not fit because they had not suffered ritualized abuse and torture. For the women for whom the ritual abuse-torture model fit, they expressed relief that the chaos of the many forms of violence they suffered could be organized and explained as torture victimizations. Also validated in the women's stories were the forms of non-State torture listed in our patriarchal divide model, figure 8. We share the women's herstorical journals in this chapter and elsewhere in the book as their first-person accounts.

The women who spoke to us at their kitchen tables were aware of their childhood victimizations. They had present-day support. One woman said she was occasionally stalked and sometimes physically assaulted by her family. She reported this to the police but no action was ever taken. We begin sharing the women's stories by introducing Carrie.

Carrie's Story

Carrie was in her early 50s, married with one adult child. She grew up with five siblings. Her father worked as a merchant seaman, then later as a commissionaire at a large plant in her hometown. She explained: "I lived within three realities at once. Our family community face reality, our family insider face reality, and my father's secret relationship with me reality."

Carrie said her father was "loved" in the community. The family insider face, though, was filled with her father's alcoholic rages. Remembering the episode of her father holding a gun to her mother's head, Carrie said, "He pulled the trigger…as I speak with you, I can still hear myself screaming… I couldn't stop."

> My father's secret relationship with me was horrendously different. I can still see my father…raping my small little body…I was six years old…he stuffed the pyjamas with little black and white dogs printed on them into my mouth…when he raped me…I remember blood running down my little legs. That night is vividly clear (Sarson & MacDonald, 2005).
>
> But, how old I was when the group ritualized torture started is not as clear. I sometimes think these may have started earlier, between the ages of four to six years. I had two pregnancies while I was still a child. I remember being so scared; I didn't understand what was happening to me. I was about 13 when the ritualized torture stopped.

The sexualized torture Carrie described involved an organized "more formal group" gathering. It included, she said, her father and about 12 like-minded friends, both men and women, including two doctors, one lawyer, and one teacher. Carrie was clear her mother was not involved.

Describing the group's organized ritualized patterns, Carrie began:

> I'm shivering and I'm feeling so cold just having to recall these hor-rific experiences. I was tied to a stand made of wooden planks. Often another little girl, Margaret, was also similarly tied up. There were two containers of blood used to smear over me and Margaret. They gave us enemas…The adults forced me to choose what to do with it, either I smeared it on Margaret or I'd be forced to eat it. I would always choose to smear it on Margaret, but then I knew Margaret would be forced to eat it. There was no way I could win. Either

decision left me feeling I had harmed Margaret. I felt so guilty, so ashamed, so humiliated, so terrified.

We, the other children and I, were forced to drink wine until we were very drunk, then the adults would laugh at us.

Then there was the stone house with the swinging gate in front! I remember my father walking me through that gate, so many times, leading, forcing, dragging me into that stone house…it was like being dragged into hell!…This is where my father took me to be raped. I got so I would just lie on the bed waiting for the old man to almost choke me to near-death with his penis. My father and other men and women would stand around the bed, watch, and laugh. There are no words to describe their sound, the tone of their laughter, and feelings I felt. Their laughter still haunts me today…I can still hear their laughter ringing inside my head…inside my ears!

Carrie spoke about the chilling, threatening experience of her father taking her and her pet kitten, Brownie, for a walk to the lake in the woods. She described how her father forced her to drown Brownie. Carrie explained her father told her she was never to tell her mother or he would kill her like she'd "killed Brownie." Carrie said, "I never told."

As a child I was constantly being told I was bad, bad, bad. This message, like all the others, seems locked inside my head, inside of me…Logically, I know I'm a good person…Being told I was bad, over and over again, also made me feel and believe it was my fault I was being ritually tortured. This sense of emotional guilt made me feel as if I was floating in the deepest sea of shame and blame, so deep it shamed my very soul.

As a child I felt my father took my heart, my body and my soul, he left me to rot in the bottom of the hole of agony. A hell hole!

How could my father and his friends, who loved and derived so much pleasure from doing what they did, ever have stopped their behaviour? I doubt such people can stop.

As children there was no one to tell…who would have listened to us…who was willing to listen…prepared to listen?

In her storytelling, it became clear Carrie suffered sexualized violence when raped by her father; in Canadian law, rape is legally considered sexual assault. Carrie also witnessed the spousal violence suffered by her mother. This, too, is legally defined as assault. When her father took Carrie to the organized secretive group, she was tortured and trafficked. The ritual abuse-torture model lists both abuse and torture crimes because this is how Sara verbalized her ordeals. Carrie also verbalized the ordeals she suffered in this way.

Carrie's father terrified and horrified her both at home and when trafficking her to his like-minded torture group. It must be acknowledged that Carrie lived every day with the realization she could be tortured. From our perspective, we believe that "abuse" needs to be considered torture when children live in a relational environment where they are subjected to torture perpetrated by a parent, so their victimization and traumatization responses will be clearly understood. Carrie said the model explained her childhood victimizations but asked what healthy caring was.

Hope's Story

Hope, like Carrie, was married. She was in her 40s with young adult children. She said she married at 19 to escape "the family." Hope's explanation of her use of the term "the family" was the same as Sara's explanation. It referred to their biological families and the like-minded perpetrators with whom their biological families had links. Additionally, like Carrie, Hope began by exposing three layers of family relationships. Hope and Carrie did not know each other; they lived in separate communities. Sara did not indicate knowing Hope or Carrie and she lived in a different community from them.

Hope explained (Sarson & MacDonald 2009b):

> My father was a veteran of the Second World War. He told me his job was removing the wounded and the dead from the battlefields. He worked in a large hospital as a care-provider while my mother worked in the home until I was about twelve, then it became my job to look after my siblings because my mother decided she'd also go to work as a care-provider. To the outside community, our family probably looked like a good family. The family went to church with the outsiders and my father bowled three times a week with the men in the community. I tried never to miss Sunday school.
>
> My mother focused on keeping a good public face. Outsiders referred to my mother as the "Mother Hen" because when they were around my mother would be touching and hugging us. What a great job she did of tricking the outsiders! But to comprehend my life within the family I need to explain two other levels of reality—the insider day-by-day relationships and the family nighttime activities. Members of the family included my parents, my mother's parents, other parents, and extended others. The family has many "relatives."
>
> It never occurred to me to run away from the family when I was young. There was no reason to, was there? My life in the family was normal, wasn't it? Even though I didn't like what was happening and fought back in many ways, even though I tried to show and tell others what was happening to me, people didn't respond to help get me out. I was trapped.
>
> When my mother did serve me food it was on a small dinner plate and if I couldn't eat it all she'd cover the leftovers with waxed paper then serve it to me cold at the next meal. I'd have to eat this before I was allowed any hot food, by then the hot food was usually all gone. And sometimes the choice was dog poop…served hot or cold…cold was better. Worms also did in a pinch.

Hope asked us to accompany her outdoors to walk her dog. She said it would be easier for her to tell what she wanted us to hear. We walked.

Hope talked. We listened. That is when she disclosed she was fed "dog poop" (Sarson & MacDonald, 2012).

Hope spoke of the crazy-making uncertainty and chaos she grew up in:

> A neighbour, Mrs. Smith, she'd come over to our house and ask my mother where I was. My mother would tell her I was in bed but I think Mrs. Smith suspected something wasn't right. I'm sure she would never have thought I was down in our basement with my hands tied together, a rope around my neck, in a cage hanging from the ceiling. My father used to put me there, at about six or six-thirty at night, with the rope placed around my neck in such a way that if I caused the cage to swing too much the noose would tighten around my neck. I used to try to get the cage to swing…Swinging helped to ease being trapped in my cage. Often my black cloak was thrown over the cage to make me even more disorientated and shut off. Sometimes before putting me into the cage, my father threw food onto the basement dirt floor, forcing me to eat like an animal or sometimes he'd put canned dog food in a white china saucer and force me to eat it like a dog. There was a bucket of pee he'd force me to drink…My caging stopped when I was about 11 or 12 (Sarson & MacDonald, 2008).

> Besides my father, my mother also sexually abused me. Being abused by women, my mother, my aunt, others, has its own terror… feelings of skin-on-skin, trapped, sucked in, surrounded, pulled into a drowning crack of an earthquake…terror…vaginal fluids…body odours…terror. That's what it was like…feeling…being consumed.

> Beatings for not being toilet trained just progressed into a routine of almost daily beatings by my mother, accompanied by her bizarre laughter…of pleasure. I was whipped and strapped mostly in places that didn't show the bruising. Beatings were given without reasons, they just were. Besides the regular nighttime beatings that were part of the family behaviours, we also had special routines, rituals and ceremonies; at least that's what the family called their ordeals of torture and horror…routines for your own good.

Rituals started in the homes of wee infants. Being orally raped started, I believe, when I was just a wee one—just like the little babies I witnessed having their eyes taped shut before they were forced to suckle the man's penis. Many men orally raped me, including my grandfather…I just accepted this behaviour and the other things he did as normal. That is, up until I was about 10 years old when he anally raped me. I was so devastated, so hurt in all ways. I remember feeling my grandfather had broken my heart. My grandfather used to give me "Tums" for my sore stomach, he said. I don't remember having a sore stomach but I took the Tums like he said. They made me so sleepy I'd have to go lay down and sleep or I remember laying down with my grandfather. I wonder now what he was giving me?

By the time I was eight I had been forced into the child pornography and child prostitution business and paid $2.00 each time I worked as a child prostitute. When I got home with my $2.00 I had to give my father a blow job and pay him $2.00 or he threatened to starve my siblings. What choice did I have?

When I started to understand my abusers and torturers, especially the pornographers and prostitutors who got pleasure when I cried, got off on seeing me suffer, I resolved never to cry again. The "Black-cloaked Man," a minister, was…responsible…for drugging me…for the most horrific acts of child pornography involving groups and animals—dogs. Led into a room for pornography…flashing lights, cameras, the man, men, dogs…oh such pain, degradation, deprivation…feces, urine, smells, taste, sounds…silence…dead silence… overwhelmed I felt like I was no more! When they were finished with me I was taken into another room to be with a man with kind eyes who wanted me to eat and do "sex" stuff.

At about 13 or 14 I was pregnant and "the family" took my pregnancy. I guess they called my abortion a ceremony. By the way, just like the outsiders have their rituals and ceremonies so too did the family. And, the preparations always seemed to include a clear warm drink from a Miracle Whip jar which always made me feel like I was floating and tired. After this ceremony I somehow fought back and never had to go to another. You couldn't win in the family because even though they let me go, they told me my sister would now suffer because of my fighting back. This left me burdened with horrendous guilt. How did I manage to cope; how does anyone manage to cope with such overwhelming atrocities? What kind of adults were they?

Being a child of the family meant I was overwhelmed in every way possible. As the terror and horror grew, when my degradation was so profound, there were times I didn't even feel human; I felt like an animal, I felt like a pile of shit. I was only a thing to my torturers so "I" didn't matter to them.

My overwhelming chaos and confusion made explaining my life almost impossible. I didn't understand my feelings or what was being done to me. Growing up and coping with experiences of ritual abuse-torture meant developing many ways of coping. Telling my story is a vital achievement in my healing, replacing fantasy with the horrific reality of evil human behaviour.

Hope, like Sara, lived in a home with parents who were both involved in the torture she suffered and the "schooling" conditioning she endured. We learned that non-State torturers not only inflict similar acts of torture, they often use similar language.

Sharing the ritual abuse-torture model with Hope at our last meeting brought this response:

When Jeanne and Linda showed me their model of ritual abuse-torture my first reaction was to fall in love with it. I couldn't believe someone had been able to organize my experiences in the family. I simply fell in love with it.

Kate and Jessie's Stories

Kate and Jessie are sisters. Kate was divorced; Jessie was married. Both had children. They lived in different communities so they told their stories separately. Kate was eight years older than Jessie, who was the youngest child in their family. Although they grew up in the same family system, the details of their victimizations were significantly different. Their grandfather was the prime perpetrator. Therefore, the variables of their grandfather's age, illness, and death impacted their descriptions of the forms of victimizations he inflicted. This insight alone brings into focus the reality that siblings can have very different experiences within the same family system, thus very different experiential memories.

Piecing together Kate and Jessie's descriptions of their grandfather's community face, this emerged:

> He was well respected, had a position of authority within the community, and was considered a good guy. He was a Nova Scotian constable of some kind; he travelled in the province, issued subpoenas, and had a gun but no uniform. He didn't smoke.

Kate and Jessie acknowledged and respected each other's distinctly different family-based victimization stories. For example, Jessie explained that seven years prior to speaking with us she had believed Kate when Kate told her about the "ritualized sexual torture within our family...there were also people outside the family involved." Both, however, disclosed their grandfather had sexually abused them. Kate explained she had also suffered sexualized abuse perpetrated by her father and a brother. It was their father, Kate said, who drove and dropped her off at the group sexualized torture gatherings led by her grandfather.

Jessie explained the violence that occurred inside the family and to her:

> My father was an alcoholic. He had been a sergeant in the army. He belonged to the United Church. My father was often in difficulty with the law and even though he spoke of how he hated his father he would always call him for help. My grandfather would do favours for him because he knew people and got my father out of trouble.
>
> My mother was Catholic and totally husband-focused. She emotionally neglected me; my father verbally abused me. He had alcoholic rages and because there were always guns for hunting around our house, things got pretty scary. When I was three years old I remember my father holding the gun to my mother's head, threatening her. I thought he was going to kill her.
>
> I don't remember exactly how little I was when my grandfather started sexually abusing me…but I do remember some things happened somewhere between 12 and 18 months of age. It seems as if many things happened when I sat on his knee when he was in his chair by the rolltop desk in front of the window. I was in diapers when he finger raped me. He penetrated my vagina with his finger and used his tongue to kiss me. He was so quick.
>
> I believe the adults in the family had a code of silence about my grandfather's sexually abusive behaviour. As I grew up we, the kids talked openly about sitting on our grandfather's knee and what that meant. We'd say among ourselves, "Grampie is a dirty old man, a dirty old man." They'd say, "He just loves children."
>
> My grandfather had the ritual of taking me alone in the car to get ice cream then sexually abusing me. The sexual abuse stopped when I was about four or five. My grandfather got sick; but even in his dying bed he still tried to sexually abuse me.

Kate's Story

Kate recalled that the sexualized group torture victimization led and executed by her grandfather began when she was an infant and continued until she was seven. She said she had dissociated from the horror. This left her with a "deep sense of little or no physical safety. As a child learning I could do nothing to stop what was happening to me or others…knowing and learning no one else was going to help me."

When describing her victimizations, Kate said that initially her memories "came as a fraction or fractions of an image and this resulted in a period of confusion. I was…unfamiliar with this way of remembering."

> The way I survived…as a child was dissociating into nothingness, feeling nothingness. [Such as when], I was on a table and at the same time I could see myself on the table from a distance. I watched as my body moved in pain. I could see pain in my arms, legs, neck, and face. I didn't feel the pain…My arm was made to do things—bad things and hurtful things. My arm was not attached to my body, to me. I thought I was bad and I was confused. I left my arm on the table and went to a place far away that felt safe.

After describing these dissociative survival responses, Kate said her intrusive memories and dissociation reached a peak when she remembered being "surrounded by German shepherd dogs."

> They were barking and somehow restrained. There was a woman (unknown) and…[other family members] with me…My [female relative] and the woman are held down on the ground. The dogs were over them. There are ropes and handcuffs. Men rape my… [relative]. I see her eyes and she doesn't see, although her eyes are open. I was then held down. Hands and objects did things to hurt me. My grandfather gave orders to these people and to me…I left my body.

Kate spoke of her grandfather and others terrorizing her to never tell what they were doing to her.

Having the privilege to hear both Kate and Jessie describe their family-based victimizations, we understood that although in the same family system, they suffered different forms of violence. Kate suffered ritual abuse-torture; Jessie's herstorical victimization memory was of sexualized abuse or assault. However, both Kate and Jessie described that their victimizations began when they were infants. For Kate, the ritual abuse-torture model fit; for Jessie, it did not.

About Siblings. When supporting other women we considered the reality that one girl child may suffer forms of non-State torture while another female sibling may not. Could it be the MO of these torturer-traffickers to only "safely" dominate and control the organized group victimization of a single daughter at one time? Was this a way to ensure they could condition one child to never tell and, therefore, never be exposed?

Women frequently describe how torturers disrupted sibling relationships. They pitted siblings against each other by scapegoating the daughter they tortured and trafficked, treating the other as "special." Sometimes jealousy occurred if one child was treated as uniquely special. Male siblings were victimized when forced into sexualized behaviours inflicted onto their sisters. This fractured the siblings' ability to be of support to each other. Women speak of how these relationships imposed various levels of fear, terror, powerlessness, aloneness, isolation, and hopelessness.

Phoenix's story

Phoenix's friends wanted to disclose what she told them about the ritual abuse-torture family she had been born into. They wanted their painful burden of secrecy to end. Phoenix had attended a Self-help group for Adult Children of Alcoholics, as had her three friends. They spoke in memory of

Phoenix following her death. Phoenix wanted to share her story but tragically died of a terminal illness before she was able to do so.

Phoenix told her friends her father was a railway worker and her mother stayed at home. Her parents attended a Christian church and belonged to local community groups. Phoenix graduated from high school. She had two siblings.

Phoenix shared that both her parents were alcoholics who verbally and physically abused her. Her father, Phoenix told her friends, had sexually assaulted her. Describing the organized group's ritualized patterns of exploitation, Phoenix told her friends the group involved extended family members and her parents' like-minded female and male friends. The dominant perpetrators were her mother, father, and uncle. The group's victimizations, Phoenix described, involved being tied up in various ways, being torture-raped, buried in a hole in the mud floor of the basement of her parents' home, and bestiality. Phoenix expressed to her friends feeling full of anger and constant terror she would be killed if she disclosed the existence of the group and their actions. Underlying her life was her ever-present terror of evil. Phoenix explained she thought her victimization by this group, whose members blended easily into the community, ended when she was seven. However, her friends said Phoenix admitted being compelled to go to the group's gathering when she was 18 to support her sibling. This was the age when Phoenix attempted suicide.

From the stories told by her friends, it appeared Phoenix grew up in an environment similar to that described by Carrie, Hope, Kate, and Sara. Terror accompanied Phoenix in life; it was with her when she was diagnosed with a terminal illness. Terrified and unable to feel safe during nighttime hours, a friend slept in bed with Phoenix when her husband was away. While she was dying, her uncle, whom she identified as one of the torturers, tried to go to her hospital bedside—Phoenix's husband kicked him out. Her friends said the model of ritual abuse-torture definitely described the victimizations Phoenix had disclosed to them.

Jane's Story

Married at 21, Jane was now divorced. She had adult children. Growing up in a family of violence, she explained:

> It was normal for my father to threaten my mother with knives…I watched him beat her. I watched as he burned her clothes, listened to him rant that women were meant to be kept in their place, in the home, and not go out. "No clothes! No getting out!" that was his motto…My mother used to climb into bed with me, to escape my father's drunken sexual demands. Sometimes this worked for her, other times it didn't. When my father came looking for her he'd climb into our beds forcing sex right there in the bed with us kids. To cope I tried to pretend I was asleep…I can still see their last fight, my father wielding a knife, my mother upsetting the kitchen table to block his raging attack.

Jane said her mother fled the house and never returned. The night her father raped Jane, she was 14 and Jane said she sobbed. At 15, "It happened again—my uncle sexually abused me three times. Forcing me to masturbate him. Sexual abuse felt terrible. I felt terrible." Jane explained how confused and frightened she was growing up.

In her marriage, there were times she was "*absolutely terrorized*," describing how her husband pushed her down onto a cement sidewalk when she was 14 weeks pregnant. Jane miscarried. Into the eighth month of her third pregnancy, her husband "attacked—whipped my stomach with a skipping rope."

She said physical beatings left her left arm looking like "raspberry jam":

> He pounded me into the wall…slapped me when I refused to use vibrators, have anal, oral sex, and sex with dogs…Even when I was

very sick in the hospital [he] would visit…forcing me to have sex in the hospital bed…Fucking bitch, whore, [and] no good are the names [he] screamed at me. I feared for my life especially…when he hunted for me with his hunting rifle…It took me 21 years to get out…I left with the help of a very caring male social worker.

On reviewing the ritual abuse-torture model, although it did not fit, Jane said, "I felt tortured in my relationship, however…I'd say I wasn't tortured—I was abused, beaten, controlled, and terrorized! Repeatedly." Did Jane experience some acts of violence that were beyond abuse—that ought to be considered human cruelty, brutality, and torture?

Three Layers of Family Criminality. All the women who shared their herstories explained they wanted to expose the layered complexities of violence perpetrators can and do inflict within family systems. They hoped their telling might help others.

Carrie, Hope, Kate, and Phoenix's friends clearly defined three layers of family organization which involved: (a) presenting a community face that appeared friendly and engaging; (b) violence within the biological family system; and (c) like-minded relationships which they referred to as the "inner circle." During the organized "inner circle" torture gatherings, criminality with actions of human evil increased, sometimes expressed in ritual dramas. This relational layering is pointed out in figure 12.

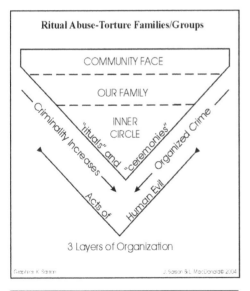

Fig. 12: Three layers of family organization

It illustrates that if society's structures and institutions are to act to protect children, the policies and practices must be informed by the layers of violence that can exist within family relationships. For us, we began the kitchen-table research project conversations to address head-on whether we and the model of ritual abuse-torture made sense. It did for Carrie, Hope, Kate, and for the friends of Phoenix. A lasting image and gift we carried away from these relationships was watching one woman rub her hand ever so gently over the surface of the ritual abuse-torture model, absorbing and embracing its validation of her lived reality.

What were we to do next?

BORDER CROSSING

We not only believed Sara, we now believed Carrie, Hope, Kate, and the disclosures described by Phoenix's friends. Their herstories were of similar victimizations, including speaking of acts of human evil. It was now the year 2000. Having achieved validation in our kitchen-table research conversations, we again needed to risk stepping further afield.

Linda's Reflection—My Turning Point

Once Jeanne and I had developed the ritual abuse-torture model and completed our participatory kitchen-table research, it was time to test this work with a larger audience who might identify as having survived such torture. Would it make sense to them?

In 2003, I learned of a US conference where we could present our findings. The next thing I knew, Jeanne and I were on a plane with our model in hand. I can remember sitting on the plane, excited about this next part of our journey, when Jeanne said, "If the audience does not agree with our work I don't know what that will mean for where we go next." This thought had never entered my mind. I call this Jeanne's "plane bomb technique," which has occurred in our other journeys. She was right! Would a rejection of our ritual abuse-torture or RAT model by a larger audience mean the end of our work? It could! My body and emotions went immediately into high stress.

When we landed, we boarded the hotel shuttle. Another woman attending the conference introduced her-Self as Jeanette Westbrook. She kept looking at us very intently and with a questioning gaze. Jeanne and I calmly chatted with her about what we would be presenting. We felt Jeanette was really checking us out to see if we were safe people. Jeanette told us later she had deliberately found out when we were landing and went to the airport to figure out who were these two women from Canada.

Our presentation was scheduled for the second day. I could feel my back seizing up moment by moment as I sat all day asking my-Self: "Will the audience agree with our work or reject it?" I poured my-Self into bed that night and by morning my back was so stiff and sore I could hardly pull my-Self out of bed. Jeanne seemed so very calm and said she would accept whatever would come. Not me. I was so worried our work would stop and then what would happen?

The time came to share our human rights framework that included the RAT model. It was a resounding success. The audience gave us a standing ovation. I was so relieved I felt like crying. Jeanette came up immediately to tell us she felt validated. She loved that we were standing to say that ritual abuse-torture was a violation of her human rights. I knew then Jeanne and I had passed the test, even Jeanette's airport screening test. How exciting! Jeanette became a friend and colleague.

Looking back, I realize this was the first public conference where Jeanne and I shared the results of our first nine years of work. It was a turning point. It launched us onto the global stage. I will forever be grateful to those who showed us this vital trust.

Jeanne's Response

As closely as Linda and I worked together, I had not realized verbalizing my perspective was experienced by Linda as my "plane bomb technique." Sitting on the plane, headed into a particular event where the outcome is unknown, I had no other distractions except thinking about the event. Obviously, we were carrying two different emotional perspectives going to this conference. As Capra said, we each carry our personal perspectives into the research we do.

When Linda and I are together with Jeanette, we often have some delightful moments of reminiscing about the day she spied on us, the Canadian women.

Presenting the Ritual Abuse-Torture Model

In 2003, delivering the ritual abuse-torture model at the US conference was a border crossing. Approximately 85 people attended. They identified as having survived various forms of victimizations, or were supporters of an adult child, a partner, friends, or professionals. The rate of evaluations returned was 29.5 percent; 80 percent were female, 12 percent male, and 8 percent identified as transgendered. From these responses, we learned our presentation was 100 percent helpful. Those who responded said torture victimization occurred, that it was a violation of human rights, a form of organized crime, and that our model helped to identify and organize the MO of the torturers. One of the evaluation questions we asked was whether the torturers' MO tactics were expressions of human evil actions. Ninety-six percent said "yes." We received these examples of positive written feedback statements:

- Keep saying this is a crime! It does take away stigma and labeling.
- I realize now it is torture and a violation of rights. You broke my denial! Abuse is a more benign word than torture but torture is the correct term for what I experienced.

- Brilliant, helpful, long-needed model that can be utilized by multi-disciplinary workers, professionals, courts, women's centres, [and] by grassroots survivor movements.

We closed our presentation by saying we had a dream of wanting to present at the UN because we realized torture by private individuals and groups was not named as a specific human rights violation. Unbeknownst to us, Dana Raphael was in the audience. She worked in a non-governmental organization (NGO). It had membership status that permitted participation in the UN Commission on the Status of Women (CSW) sessions, held every year at the UN Headquarters in New York City. Following our presentation, Dana introduced her-Self. She told us she had the authority to invite us to participate in the UN CSW session.

Jeanne's Reflections

Decades ago, my cousin took me to the UN in New York City. I remember looking up at the building and thinking how I would one day like to work there. This "dream" got lost. I was graduating from nursing; I needed a job; I lived in Nova Scotia, Canada. Life events and adventures filled the years. This decades-old memory of a "dream" jumped into me as I prepared the overhead slides for our presentation; it hopped onto the closing slide. It, like Sara, would change the course of my life, Linda's life, and the lives of our families. They would see us travel the world in our activism and push for the global recognition that it is a human right of women and girls of all ages not to be subjected to torture by non-State actors.

Another Conference in 2004

At another conference in 2004, our presentation focused on torturers as human traffickers. Following our presentation, we facilitated a focus group side-event discussion on human trafficking. We received evaluative feedback from 38 respondents which represented 70 percent of the attendees. We posed three yes or no questions, asking whether they considered:

Survivors (n = 18)	YES	NO
Torturers seen as traffickers	55.5%	44%
Child as trafficked victim	66%	33%
Adult as victim	50%	50%
Professional experience (n = 8)		
Torturers seen as traffickers	62.5%	37.5%
Child as trafficked victim	75%	25%
Adult as victim	75%	25%
Others: Supporters, partners (n = 11)		
Torturers seen as traffickers	36%	63.6%
Child as trafficked victim	45%	54.5%
Adult as victim	36%	63.6%

Fig. 13: Feedback and evaluation 2004

(a) that these torturers were also human traffickers, (b) that a child who was taken or transported to the group gatherings was a victim of human trafficking, and (c) whether a woman or man who is "used," exploited, and victimized is also a victim of human trafficking. These questions correspond to the section labeled "exploitation & other criminal acts" on the ritual abuse-torture model. The feedback and evaluation responses are shown in figure 13. Apparently, the invisibility of these torturers as perpetrators of human trafficking of adults and children was a concept supporters and partners had not fully considered before.

That same year, 2004, we presented to a criminology class at the University of Indiana. Twenty-seven students attended. They provided feedback about the ritual abuse-torture model. Their responses informed us the model had organized and identified the torturers' MO. This was, they said, a paradigm shift for them. They said the torturers' MO revealed that such groups perpetrated a form of organized crime, including human trafficking. Students said they agreed these were human rights violations. And 24 considered the torturers' actions were expressions of human evil. Overall, 26 students, with one declining to answer, said the presentation was beneficial.

We have never looked back. We have never again debated with each other whether our developing knowledge made "scientific" sense to others. We own our developing knowing. We believe Capra would agree!

CHAPTER 7
DECONSTRUCTING WOMEN'S EVILISM ANXIETY, FEAR, AND TERROR

────────

ANXIETY, FEAR, AND TERROR: TORTURERS' ACTIONS OF HUMAN EVIL

Often when we do presentations, the audience easily defines torturers as perpetrators of acts of human evil. Sara, Carrie, Hope, Kate, and Phoenix's friends voiced that the family-based torturers committed actions of human evil. This has been true for other women we have supported since 1998. This persistent reference to the torturers' actions of human evil illustrates a pattern of women's shared personal or subjective ordeals. In other words, women were telling similar stories about being subjected to actions of human evil. This process was consistent with Capra's scientific fundamentals as discussed in the previous chapter.

Realizing women so tortured needed direct conversations about their concepts and emotional responses to the perpetrators' actions of human evil, we asked if they experienced evilism anxiety, fear, and terror. Women welcomed this naming. It offered them the opportunity to tell all.

Working with Sara was intense, and required deconstructing the torture-based evilism conditioning she was forced to internalize. This blocked her recovery. It required us to dig deep into the need to confront her values, perceptions, and responses to the concept of human evil actions.

Model of Evilism Anxiety, Fear, and Terror

As a result of our conversations with women, we developed the evilism model shown in figure 14. It names six common destructive thematic issues relating to women's subjective beliefs or perceptions about their internalized evilism anxiety, fear, and terror. These thematic issues were:

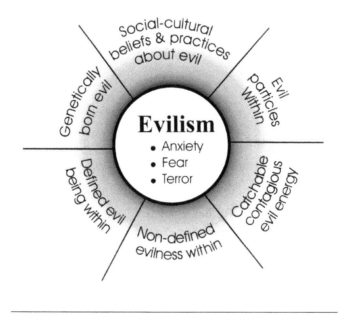

Fig. 14: Model of Evilism Anxiety, Fear, and Terror

1. Social-cultural beliefs and practices related to evil

2. Evil particles within

3. Catchable or contagious evil energy

4. Non-defined evilism within

5. Defined evil being within

6. Genetically born evil

In the following paragraphs we discuss these six thematic issues and share women's detailed ordeals.

Carrie: Evilism Anxiety, Fear, and Terror

When I was in my 20s…I mentioned to a lady…I was having night terrors related to evil…the next time she came to visit me she simply told me we were going somewhere.

We ended up at the manse where the pastor and his wife were waiting for us…I became frightened and stated I wanted to go home. I was trapped…a very large woman blocked the doorway. Surrounded by the pastor's wife, also a huge woman, and the pastor, who was overpowering physically, who with a bible in his hand came towards me, telling me that I had demons inside of me. Coming at me… placing their hands on my shoulders overwhelmed and terrified me. I fainted. I remember the feelings that came…I felt like I was six years old again…facing evil-doers.

When I came to I was lying on the floor with the three of them surrounding me. The pastor was the only one speaking, asking, "Do you see the demons coming out of you? Do you feel the devils coming out of you?" I was so terrified I said, "Yes." I felt less than a speck of dirt. I felt as if I was less than nothing. Feeling powerless…All my evilism fears were exploding.

Spiritually, my pain was extreme…When I got home I was so nauseated I vomited…telling my husband I had the flu. I know now that wasn't true. My responses were directly related to the intensity of my fear and terror of believing I must be evil. After all, I had been victimized by evil-doers and the church had taught me about being evil and about going to hell…Believing as I did about evil and evilism it was as if this exorcism experience condemned me to hell. Thinking I might as well die…I decided to commit suicide.

I often think of the events that followed. At the time my husband and I were renting out an apartment to a woman who usually paid her rent without contacting us. On the day I took the overdose of pills, she phoned about the rent. Hearing my voice, she knew instantly I had overdosed and came right over…and took me to the hospital… She explained she had attempted suicide once and someone had helped her…She saved me!

After the exorcism my nightmares and night terrors…attacked me. I ended up crawling on the floor on my hands and knees trying to get away…from the reality…of the horrors. These people who did the exorcism held me there…for about an hour. This felt like the worst experience of my life…that is, after I had gotten away from my perpetrators. It was so spiritually damning and caused me to be stuck with evilism fears and anxieties ever since. This is the first time I have ever dared talk about this exorcism experience.

I realize how strongly I feel when I say how dare the clergy believe they have so much power that they can decide, they can think they can excise demons! How dare they! I want people to know that such beliefs and ignorance are harmful. My body healed but healing the spiritual assault has been, until now, a reality I did not dare speak to anyone about. I have been locked, trapped in a belief and been carrying emotional evilism, anxiety, fear, and maybe even evilism terror about my-Self all these years…I know how good I feel when I speak…I know the power speaking brings.

Carrie's ordeal included the social-cultural beliefs and practices about evilism related to the pastor's religious-based doctrines of "demons within." When his beliefs were imposed onto Carrie they reinforced her fear she had non-defined evilism within, given she said she had been "victimized by evil-doers." She also thought having been victimized by torturers' evil actions meant she may have had a genetic or contagious form of evilism within. This "exorcism" victimization magnified her internalized evilism anxieties, fears, and terror, triggering a life-threatening suicidal response.

Living in environments where the infliction of acts of human evil was the norm, other women remarked on feeling the perpetrator's evilness. Consequently they, like Carrie, feared evilness might be genetic or contagious, and could therefore reside within them. Unable to trust, and fearful others might respond with repulsion, women's evilism anxieties, fears, and terrors remained unchallenged in their belief systems. Carrie's statement, *"I know how good I feel when I speak…I know the power speaking brings,"* reinforces our experiences that women need the healing freedom to tell all, including about their evilism anxiety, fear, and terror. It was our privilege to be trusted by Carrie to speak freely about her terrifying exorcism ordeal and express how important this was for her.

Lynn: Evil Particles and Non-Defined Evilism Within

Earlier we introduced Lynn who shared being held captive, tortured, and trafficked by her husband and his three friends. She was also tortured by the buyers. Speaking of her fears, Lynn perceived she had swallowed evil when the torturers forced their body fluids down her throat. She perceived these body fluids remained clustered like grapes on her internal body organs or remained undigested as evil particles inside her body. Other women also voiced these same perceptions and fears.

Lynn, and other women, expressed that these evilism fears were heightened whenever they felt nauseated. If they vomited they feared they would expel evil matter or a non-defined form of evil within. Healing meant learning the human gastrointestinal tract was an organ system that processes and eliminates ingested substances over several days, and the forced ingested body fluids do not collect on their body organs. This science offered women an opportunity to consider shifting and letting go of their evilism fears that evil particles remained clustered inside their body.

Sara: "Monster" Fear

Sara's forced belief was that sexualized tortures involving bestiality meant she would have monsters, half-human and half-animal, evil babies. Sara's parents repeatedly told her this would occur. Our nursing backgrounds were always beneficial when responding to such disclosures. Women often told us our nursing backgrounds in anatomy, physiology, and biology were a benefit to them. It made explaining the human body easier. Explaining scientific facts that she would not have monster babies was a critical healing intervention for Sara. Her healing also required her to realize her parents' MO had been to intentionally lie to her when she was a child, thereby creating her evilism fear of producing evil monster babies.

Alex: Evil Being Within

Torturers utilized whatever distortion they could to terrify and manipulate the women, when they were children, into believing they had a defined evil being within. Self-harming such as Self-cutting can sometimes be a response to being forced to believe an evil being is growing within their body. Alex tells her story next.

Alex, a Canadian woman who fled Western Canada to escape her father and his like-minded friends' torturing ordeals, reached out to us in 2009. She said, "I want to share something with you. I mentioned how my dad told me I had evil inside me that would never come out." Alex shared her 1992 drawing, "My Reality," to illustrate her fear of the impact of the torture, horror, and enforced belief of an evil being contained within. Her disclosing art is in figure 15. She said:

> Attached is a drawing I did called "My Reality." Got pregnant by one of the men when I was 12 years old. They did an abortion on me, saying they were trying to get evil out of me. I was grateful for them helping me...at the same time wanting to die because the pain was

Fig. 15: "My Reality"

excruciating. After they finished they cut up [what]…they aborted and made me eat some of it. I was confused and believed I just ate evil…I believed there was evil inside of me. I did not want it to grow. I stopped eating, thinking if I don't eat, the evil won't grow. If I eat, the evil will get bigger. By 12 years old I had stopped eating unless forced. I didn't know anything about anorexia, however that is what developed. My goal was not to feed the evil inside. If I ate, the evil inside would grow and would explode out of my stomach breaking through my skin and come out of my mouth and stomach. People would know how evil I was…I wanted to get smaller and smaller and just completely disappear.

I was desperate to get the evil out of me. I felt possessed, having something alive inside. I cut along the veins from my wrists to my elbows. I cut X's on my arms because I felt dirty inside. I tried to cut deep enough to get to the evil and yank it out. Each time it didn't work, I cut deeper. I believed that was the only way to get clean. I cut the vein in my groin after the other cutting didn't work to get the evil out. I wanted to die. Getting clean meant someone might think I was worth helping. I thought it was me who was evil.

Women: Genetically Born Evil and Catchable or Contagious Evil Energy

Women spoke of fearing they may have been genetically born evil because of the torturers' evilness—because of the torturers' evil actions. Sara and other women also feared the torturers' evil energy was catchable or contagious. We understood this fear because women's horrific memories brought bone-chilling responses. However, women needed to reflect on the meaning of their own words when they said, *"I'm not like them."* If they are not like them, then they were not born evil and the evil energy was not catchable or contagious.

Challenging internalized evilism beliefs is essential to help women heal Self-hatred responses—hatred of their bodies, hatred of their "bad parts," to help heal Self-blaming for having a vagina, and physical Self-harming and suicidality responses. Women can develop a clear separation of their thoughts, values, and beliefs from those of the torturers, by clarifying their own rationale for what they think and believe. The intervention of establishing belief boundaries as discussed in Chapter 4 is helpful. This assists women in nurturing their relationship with/to/for Self. Letting go of the destructive, intentional, manipulative deceptions of the torturers is essential healing.

DRAWINGS AS EXPERIENTIAL STORYTELLING

Drawings by Alex, Sara, and other women are ways of telling their stories. Drawings make women's non-State torture and human trafficking memories visible; this can break their years of isolation and aloneness because others can "see" what was done to them. Women can then share in words what their drawings mean to them.

Unsilencing atrocities via drawings is effective for many. When Myra Balk traveled to Nepal in the late 1990s, she met Nepali women, many of whom had suffered sexualized human trafficking victimizations (Tomlinson, 2002). She handed paper and crayons to the women who had never held a crayon before; the women began drawing their testimonies and talking. We attended the art exhibit of the women's art testimonials (Parker, 2002) and were able to witness the power of their art to explain the impact of the sexualized human trafficking they survived.

Similarly, in 2016, Toronto's Sick Kids hospital exhibited 22 pieces of art by Indigenous Canadian children and youth from four Maritime First Nations communities. In efforts to understand how Indigenous children and youth interpreted their physical pain, researchers asked the children to use art to paint—to tell—what their physical pain and hurt looked like. The rationale was that Indigenous children are culturally socialized to be stoic about such pain because showing physical pain indicates weakness (Roussy, 2016). The children's art told of their emotional pain, of their feelings of loneliness, sadness, darkness, bullying, and hopelessness. This surprised the researchers as they were asking about physical pain.

Just as Indigenous children were taught to be stoic about physical pain because showing it was considered a sign of weakness, Sara said she was torture-taught never to show signs of physical pain. She said, "the family" indicated this was a sign of personal weakness. Consequently, Sara explained how she tried "to do good" at withstanding the torture-pain so "the family" would love her. To "*do good*"—to show no weakness, Sara shared her "must not let anyone know" drawing in figure 16. Sara was forced to believe that feeling the torture-pain meant that she was weak. This belief kept her silent. This belief protected the torturers.

Drawing atrocities as a form of experiential storytelling is done by many. For instance, the drawings of children who were forcedly turned into child soldiers can be considered unsilencing testimonies of the atrocities they suffered (Amnesty International, 2001). Drawings by Bongane, aged 11, and Gerald, aged 13, told of police violence directed specifically against children (Wood, 1995). Children's testimonial drawings recorded the atrocities inflicted by the Janjaweed

Fig. 16: Sara's silencing statement

militias in Darfur (Human Rights Watch, 2005). Similarly, Rwandan children's art told of the human rights genocide they witnessed (Salem, 2000). Given the opportunity to draw, children used their drawings to express their terrifying experiences of surviving the tsunami in the Maldives (UNICEF, 2012). *Children of the Wind/Les Enfants du Vent* was a children's rights project wherein children from nine countries told about their lives (Dale, n.d.). Children's drawings can also expose insights into their Self-image and developmental delays (Wilson & Ratekin, 1990), which, we suggest, can be consequences of the atrocities they survived.

The above experiential stories expressed in the art of Nepali women and the art of children of many countries are valued. Women's non-State torture-based testimonial art must be equally valued. However, this is frequently not the case. Therefore, we inserted their drawings throughout our book because we could not adequately tell of our journey with Sara and other women without sharing their drawings. Their drawings tell their stories in ways words cannot. Valuing storytelling drawings is the way to show respect for the drawer's autonomy (McCurdy, 1990). This freedom to draw and tell is one of our core practices in our support of women who have been non-State tortured.

In 2003, scientific researchers revealed that being excluded or rejected by others caused emotional pain similar to physical pain (Eisenberger et al., 2003). Sara and other women speaking out in our chapters fear that if the community discovers they have survived torture—survived acts of human evil—the community's disgust would leave them rejected and ostracized, especially because the community may also harbour its own evilism anxieties or fears. When a society fails to respect unsilencing testimonies of non-State torture victimization art, an ongoing social, legal, exclusionary, and harmful norm is inflicted. This increases women's suffering.

DECONSTRUCTING SARA'S CONDITIONED EVILISM BELIEFS

We begin by sharing a transformative moment that occurred in April 1994. Sara's doctor wanted her to have a vaginal exam. Terrified, Sara asked that we accompany her to explain to the female specialist what Sara's response might be to a physical examination using a vaginal speculum. Sara feared she would scream. She did—loudly. When the examination was completed Sara received healthy news. Amazingly, Sara learned her vaginal reproductive organs were normal. This information was Self-validating for Sara. She responded by saying, "I already feel like a woman, different than before."

This result helped alleviate Sara's lingering evilism fear that her insides were damaged because of the "things they put inside" of her. This included the bestiality torture victimizations she described surviving since the age of two. Her parents, Sara said, trained their pet dog to participate in the sexualized torture of Sara. Such acts are not the norm for a dog unless human enforced. We consider bestiality human-animal cruelty, as both

Sara and the dog were victimized. Animal cruelty is listed on the ritual abuse-torture model.

Other women report that forced bestiality was a common MO inflicted by family-based torturer-traffickers. They and larger animals such as horses were victimized. Evidence that such human-animal victimization is real was reported by Corporal Pierre Lemaitre of the Burnaby, British Columbia, Royal Canadian Mounted Police (RCMP) detachment. He described the seizure of 100 "loathsome and unspeakable" DVDs of pornographic crime scene images involving children, dogs, and horses (*The Chronicle Herald,* 2004). Although these crime images came from the Philippines, such atrocious victimizations are a MO of family-based torturers. Sara was also taken to a farm, treated like an animal, forced to drink out of the animals' water trough, and forced to stay in the barn. We use the term animalization to express this form of dehumanization torture, and the torturers' action of human evil. Animalization is listed on our patriarchal divide model, figure 8.

In the early days and months, the meanings of Sara's messages were generally difficult to decipher. Only after extended periods of perseverance, time, and support did these messages become understandable. Having evil within was a recurring fear of Sara's. Even though Sara had been told her vaginal exam was normal, this did not eliminate how Sara's thematic victimization memories surfaced. For instance, on an October day in 1994, Sara arrived holding back what she needed to share. With encouragement, she eventually wrote the following message, expressing her sense of having been harmed by evil and having an evil being within, figure 17.

> I cannot tell it is too embarrassing. Last night! That's why I am tired. Listen...On me whole bunch!!! Will not come off some hurt... Hurtful, scary, some have colour red/black...Can you, Jeanne only come...and I'll try to show you. I don't feel safe now. I didn't feel safe all day because of the proof.

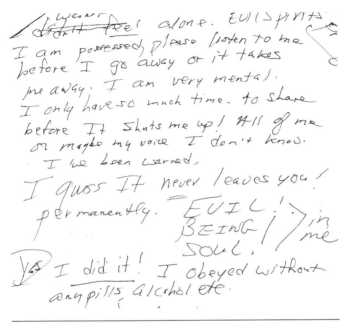

Fig. 17: Sara revealing her evilism within terror

As a stand-alone message, this made no sense to us. Eventually, Sara asked me, Jeanne, to enter the washroom with her. In the washroom, Sara showed me her body, front and back. It was covered in markings. It was impossible for Sara to do these markings as she could not have reached the middle of her back. Sara eventually explained she had been trigger-conditioned to go back to a torture group gathering where she was revictimized, including having what she perceived as *"evil markings"* written on her body.

To us, the markings could be described as graffiti—body graffiti. Sara saw the markings as evil. She was terrified. Sara's journaling and her verbally confusing message suddenly made sense. Since we were not fearful of the markings, Sara's terror eased. Our intervention with Sara was to assist her to comprehend the markings were done by individuals she had previously identified as torturers. This meant the markings were done by real people, not by evil spirits. This brought some realism back into Sara's awareness.

Body painting or markings is an objectifying tactic of some perpetrators. Having one's body marked is about being treated as an object, a thing. Sara perceived her-Self as "a thing" or an "it," which further explains why the torturers' MO of marking her body was so emotionally harmful. Over time, Sara would explain how, as a child, she was *"schooled"* to believe certain shapes or markings meant evilism. As long as these markings were on her body, Sara internalized these as indicators of her non-defined evilism within fear.

Repetitive evilism themes and symbols were constantly showing up in Sara's journaling. For instance, on December 6, 1994, Sara drew symbols on her journaling sheet as shown in figure 18. Symbols were often drawn but left unexplained. We were constantly committed to supporting her psychological safety. We were mindful she could only integrate reality at the rate she could handle safely, to prevent creating a critical incident that could trigger her into dying by suicide. It was too early in her recovery to ask about the meanings of these markings. Deconstructing Sara's internalized fears and terror of evilism would demand innovative interventions to develop her trust and awareness of her goal to heal. Perseverance was essential. It took years for Sara to heal the destructiveness of the evilism conditioning she had been subjected to, beginning when she was a preschooler. The following are examples of evilism conditioning that were the easiest for us to help Sara deconstruct.

The Moon

Not looking at the moon was a conditioned evilism fear. The torturers' MO had instilled in Sara as a toddler, that the moon had evil powers if she looked at it. This is why the quarter-moon shape appeared as an image of evilism on her journaling sheet in figure 18, as it displays what she had been conditioned to believe were evilism markings and symbols. Helping Sara let go of this fear meant scientific discussions about planets. But the most significant intervention was being outdoors when the moon was visible. Sara had to trust us, plus test her-Self about what would happen if she looked at the moon. Terrified, she looked—nothing happened. Sara's internalized evilism fear kept evaporating.

Number 11

For Sara, the upright door framework represented number 11. She had been torture-conditioned to believe any representation of "11" was evil and immobilized her. When placed in the upright door framework Sara believed she could not move until told to do so. Such immobilization torture is also known as a form of stress-positioning torture utilized by State torturers. It enforces the submission of the person being tortured and controlled. Our interventions included asking Sara to stand in a doorway for a few seconds, then to step right and left out of the doorway, to breathe, and stay present to see if evilism dangers would somehow occur. We role-played becoming mobile with Sara. This meant we walked in and out of the door frame to show that nothing "evil" happened. We encouraged Sara to do the same, and nothing happened to her. This evilism belief tactic began disappearing.

Fig. 18: Sara's journaling of evilism markings and symbols

666

Sara eventually revealed she believed the numbers 666 were branded on her forehead. This was based on "the family's" tactical use of the superstition that 666 meant the sign of the devil. This convinced Sara she was evil. Sara described that she had been forced to look into a mirror, to repeatedly agree the presence of 666 branding existed on her forehead. Sara believed in the torturers' omnipotence and would not risk going against them for fear of being tortured. To hide the perceived branding, Sara wore heavy hair bangs.

Because Sara worked for years as a professional in daily contact with people, we queried how many people had asked her about this so-called 666 branding on her forehead. Sara admitted no one had ever said they saw 666 branded on her forehead. Answering this question invalidated what she had been forced to believe. This was also an intervention aimed at assisting Sara to begin to establish her own beliefs as being very distinct and separate from those of the torturers. Sara clarified her own beliefs and this evilism belief tactic evaporated.

"Franklin the Turtle"

Sara told us perpetrators had placed plastic animal figurines, such as the "devil's goat," throughout her apartment. She believed these had the power to "see" all she did. The dominant controlling plastic figurine was "Franklin the Turtle," named after author Paulette Bourgeois' Franklin the Turtle stories, illustrated by Brenda Clark. Sara had been psychologically torture-conditioned to hold a belief that Franklin the Turtle controlled her. This kept Sara in a state of being accessible to chronic revictimization—to be tortured and trafficked by what Sara described as a group or network of violent professional women perpetrators. One perpetrator, Sara said, was called "Mama Franklin." When Sara was contacted by this woman using the phrase "Mama Franklin," Sara was triggered into a dissociative state. She would then connect with the woman. Sara eventually described, in very graphic terms, the tortures "Mama Franklin" subjected her to. This situation demonstrated the dangers of maintaining a dissociation response.

In the earlier years, Sara made it very clear she did not want to be dissociative or labelled "*as multiple*."[7] This made helping Sara heal her dissociative responses somewhat easier. Integration of women's victimizations and helping them to heal from the consequential traumas are part of our caring healing framework. If Sara had indicated she wanted to work on healing her-Self "as multiple" we would not have been able to help her; this was not our caring knowledge.

Fig. 19: Destruction of "turtle power"

To dissolve Sara's vulnerable state of dissociative revictimization, we first asked for her willingness to bring Franklin the Turtle and all the other plastic figurines to one of our meetings. We then negotiated. If she was to end her ongoing revictimization, our final intervention would be to take scissors and cut the plastic figurine Franklin the Turtle in two, as our photo shows in figure 19.

Kurt Lewin's Change Model. From a theoretical perspective, this intervention and previous interventions that addressed the need to deconstruct evilism beliefs were based on Kurt Lewin's three-step change model of unfreezing, changing, and refreezing. This knowledge was incorporated into Jeanne's nursing studies and practice (Tappen, 1983). To unfreeze a

---

7   Sara's reference to not wanting to be labelled "as multiple" refers to the psychiatric disorder of multiple personality disorder (MPD), now called dissociative identity disorder (DID), found in the American Psychiatric Association *Diagnostic and Statistical Manual of Mental Disorders*.

person from a present unmoveable place, one often has to undertake an unexpected or unusual action. This will help a person shift or unfreeze from their present position, which then provides the opportunity to stabilize, change, and develop a new way of knowing. This is what occurred. With much support, Sara stayed present as we cut the turtle figurine in two. Hyperventilating and filled with evilism fears, Sara watched the destruction of "turtle power."

A perpetrator can inflict later-in-life victimization conditioning by utilizing a person's earlier-in-life conditioned vulnerabilities. Sara was full of deep-seated childhood evilism anxieties, fears, and terrors. "Franklin the Turtle" conditioning, Sara explained, was inflicted in adulthood by "Mama Franklin," the woman from whom she sought professional counselling. Both Sara's childhood conditioning and the later-in-life conditioning made Sara's efforts to not die by suicide difficult. Dismantling evilism tactics with interventions such as those we just described were easier because they were more tangible or behavioural-based interventions.

Social Cultural Rituals

Everyday social-cultural rituals can reinforce a girl child's sense of evilism when born into a family system with parents who committed actions of human evil. For example, Sara said her parents practiced looking good at Christmas by taking her to visit Santa Claus. Sara explained this cultural ritualized experience:

> I told Santa I wanted a happy family…I see him in Newfoundland… at the Hudson Bay Store…I didn't get nothing I wished for from Santa…Nobody came, nobody tucked me in bed, nobody cuddled me, nobody took me out of the family…I felt I was bad and evil.

It was not until July 2000 that Sara made this testimonial drawing of the meaning of a Christmas ritual holiday, figure 20. Sara explained she was the "*Christmas present,*" suffering grievous torture victimizations. Such acts of physical and sexualized torture were accompanied by verbal dehumanizing degradations, being told she was nothing, bad, evil, and deserving of such harms. Such holidays provided torturers with extra days of inflicting torture and staying invisible. Sara now understood why, as a tiny child, she had told "Santa" she wanted "a happy family."

Fig. 20: "Christmas present" victimization

Sara kept going deeper and deeper into how she had been "*schooled*" and conditioned by the torturers' actions. At one meeting Sara declared, "*I am satan.*" Sara's seriousness in stipulating this message created a ripple effect that required personal Self-reflective evaluations.

Linda's Reflective Notes

We, three women, sat on the floor as Sara struggled to tell her story about why she thought she was evil. Jeanne and Sara were facing each other. I was sitting facing both of them, witnessing their exchange. Jeanne was very clearly disagreeing with Sara, who believed she was evil. In my head I was agreeing with Jeanne, knowing Sara could not be evil as she was so traumatized and agonized about others who were harmed as well. As Sara became more and more stressed, I could feel my emotions escalating and I was not really asking my-Self why this was. All of a sudden, I heard Sara tell Jeanne, "I am satan." Of course I knew this was not true, but despite my logical thought, I could feel my fear level shoot up through the ceiling. I spent the rest of the session trying to talk my-Self emotionally down off the ceiling, as shown in my drawing of figure 21. My fear level was so high and so loud I heard very little of the rest of Jeanne and Sara's conversation.

up on the ceiling
Linda MacDonald 07/05

Fig. 21: Linda on the ceiling

After Sara left Jeanne asked me, "Where did you go, Linda? What are you feeling?" As I talked it through with Jeanne, I came to learn that even though I did not believe in satan, as a child, I had been brought up Roman Catholic. I was very specifically taught that the devil was real and I would go to hell if I was a "bad girl." Obviously, I was stuck back to that little girl state of emotion where I still felt fear about this indoctrination. I felt terrified. Once I became aware of this blind spot I could let go of the old fears about being taught there was a devil. I moved forward with supporting Sara in her healing, reassuring her, as Jeanne did, that I did not believe she was satan or evil. This experience taught me a great deal about how I had to be ever-present in my Self-assessment about my own emotions when supporting others in healing from their fears of evilism. I never was terrified again when women expressed their fears of seeing them-Selves as evil.

There was another fear I lived with and had to overcome. I had read that one of the common tactics used by torturing groups was to frighten helpers by leaving a dead cat on their doorstep. For years, I had this frightening image in my mind that I would come home one evening after work and find a dead white cat covered in blood, lying on the floor of my front hall. I worried how I would explain such a gruesome image to my children. And I worried my husband would become even more insistent I stop this work because he was frightened I was putting our children at risk. The dead cat never happened. I realized I had blown this out of proportion because I was feeling overwhelmed with the emotional demands of working with Sara.

A final fear was when Jeanne and I realized we were dealing with perpetrators of organized crime. With the realization of naming organized crime, I became instantly terrified I would be shot in the back or my family could be harmed at any moment. I talked this out loud with Jeanne and she helped me understand this was not the MO of the non-State torturers. They work very hard to stay invisible. Calling attention to them-Self in such a public way was not their pattern. My fear immediately dropped and I quickly moved on.

I wish I had discussed my fear of the cat out loud too but it got stuck in my "inconscious,"[8] with all the demands of the work. It was years later before I told Jeanne about my past fears of the dead cat. Talking my fears out was crucial for my survival, for coping, and being effective in my caring support of Sara.

Jeanne's Reflections

The reason I asked Linda "Where did you go?" was because I felt she had left the room emotionally. I knew she was not present at this moment in

---

8   We use the term "inconscious" to express that a concept in our mind is not totally unconscious, rather that we are somewhat aware of a specific thought but have not processed it to the extent that we are totally cognitively aware of our perspective.

time when Sara said "I am satan." Sara said she would take me to satan. I had long ago sorted out my religious beliefs and was unafraid.

When my mother fled my father's cruelty, never to return, I was about nine. My mother had been raised Roman Catholic. When she left we moved to the town of Yarmouth, Nova Scotia, and I remember the priest arriving in his big car. He came to tell my mother she was a sinner for abandoning her marriage; he told her she was not allowed the ritual of "communion." His arrogance, his privilege, and his condemnation of my mother began my break with any religious-based beliefs I had.

Then, when I was a teenager, at the request of my mother, I went to talk with the priest about religion. He was so biased about the Catholic religion being better than any other religion I left. I never returned. For me, religious-based beliefs are like that. Beliefs are what a person chooses to believe. So, when Sara said she was "satan" I was not disturbed. I knew her torture-conditioned beliefs in evilism were foundational to her misery. And recovery from "the family's" use of evilism conditioning would be prolonged and painful. Sara would eventually have to decide on her own belief boundaries, she would need to separate her beliefs from the evilism beliefs she had been manipulated into internalizing. There would be many challenging interventions which Sara, as revealed in Chapter 4, came to call "C word" interventions. She learned that being challenged was about caring—caring also begins with a "c." Why would we work so hard at finding helpful ways to challenge her if Linda and I did not care about her? This was a new concept for Sara. She would learn she needed to be challenged and to challenge her-Self for her own continued recovery.

The reason I so quickly understood that organized criminals and "the family" would not want to draw attention to their existence was intuitive as well as experiential. This came from watching my father's ability to switch from being a totally violent man to being the nicest guy one would ever meet. This always happened when our neighbour Sally called the police, when she thought my mother's survival was precarious. When the police arrived, they were presented with situational non-truth versus situational truth. My father became a great guy. This was his ability to exert psychological manipulation. He was good at it. He did not want to expose his infliction of cruelty and in my opinion, neither would non-State torturers. Killing Linda or me would have established their visibility. Their maintenance of invisibility was a prime strategy, evidenced by their repetitive tactics to ensure women as children never told. It was their prime decree—never tell on "the family."

My favourite reading material as a child was true crime. From these books I learned criminals do not advertise their intended crime, rather they prefer to be invisible. I deduced that if "the family" shot both of us, it would expose them. Doing the opposite would be to ignore us, while attempting to break the relationship we were developing with Sara, such as repeatedly harassing her, placing a traitor notice on her car windshield, triggering her into dissociative responses, and revictimizing her. Sara was pulling away, inch-by-inch, not only from "the family" but also from the group of violent women Sara described as torturing and trafficking her. Losing the pleasures they derived from victimizing Sara was infuriating for all these perpetrators, but staying invisible was elemental.

It would be years before Linda spoke about her fear of finding a dead cat in her front hall. This was never a thought that ran through my mind. At the time, my sons were in their early 20s. One evening they wanted to have a conversation about human evil. They needed to know if human evil could overpower human goodness. They asked this question because in Sara's desperation to end the chronic revictimizations she was enduring, and to try not to die by suicide, she would call my home telephone. If I was not home, they answered and sometimes tried to be of support, as did my partner. For instance, pulling out a file dated 29 October 1999, I saw that Sara called 43 times because every moment was an emergency. I understood this. But the calls to my family phone were creating distress for my family and adding to my massive stress. I had to place a consequence on Sara. I informed her I would have to block her number if she continued calling my home phone. I explained I needed to Self-care by setting this boundary.

In 2019, I asked my sons if they remembered this conversation. They did not. However, watching them manoeuvre through tough unjust work conditions and relational experiences, I realized they had learned from Linda and my support of Sara. Our caring work had role-modelled ethical stances. This became another motivation to continue doing the work this book discloses.

Supporting Sara's recovery altered my worldview forever. I repeat this because every day our work transformed how I see reality. Every possible layer of society is now viewed through bifocal lenses. I now accept the daily possibility I may be in contact with those who live, work, play, and volunteer among us, who could also have the hidden agenda of deriving pleasure by inflicting actions of human evil. But human evil actions can only thrive when there is no detrimental deterrent. Unsilencing women's stories is a powerful deterrent.

CHAPTER 8
CONFRONTING ACTIONS OF HUMAN EVIL

_____

INSIGHTS ABOUT ACTIONS OF HUMAN EVIL

Since 1993, when Sara first sought our support, she, as well as other women, have been clear in expressing the torturers committed acts of human evil. Their persistence meant we needed to secure our personal views and be watchful for literature that spoke about actions of human evil. We gleaned support from the works of the following authors.

Ervin Staub

One important resource was Ervin Staub's 1993 book, *The Roots of Evil The Origins of Genocide and Other Group Violence*, in which he defined *"evil"* as human *"actions."* He wrote that evil actions devalue and destroy another individual human being or groups of human beings, diminishing their human dignity, their happiness, and their ability to accomplish their basic material needs. This is precisely how Sara presented. We were working day and night because Sara's recovery meant finding ways to help her heal and end her ongoing victimized destruction. We needed to explore activities that improved her ability to manage daily living and also present experiences that promoted forms of happiness.

Staub also said the intentions of those who commit acts of human evil were not necessarily to kill those they harmed; this was Jeanne's and eventually Linda's basic perception. Women's testimonial evidence suggested torturers' pleasure was having a live girl or woman to torture. Terrorized, horrified, and threatened as a tiny child that she would be killed was also their pleasure, and Sara carried this torture-conditioned belief into adulthood. Reinforcing Sara's belief that she might be killed occurred when she was a very sick toddler. She described a situation whereby she could have died. Her death might have been considered "accidental." This ordeal will be covered in Chapter 12: Part 3 under the section "On Killing." Nonetheless, the situational reality was if non-State torturers had wanted to kill Sara, it seemed to us they would have done so ages ago, not when she became visible by seeking our support. However, it also seemed likely the torturers were relying on their conditioning of Sara to die by suicide, thus their escape from responsibility for her death. We named this specific MO suicidal-femicide conditioning (Sarson & MacDonald, 2018c); femicide refers to the misogynistic killing of women and girls.

Nevertheless, Sara and other women do describe witnessing killings covered up as "accidents." Women told of specific horrors of witnessing the murder of a marginalized street woman and a trafficked street child, both socially invisible persons.

It was also Staub's opinion that perpetrators of acts of human evil hide their true intentions from them-Selves. However, women's disclosures to us do not concur with Staub's opinion. The non-State torturers we have come to understand are well organized, leaving little doubt they know exactly what they are doing. It may be that there is a difference when a whole society condones massive brutalities, but the torturers known to us were and remain highly skilled manipulators. They function within their professions and mainstream society while maintaining their ability to keep their violent co-culture intact and invisible.

Staub discussed that other authors said perpetrators' motivations for committing actions of evil were to satisfy their own Self-interests and exert power over others. This perspective would apply to Sara's and other women's descriptions of family-based non-State torturers' actions.

Family-based torturers satisfy their own Self-interests and exert dominating power over others. During our kitchen-table research interviews, Hope explained the torturers' intentionality, organizational skills, and the Self-interest displayed during a *"beating ritual."* She said usually other people were present to supervise the *"adult beater."* They knew when to stop the beater so there would be no visible marks or marks clothing could hide. Hope described the beating ritual she suffered as:

> Once when I was about eight or nine years old, I was being beaten but no guard was present to watch over this beater. The man just kept beating and beating me. We were in a room and I remember spotting the closet and thinking I'd have to make it to the closet if I was to survive. Digging my fingernails into the floor, I crawled and crawled towards the closet while the man kept pounding me...I did make it into the closet and the man stopped battering me.

Concerning groups, Staub wrote that belonging in a group can diffuse personal responsibility, repress dissent, and enhance the group's potential for inflicting acts of human evil. Ritual behaviours can foster groupthink (Sarson & MacDonald, 2009b). Hope's "beating ritual" is an example of this. The "adult beater" was part of "the family" group and the "ritual beating" was normalized as acceptable by naming it a "ritual" of "the family" group.

When addressing the "role of victims," Staub said that as violent destruction progresses, victimized persons "give up hope." Women did say they thought many times there was no way out. Sara said she "borrowed" our hope. We suggest that women we came to know never gave up hope; even though they may have felt hopelessness, they kept searching for help or a way out. Staub also mentioned bystanders can significantly influence the outcome for the person being victimized. Women frequently asked why bystanders did not help them when they were children. Sara's opinion was:

> When I think of how many times I went to school unable to sit without pain, how many times I couldn't bear a teacher's hand on my shoulder because of my physical beatings, and the time I was orally raped just before being dropped off at school and threw up right on the classroom floor, I wonder how my plight was missed. Couldn't the teacher see, smell I had vomited semen? I couldn't tell on the family but maybe if people had consistently reported and reported and reported their concerns eventually I would have been taken out of the family.

Simon Baron-Cohen

Neuroscientist Simon Baron-Cohen speaks of evilism as acts of human cruelty inflicted by a person who lacks affective empathy. He says this relates to the functioning of the brain's empathic network (Denny, 2012). This is partly genetic, partly from the parenting one has received, and also influenced by social conditioning (Denny, 2012). In response, it remains a wonderment that the women we have supported, who have been tortured by parents and others for years, and some for decades, are empathic, kind, and caring of others.

Why did Sara as a child often say to the torturers: "take me, take me," in her efforts to try and save other children from harm? In Simon Baron-Cohen's view, when acts of human evil are committed, the person victimized is objectified to a thing—to a non-person (Denny, 2012). With this, we agree. Many women have stated their torture ordeals left them with a conviction they were "a thing," "a nothing," or "an it," or even unaware they had a body or skin. Sara worded it this way: "One thing for sure I never knew I was human."

We do not support that women we know ought to be fearful they could potentially be like the torturers. If they were told they could have genetically inherited a tendency towards inflicting acts of human evil, this could risk their recovery or trigger suicidality, given that genetically born evil may be one of their evilism-based fears.

Michael Welner and Co-Authors

In 2014, we joined 40,000 other individuals in the first forensic research project involving general public participation (Sarson & MacDonald, 2020b). This work by Michael Welner and co-authors focused on developing the "Depravity Standard" (Welner et al., 2018). The Depravity Standard aimed to promote fairness and evidence-based decisions when addressing the worst of crimes frequently described as acts of evil, or as "heinous," "atrocious," or "cruel." The Depravity Standard is not meant to define who is depraved rather it is meant to consider the depraved motivations, behaviours or actions of the perpetrator. The Depravity Standard's 25 specific items are listed under intention, actions, attitudes, and the perpetrator's choice of victim(s), as shown in Figure 22.

These 25 items can be used to evaluate the evidence of the presence or absence of depravity of the perpetrator's actions of their committed crime. Welner and his co-authors suggest the Depravity Standard is adaptable to evolving societal attitudes. We advocate that the evolution of societal attitudes demands socio-legal acknowledgement, visibility, and understanding of organized criminal groups such as the family-based torturers into which Sara describes being born. It was the socio-legal invisibility that confronted us, and Sara, when she reached out for help in 1993. For instance, in Canada no law criminalizes torture perpetrated by private individuals or groups. This adds to the invisibilization of the torturers and their depravity. When there is no law there is no crime, no legal cases, no acknowledgment of the individuals who endured non-State torture, and that there are no perpetrators of such human evil actions identified. This is a socio-legal falsehood that must be unsilenced.

Depravity Standard			
INTENT	**ACTIONS**	**ATTITUDES**	**CHOICE OF VICTIM(S)**
1: emotionally traumatize the victim, maximizing terror, humiliation, or create an indelible emotional memory of the event	12: Disregarding the known consequences to the victimized person	21: Pleasure in response to the actions and their impact	5: Targeting victimized person who are not merely vulnerable, but helpless
2: maximize damage or destruction to victimized person(s)	14: Prolonging the victimized person's physical suffering	22: Falsely implicating others, exposing them to wrongful penalty and the stress of prosecution	6: Exploiting a necessarily trusting relationship to the victimized person
3: cause permanent physical disfigurement to victimized person	15: Unrelenting amount of physical and emotional victimization	23: Projecting responsibility onto the victimized person; feeling entitled to do so	13:Intentionally targeting victimized person based upon prejudice
4: excitement of the criminal act	16: Exceptional degree of physical harm; amount of damage	24: Disrespect for the victimized person after the fact	
7: Influencing depravity in others in order to destroy more	17: Unusual and extreme quality of victimized person suffering, including terror and helplessness	25: Indifference to the actions and their impact	
8: progressively increasing depravity	18: Indulgence of actions, inconsistent with the social context		
9: terrorize others	19: Carrying out crime in unnecessarily close proximity to the victimized person		
10: gain social acceptance or attention, or to show off	20: Excessive response to trivial irritant; clearly disproportionate to the perceived provocation		
11: Influencing criminality in others to avoid prosecution			

Fig. 22: Depravity Standard from Welner and co-authors

In summary, the four categories of intent, actions, attitudes, and choice of victim(s) of the Depravity Standard apply to Sara's disclosures, and to the torture voiced by other women in various chapters of this book. For instance, women, and women as children, have been terrorized, have suffered destruction, have spoken of the torturers' excitement and pleasure, have been forced to inflict harm on others being victimized, and have been horrified. This is intent. The torturers all participate in their collective crimes. They force those they victimize to cause harm to others including, for example, pets, such as when Carrie, as a little girl, was left terrorized and feeling she was a "bad" person after being forced to drown her pet kitten, Brownie. Feeling so bad, she never spoke of the harm she was forced to inflict. This quick review of the items listed under intent can be applied to the non-State torturers.

Item number 3—the intent to cause permanent physical disfigurement—might initially be considered not to apply. However, from a woman's perspective, it does. Women have suffered internal reproductive damage. They required hysterectomies or suffered damage that left them sterile. These are invisible physical disfigurements that only become visible by listening to women's disclosures.

Women's Invisible Physical Disfigurements

Carrie's story

From Carrie, who participated in our kitchen-table research, came this insight about invisible physical disfigurements. She described:

> When I was in my late 20s doctors did a hysterectomy because my insides were so mangled I couldn't have children. The doctors didn't ask why my insides were like they were. So many clues and no one asked me any questions. Why?

Lynn's story

Lynn, who escaped after four and a half years of captivity, torture, and exploitation through prostitution organized by her husband and his three "goons," discussed her insight into a physical disfigurement. She said this came about because of dental surgery:

> I remember…feeling the numbing pain on the left side of my face and bottom jaw when I'd had my face smashed in; and after the clients orally raped me I'd have more pain in my jaw joints, especially along the left side of my face. After I was back home the pain in my jaw bothered me so much the dentist took all my bottom teeth out, thinking my teeth were the cause of my pain. No questions about violence were asked of me. These bouts of pain never went away and I had no bottom teeth…Now I'm realizing it couldn't help—the reoccurring pain was physical memory pain. Memory pain—phantom pain…Having my bottom teeth pulled never helped and left me feeling I must be crazy. Additionally, I've realized how unjustly I've thought and felt about myself and how my fear of having evilism within diminished my sense of spiritual goodness.

During the two years we volunteered to support Lynn in her recovery, the pain did go away. She made the link that her body stored a cellular memory of all the physical and sexualized torture pain inflicted on her jaw. Once she understood this, the pain did leave, as did her Self-concepts that she was crazy or had evilism within. This was an invisible injury. It was never acknowledged that Lynn's dental loss was a consequence of torture victimization.

Lynda's story

Lynda is a Western European woman who said her non-family torturers intended to cause her permanent physical disfigurement. These were not visible until she needed medical attention. Lynda said:

> He cut my insides very badly and badly damaged my breasts with biting and removed a nipple…The gynecologist was shocked at the injuries both externally and the amount of scarring internally. I didn't explain a lot of what had happened—just that I had a lot

of abuse in the past and my GP had confirmed this in my referral. She asked at one point "what kind of monsters could do this sort of thing." I couldn't bring myself to tell her "my family."

The Depravity Standard list helps answer the question often asked by women so victimized: Was it my fault? The Depravity Standard items clearly demonstrate it was never their fault; the responsibility belongs solely to the non-State torturers.

Another example, number 11, influencing criminality in others to avoid prosecution, could range from a parent torturer forcing their child to sell drugs at school or using the child as a decoy for the victimization of others. Women detailed both of these experiences.

There is not one of the four categories of intent, actions, attitudes, and choice of victim(s) of the Depravity Standard that we can discount. Attitude category number 22 of "falsely implicating others, knowingly exposing them to wrongful penalty and the stress of prosecution" is one depravity standard that impacted us professionally and personally. Once, Sara said, "I have to tell you something. I feel so terrible and guilty and this has haunted me for several years, but I have to tell you." She then dropped a bombshell that rocked us to the core.

Sara's Bombshell

She said, "I was forced to write a suicide letter blaming you for my suicide. The letter said something like this:

> I, Sara, take my life today because Jeanne Sarson and Linda MacDonald have destroyed me. They pretended to want to help me but instead abused and tortured me. I cannot take it anymore. This is the only way out for me. I need peace and freedom. I just want you all to know this and beware of these women…Truthfully, Sara.

Sara went on to explain this letter was placed in a little metal box inside the bank of one of the women from the women's torturing group. She explained:

> I was with her. It was placed in a little box that was in a little room that had lots of little metal boxes. I've never seen a room like this in my bank and didn't know such rooms existed.

Sara also explained that this violent women's group had pictures of us. These, Sara revealed, were used when Sara was being victimized as a MO to attempt to force her to believe we were like the women torturers. Because this occurred early in Sara's relationship with us, it left her extremely confused. Even though she was progressively improving, she persisted in being fearful and uncertain about trusting us. It made our support of Sara even more difficult and painful, and we did not know why. Not until Sara revealed these attacks against us, did we understand. These attacks were efforts to stop Sara from seeking our support because she was pulling away from being victimized and they, "the family," wanted her back.

There were days Sara arrived at meetings physically brutalized. She did not comprehend that being beaten was relational violence. Even though Sara was still being harmed, we kept working at helping her understand she was a person with human rights that were being violated. We had the *Universal Declaration of Human Rights* as a visual tool to illustrate this fundamental global educational standard. We were saying to Sara, "Sara, this is not only our opinion that your human rights are being violated, it is a global opinion." She said, "I didn't know I was a person until you told me." But we knew!

Sara eventually had to let go of her professional career. This was a loss and grief for her. As part of our *advocacy caring*, we arranged for Sara to meet with a member of parliament who believed Sara's disclosures. He and his office challenged the political system. Sara was awarded a disability pension.

Sara was deeply in debt. She eventually revealed all her income was taken by "the family." Sara did not understand that her wages belonged to her; without a salary she used her credit cards, as did her family. These totalitarian MOs created her huge debt. It took Sara years to become financially stable because she used shopping to cope with her lifetime of deprivations. Impulse shopping remains an infrequent issue. "The family," Sara disclosed, also decided whether or not they would buy her food, and how much food they would give her to last the two weeks between the paycheques they stole from her. Sara's nutritional intake suffered, adding more challenges to her strength to recover. When Sara began keeping her money, we took her food shopping.

It would take Sara almost seven years to physically exit "the family." It was a two-step forward and one-step backward process—although some days felt like three steps backward. Even after the seven years, there would be several occasions Sara went back to "the family," thinking she would be safe or she could convince them to change. Each time she reported being severely physically and sexually harmed. This included, she said, a group her father had gathered to hide in the house waiting for Sara to arrive. Despite this, one day Sara was going to see her father to borrow money.

We respected but strongly discussed with Sara that we disagreed with her decisions. The best solution she and we had was to agree to disagree. Even though we explained to Sara these ordeals kept interfering with her healing, Sara kept holding on because, as she said, "I wanted a family." Violent ordeals such as these created intense crises. When Sara was in crisis our phones rang constantly. We had to set firm boundaries that held Sara responsible for the decisions we agreed to disagree on. A *caring healing intervention* meant challenging Sara. She needed to learn

Self-responsibility and problem-solving skills. These were indispensable skills, absolutely crucial for Sara to counter her learned behaviour of having her life totally controlled by "the family." Sara needed to learn Self-confidence and Self-trust, and to embrace control of her life.

Sara informed us she was chronically stalked, harassed, and threatened. Once, when leaving an appointment, she reported being pulled into a van, in a parking lot, and sexually assaulted by "the family." She was followed when driving, including being driven off the road several times. Perpetual crises went on for years. They kept Sara in a hypervigilant state, challenging her newly developing belief that escape was possible. These harmful and violent events repeatedly taxed our energies, but persevere we all did!

As for us, we had to stay focused on working to keep our day jobs and our families intact. Our jobs were the financial security of our families and our careers. Our work with Sara was pro-bono.

THE PRINCIPLE OF DOING THE OPPOSITE OF WHAT THE TORTURERS DO

For years Sara filled flipchart pages with the torturers' destructive use of evil actions and suicidal-conditioning tactics. Eventually, Sara explained she had been taught to believe she had to take her own life—to "*sacrifice*" her life—as a gift to "the family." This was one reason Sara was constantly feeling suicidal. Learning this information also helped to explain Sara's desperate late-night call back in August of 1993. She believed she was going to die in four days at "the family's" organized group gathering. Debunking this bizarre distortion was vital to Sara's recovery.

The "C Word" Intervention

There was a need to constantly challenge Sara. As previously mentioned, in Chapter 4, on November 30, this became known as our "C word" intervention. This intervention was required many times so Sara could unlearn constantly asking for and following the opinions of others. This was a result of being forced as a child to do as she was told to do by "the family." As she said, "I have lived my life doing what others wanted me to with the hope they might love me or come to care for me even a little."

Working to deconstruct Sara's torture-inflicted psychological violations meant critically examining distorted concepts she had internalized as truthful beliefs. At first, Sara thought we were challenging her because we disbelieved her. Encouraging Sara to critically rethink her internalized beliefs, we challenged her to recall that her father had told her as a preschooler to bang her head on the wall because the bruises made her pretty. We then asked Sara how she would justify teaching every preschooler in daycare to bang their heads on the wall to make them pretty. Sara would never justify such an action. She cared about children. Not able to justify her father's statement offered Sara the opportunity to begin dismantling one after another of the torturers' psychological MOs. This was an illustration of the problem-solving Sara needed: to learn, question, and critically examine what she had previously internalized as truths or beliefs.

Critical analysis was essential to deconstruct the MO of the torturers' bizarreness. It was needed for Sara's recovery. As an adult, she had harmful head-banging re-enactments; she would run and bang her head into the wall, hurting her-Self, and dangerously impacting her physical safety and recovery. Deconstructing torture-instilled distorted beliefs was required. Assisting Sara to consider the principles of critical analysis promoted her ability to do the opposite of what the torturers had tricked her into doing. She worked to end her conditioned head-banging re-enactments.

Jeanne's Reflection about Bizarreness

As to the bizarreness the torturers incorporated into their MO, bizarre behaviours were not unfamiliar to me. My father acted bizarrely. For instance, he had a German shepherd dog which he "loved" at one moment and tormented the next. I can still "see" the dog running down the driveway with its tail tucked tightly between its hind legs. Because the dog had not been inoculated for distemper, it eventually became sick. My father put the sick dog on the kitchen floor, tucked halfway under the kitchen sink. The dog lay there dying for several more days. After the dog died it remained there for another few days. My father would sit on the floor, cradle the dead dog, and sob. My mother, my brother Raymond, and I looked at the dead dog, skirting around its dead body for more days, as we manoeuvred around the small kitchen. I think I was around six as I remember Raymond was not yet in school. As a young child I knew my father's behaviour was bizarre.

I knew another form of bizarreness was that my mother had to climb into bed with the man who battered her. I would lie in bed and think of this. This bizarre event happened every night until she finally left when I was nine.

Doing the Opposite from the Torturers

The principle of doing the opposite of the torturers was the core essence of our interventions. Torturers aim to destroy a person's sense of being human or, in our wording, to destroy the relationship a person needs to have *with/to/for Self*. The MO of "the family" had already destroyed Sara's sense of being human—as she said, "*I didn't know I was a person until you told me.*" We were working hard at creative ways to help Sara rebuild her relationship with/to/for her-Self. As Staub noted, torturers' actions of human evil destroy happiness. We wanted to help Sara restore the possibility of happiness, to provide interventions whereby she could learn to appreciate beauty, and find happiness in the world.

Outdoor Interventions

Gaining a sense of beauty and happiness included outdoor interventions.

- Sitting outdoors one day, Sara suddenly realized for the first time that autumn leaves were changing into beautiful fall colours. She was in her 30s. Sara shared she had only seen in black and white. This meant she had not been able to take in such beauty before, because her physical sensory system had shut down in order to survive. This was a "*wow*" moment for Sara. She was enthralled, absolutely spellbound!

- Sara had been tortured in the woods. We needed to provide opportunities for her to learn the woods do not harm—it was the torturers who used wooden branches to beat her who were dangerous. We went for walks in the park, progressing to learning that barks on trees were different, learning to touch and feel those differences, and eventually hugging a tree.

- When walking in the park we talked about the vibrant colours of the beautiful flowers and suggested she stop and smell them.

- Sara also experienced looking at the early evening stars and the moon, to learn these were not under the torturers' control but were planets in the galaxies.

Outdoor interventions made for *transformative healing* which nurtured Sara's appreciation of nature.

To assist Sara in beginning to perceive her body anatomically and holistically, we would go to a park, lie on the grass, and sing the "Dry Bones" song. Its lyrics were about how all our bones are connected, one to the other. While we sang this song as fun, its meaning was very serious. Sara had shared her drawing of how she perceived each part of her body separate from every other part. For example, her hands were disconnected from her arms; her arms detached from her body as shown in figure 23 (Sarson & MacDonald, 2018a). This was a survival response. Sara needed to reconnect with her body.

September 28, 1994

This was one of our many outdoor meetings. Whether indoors or outdoors, we always had paper, pens, pencils, and coloured markers handy. We never knew when Sara needed to write to "get it out," or when we would need to write as she spoke. We planned our interventions

Fig. 23: Sara's physical Self-concept

to help increase Sara's Self-awareness and to assist her in learning that "outsiders" would not "contaminate" her, as she had been conditioned to believe. By experiencing outdoor interventions Sara gradually learned to develop relational trust. For example, at this meeting the objective was for her to list experiential transformations she had achieved while working with us over the past year. Sara's transformations, she said, included:

Visions of noticing coloured trees, clouds,

sunrise, and rainbows is too much

Able to play with a dog

Felt the sand on my feet this summer, noticing the heat of the sand

Noticing saltwater and the difference between salt and fresh water

Feeling my body in the water

Feeling the rain

Hearing the wind

Feeling the breeze

Noticing the scenery as I drive by as not dissociated

Noticing my apartment untidiness

Noticing the feeling of my cat

Plants look different

Burning in my feet is gone

Eyes in the front of my head

Able to cry

Able to recognize feelings

Many, many changes

We detailed Sara's responses to help her identify her body's increasing ability to regain physical sensory responses, which her body had shut off when dissociating. Working outdoors helped bring wonder into Sara's life. Sara's list identified many sensory transformations.

Reshaping and Re-Experiencing Everyday Events

We offered Sara opportunities to reshape and re-experience everyday events. For example, Sara described how her father and mother would take her to a restaurant, sit in a booth, and her father always ordered her food. This looked like "manly" respect, but the reality was, Sara said, that her father would finger-rape her as she sat in the booth. Therefore, doing the opposite meant we needed to encourage Sara to trust going to a restaurant with us, to sit in a booth, to read the menu, to make her own decisions on the type of food she wanted to order, to be responsible to know what she could afford and to experience that being in a restaurant meant not being finger-raped. This intervention was done repeatedly. It offered Sara the opportunity to adopt a new way of experiencing a relationship *with* her-Self, deciding what she wanted *to* do, then doing *for* her-Self. This gave Sara the opportunity to reframe the "outsider" world she had been taught never to connect with. As time went by it was always a thrill to see Sara easily manage this everyday skill.

In order to develop a relationship *with/to/for Self,* interventions were needed that touched all aspects of Sara's life. Once we knew the torturers' MO, we could create ways in which to do the opposite. As another example, Sara had been conditioned to believe that when she saw the sun shining a "path" on a lake, she could walk on it. This was the torturers' conditioned suicidal-femicide MO of drowning. To counter this perception, we took Sara to visit a lake, *to* see *for* her-Self the sunshine shimmer on the lake surface. She could critically analyze *for* her-Self what her belief was; *to* learn *for* her-Self that she could not walk on the water. This was an opportunity to decide what psychological distortions she wanted to dismantle *for* her-Self.

Some meetings would involve Sara writing—getting it out—as shown in journaling sheet figure 24. Part of the statement "the value of memories" at the top of Sara's journaling sheet refers to the concept that clarifying memories provided her with explanations for her suffering. This statement also expressed that when memories are released, it is one's body attempting to heal. We would say to Sara, when she re-remembered her victimization memories, that these were, in fact, her "friends." Memories gave her information about the torturers. Sara would easily be revictimized if she remained dissociative or lacked the awareness of the meaning of her memories and who the torturers were. In the early months, she could only realize she was violated after it occurred. Healing her dissociative responses and integrating an understanding of her victimizations took time and many years of "getting it out." She could then learn *to* take action *to* keep her-Self safe, which was about healing her relationship *with/to/ for Self.*

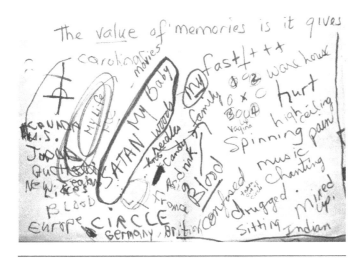

Fig. 24: The value of memories

Sara's flipchart sheets always revealed violations, as shown in figure 24. These violations included being drugged, being hurt, having pain, the use of music and chanting by the torturers, and symbols that inflicted emotional evilism terror. Writing "satan, my baby woods" referred to the forced abortion committed in the woods. This was a memory Sara would need to get out numerous times to clarify *for* her-Self the victimization suffered. And "satan" was a term used for various issues; in this agony, Sara was referring to the man Lee as "satan," who she said took her into the woods.

Sara asserted she had been trafficked across Canada, the US, and Europe, as written on her journaling sheet. Sara suggested she had been taken out-of-country and placed in a brothel when she was a preschooler. Sara called being trafficked *"rented out."* This was her relational norm. In later disclosures, Sara said like-minded torturers *"visited"* Nova Scotia for torture-group gatherings. These resembled everyday family gatherings. Covering up family-based criminal activities was easy when the dominant social stance was to deny the existence of family-based non-State torturers who trafficked their daughters.

SARA'S INSIDER SCHOOLING AND EVILISM CONDITIONING

The meaning of many of Sara's flipchart journal writings fell into place when she described her *"insider schooling."* To unfold the insider schooling demanded intense critical analysis from us plus staying present with Sara until she could relationally assist us to decipher the organized family-based criminal co-culture. Sara's insider schooling must be read from the perspective of detailing adults perpetrating non-State torture crimes against a girl child—against Sara.

The easiest way to comprehend the family-based criminal co-culture is to think of this statement: *This is the way things were done around here!* So how did they do things?

In the ritual abuse-torture model, we identified three goals of "the family." These included ensuring "the family" remained closed and secretive—goal one. To do this "the family" had to take actions that maintained totalitarian power and control—goal two. The adults' actions provided pleasures, entertainment, and, at times, financial or other benefits if involved in, for example, trafficking or other forms of exploitative crimes—goal three. These three goals begin to capture the four Depravity Standard items listed by Welner and colleagues. "The family" groups' intentionality, actions, attitudes, and choice of victim(s) begin to be more deeply revealed.

We recorded the following insider schooling ordeals as Sara re-remembered her childhood. When Sara released a flashback or worked at getting it out, she more or less spoke in the tone of the age she was when she internalized the ordeal she was re-remembering. But her language or words were a mixture of her childhood recall and adult concepts. She also re-felt the emotions experienced at the time of the ordeal. Knowing this "time-travelling" was a normal response that helped Sara to let go of her fears that something was wrong with her. Although Sara generally spoke in the tone of her memory, she did not act in the age she was when victimized.

As we listened intently to her, we also spoke to her as the adult she was, saying, for instance, "Sara, you will be okay."

The following paragraphs describe Sara's flashback insider schooling memory, as she told it. It is intermingled with our statements and paragraphs critically exposing the torturers' intentionality, actions, attitudes, and their choice of Sara as their victim. Sara began:

> I see mySelf going to the little school which was a little building in the woods, across the road, and down over the hill from our house. I went to this little nighttime school first, then when I was older I had to go to both a daytime outsider and "the family" nighttime insider school.
>
> The trainers and teachers were adults of the family, including my mom and other women. We were taught to stand by the desk, for a long time [MO: Immobilization torture]. Sometimes the police come, different policemen, policewoman, sometimes my dad, come to the little school. They had a stick and when they touched you, you got shocked [MO: Electric shock torture]. If you jumped, you get shocked again. Have to stand real still, do it just right [MO: Immobilization torture]. I didn't scream. The kids wouldn't scream. You practiced hard not to jump when they poked you with the police stick. Knew the police, they come to our house and to the store, they had guns…If I don't get learning the first time, Dad would get very angry, I got locked in a room, or in the little basement, or in the basement with the rats [MO: Confinement torture].

Furthering her recall, Sara said:

> First comes the animals in the middle of the circle, little cats and dogs, then our little white lambs called Pork Chops. Poked them all with big long sticks, we did, I did [MO: Forced participation in harming]. They turned red all the time. I wanted to be perfect. I just wanted to be good. Used a big stick with a knife at the end. Adults were happy, said "very good," "excellent," "great" if we got red stuff. Lamb was walking at first, then red, sacrificed [MO: Coded language

use of "sacrifice"]. All the children go around in circles. The circle can't be broken. Animals in the centre of the circle then eventually a child. The big people wanted you to do it to them. I hesitated to do it to them, sometimes they'd smile at you but then they'd have red stuff coming out of them [MO: Forced harming of others].

This paragraph about using a "big stick with a knife at the end" was a MO that not only terrified Sara but also horrified her. She clarified how she and other children were conditioned to harm animals. Her use of "red stuff" referred to blood. This was wording she did not have nor understand at that time. Psychologically, these torture ordeals of apparently killing animals or hurting other children were strategies used to condition Sara to think she was like the torturers. From a critical analysis perspective, there is no way to examine how much distortion and trickery were used. Based on the many stories told by other women, we do accept trickery was a MO used to distort children's concept of reality. It became clear why Sara had internalized that she must have evil within. When Sara sought our support, she had a grave fear she was evil like "the family." Also, this paragraph begins to reveal the MO of the torturers' coded language when naming the perceived killing of the lamb as a "sacrifice." What we and Sara learned was the term "sacrifice" versus "killing" distorted her understanding of reality as an adult. She still believed if she died by suicide this was a "sacrifice" for "the family." Explaining further:

> Before the age of five, the other children and I had to know how the outsiders acted so we could learn to mimic them—you. We had to know how you acted before we started regular school so you, the outsiders, wouldn't catch on to the family. I was taught outsiders were stupid, too stupid to catch on to the family because we did things right in front of your face and you wouldn't even notice. We would make fun of you, the outsiders. And, when we saw outsider children crying it was because they were weak. And if children said they got hurt when they were sexually abused that was again their

fault because they were weak. Sex stuff in the family didn't hurt, they said so. Even when you were little and if it hurts there was something wrong with you because they said you were supposed to like it [MO: Intentional distortion of child-adult relationships (Sarson & MacDonald, 2009b, 2018b)].

"The family's" intention was to condition Sara to blame Her-Self for being weak if she suffered pain when torture-raped; it trained her to be silent when being victimized. If she could not withstand any of what she later called "*torture tests*" the torturers' MO was to degrade her, by telling Sara there was something wrong with her. This conditioned Self-blaming. For many years Sara also reported having no sensation when touched. She would ask us to touch the skin on her hands, for example, and be distressed when she could not feel the touch. An aspect of healing for Sara was to eventually regain some sensation of gentle touch. Sara also described having no sensory connection to her pelvic region. Dissociative survival responses occurred to protect Sara from feeling sexualized torture-pain.

The ideology of the superiority of "the family" written in the inner circle of the ritual abuse-torture model became evident. Sara's indoctrination was that outsiders were stupid and weak but also dangerous. This made our interventions with Sara more complex. So often it felt that Sara resisted our efforts to assist her to be safe and heal. However, when we observed this feeling of resistance, we also understood why, because we heard Sara explain:

> I was also taught never to talk to the outsiders because they, you, are the enemy so I never was to tell them about the family. If I spoke to or befriended an outsider, I'd be a traitor. I'd be contaminated. Once I was contaminated I would contaminate the family so would have to self-sacrifice and make it look like suicide. I was taught to just do and never ask why. I was like a zombie.

The message of becoming a traitor is shown in figure 25. Included is the backward written sentence that says, "You belong to us. We are one." Sara explained this sentence reinforced her sense of evilism and her suicidality expressed as "You deserve to die." This was a MO of intentional and purposeful deadly suicidal indoctrination.

December 15, 1998:

Organized Adult Crimes

against Sara, a Girl Child

Sara's healing had advanced to the point of having the strength to clearly verbalize, and gradu-

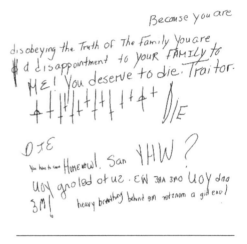

Fig. 25: "The family's" traitor message MO

ally deconstruct, how she had been conditioned into believing she was evil and connected to "satan." She explained:

> I had to know everything before the age of seven because we children become adults at seven. I was constantly fearful I might be doing "it" wrong, that I might not be good enough and, I might not please satan. I was terrified constantly. Taught to hit my forehead left side and say a whole bunch of times:

> "natas sevol em." "natas sevol em." "natas sevol em."

Deciphering this repeated, backward sentence meant: "satan loves me." Sara continued:

> And it's written on the nighttime insider school board and had to put it in the scribbler. We had to practice writing. The family and the trainers and teachers taught me and other children about satan. The family taught me how to worship satan and satan's precious blood, which was black. Black candles were used to signify the power of

satan's blood…when I was placed within and surrounded by the triangle of three black candles I was taught not to move. I couldn't move. I know because I became frozen. Frozen in satan's triangle. I was in satan's complete control [MO: Spiritual distortion used to inflict powerlessness].

The MO of a triangle of black candles conditioned Sara into powerlessness, terrifying her into believing she was evil. To undo this victimization response, with Sara's consent, we role-played the torturers' MO, based on Kurt Lewin's Change Model theory. We brought three black candles to the office. Sara agreed to sit on the floor, and three black candles were placed in a triangle around her and then lit. At first, Sara sat paralysed, waiting. When nothing happened, she took the risk to move in and out of the triangle. Still, nothing happened! This ended her distorted belief of powerlessness created by the black candle triangle. It introduced Sara to her need to develop a critical analysis of the torturers' use of deception. This was doing the opposite of what the torturers did. Sara, with support, was provided with the opportunity to decide for her-Self if the MO was a truth or a lie. Moving on, Sara said:

> I was taught to believe I was one with satan and that I must submit to him because he is my father. "My father is satan—satan is in me; satan is my controller…my brain…my master…satan owns me," that's what I was taught. That's why I was given the name Santana. Santana, the daughter of satan; Santana, the Chosen One, was my insider name…I be in a consummation ceremony…a marriage to my father.

We asked Sara to detail what she meant by a "consummation ceremony." Eventually, she clarified "the family" used this coded term to cover up intentionally organized gatherings for the purpose of inflicting pedophilic, psychological, sexualized, physical, and spiritual torture victimizations on Sara (Sarson & MacDonald, 2016b). Listening critically to Sara's recall exposed the organized family-based trafficking of Sara:

> It was daytime and I waited in the store with my dad until the man came in the car to pick me up [MO: Father as trafficker]. Walking with my dad to the man's car, I get in the back seat with a blanket [MO: The man was the "buyer" of Sara]. The man gives me a lollipop bottle. It is made of glass so I have to be very careful not to break it. It has red Kool-Aid in it. I have to practice sucking on the lollipop bottle so I can do good sucking on lollipops [MO: Use of the coded word "lollipops" for erect penises]. And soon I'm slowly falling over onto the back seat. I'm very tired, very sleepy [MO: Chemical drugging torture using the coded language "Kool-Aid"].
>
> It was dark time when I was at the ceremony [MO: Use of the coded word "ceremony" for a group perpetrator torture gathering]. I'm on my knees, dressed in my little white dress with white socks and black and white shoes in the middle of a circle of big people. The big people are my family, they love and protect me; the circle keeps you safe so you can never break the circle or you will die [MO: Conditioned psychological captivity, death threats, and distortion of child-adult relationships].
>
> I'm cold but I say over and over, "Father, I love you forever, I promise." You have to say it just right like I was taught at the family school… when the big people make a little break at one end of the circle… my father walks through wearing a black robe with a little red on it, bare feet, sandals, repeats "Santana, Santana" [MO: Intentional psychological conditioning to distort adult-child relationships and the use of dogma and ritualized drama to distort criminal reality].
>
> When my father satan is standing in front of me I have to look way up…my father says "Santana, welcome home. You are home." I smile because that's what the ladies in the family school taught me. They prepared me for a long time so I would know how to do this. I say "Yes, Father, I glad I finally home" [Again, the MO is: Intentional

psychological conditioning to distort adult-child relationships and use of dogma to distort reality].

My father has to make two cuts, one on my wrist and one on his wrist. I have to give my father blood. He sucks on my cut and I suck on his cut. Sometimes I have a dribble of blood on my chin but not allowed to wipe it off. I was also taught this in the family school. My father gave me his lollipop to suck [MO: Coded language for oral torture-rape]. And it goes in you and stuff runs from my father right into me.

My father takes me out...to the cabin for the rest of the consummation ceremony [MO: Use of coded language "consummation ceremony" as a cover-up for organized pedophilic torture-rape of Sara plus organized voyeurism by the group]. That's a big word I learned and there's only me and my father in the cabin. On the bed my father goes home in me [The repeated MO: Coded language of "home" for vaginal torture-rape] and puts cream from a little jar on his lollipop and puts his lollipop in the house and in the dog house [MO: Coded language of "house" for the vagina and "dog house" for anal torture-rape]. He's breathing funny and falls over on his back. I stay there, be very still. I have no clothes on and I'm so cold. It's dark and I'm very scared [MO: Deprivation tortures of forced nakedness and cold temperature with emotional fear].

I say to me, "I be in a marriage to my father. I have duties now, I be seven and all grown up. I be an adult, the lollipop stuff be inside of me forever" [MO: Conditioning and violently distorting Sara's concepts of adult-child relationships by instilling spiritual distortion that semen means she had evil within and the perpetrator was her "satan father"].

I just lay there because I'm tired and my arms and head are heavy. I'm sore in the home and in the mom. I feel my home [MO: Taught coded distorting language, use of words "mom" and "home" refers to mouth and vagina] is bigger but it will go little again and will get bigger when my father comes again [MO: Normalization of pedophilic torture-raping and intentional distortion of adult-child relationships].

Prior to this memory, we had taught Sara about her body using anatomical names. This knowledge helped Sara examine her memory and clarify how coded language had been used to deceive her and protect the torturers. The torturers taught Sara as a child to use their coded language, which prevented her from exposing the organized criminal family and group. If Sara said, "Dad came in the back door" or "Dad is in the dog house," both of these statements would generally be misunderstood by outsiders. This is one reason we strongly advocate for children in school, from primary onwards, to become familiar with anatomically naming their body parts. Sara, and the women who connected with us, mentioned if they had received this informational education in school they may have realized what they were suffering, and tried to tell and be believed. Non-perpetrating parents must begin this awareness, protection, and prevention education from day one.

Our outsiders' look into the insider family-based organized gathering which aimed at trafficking and torturing Sara, must be clearly understood. Sara's story is of adults who inflicted organized crimes against her when she was a child. Welner's work on the depravity standard captures their intentions, actions, attitudes, and Sara as their "choice of victim." Staub describes that actions of human evil devalue and destroy another individual human being. This fits the torture the adult group inflicted against Sara.

Sara, as an innocent toddler, preschooler, and seven-year-old was manipulated, deceived, tortured, and trafficked by multi-perpetrators. They intentionally, purposefully, and discriminately altered her reality in every way possible, to create the "perfect victim." They further distorted her relationship with/to/for Self by forcing her to believe she was "special," she was "the chosen one." They coated Sara's indoctrination intentionally with spiritual evilism distortions of "satan's child"—falsifying the truth that "satan" was coded language that, for example, referred to an erect penis (Sarson & MacDonald, 2008).

When Sara and her family moved to Nova Scotia from another Atlantic province, Sara told she was again identified as "satan's child" and "Lee" was her "satan father." She revealed this in figure 6, on thoughts and beliefs, in Chapter 4. Sara's journaling sheets revealed Lee's brutal and horrifying serial torturing of Sara using these terms.

Canadian Centre for Child Protection

Research by the Canadian Centre for Child Protection on the internet reveals images of the sexualized victimization of children (Bunzeluk, 2009). Fifty-seven percent of the crime scene images were of children under eight years of age, and the most extreme sexualized victimization was inflicted against them, with many crime scene images showing infants or toddlers being victimized;

1. The extreme crime scene images involved torture, bondage, bestiality, and degradation, such as being defecated upon;

2. Eighty-three percent of the crime scene images were of the girl child; and

3. Parents and those known to the children were the most common perpetrators.

Further evidence of depravity was described in an article that stated employees of the Canadian Centre for Child Protection noted there was a 12 percent increase between 2013 and 2014 in the depravity of "torture" and "bondage" of children (Cribb, 2015). These crime scene videos provide actual evidence and knowledge to support Sara's childhood victimization reality. As well, this evidence demonstrates to Canadian political and legal groups that such crimes are real. Canadian members of parliament have, however, persistently refused to criminalize torture committed by private individuals or groups as a crime of torture.

The Organized Adult Crime Against Sara Continued: Women's Involvement

Sara's retelling of this specific torture ordeal exposes that her parents had connections with like-minded others. Although Sara does not know what benefits her parents derived from planning and "preparing" her to be transported to this organized torture group, Sara's ordeals reveal her parents were human traffickers as well as torturers.

Before and after Sara's torture-trafficking ordeal, Sara said women were involved (Sarson & MacDonald, 2016b). She described the women's MO involved "*purification*" and "*cleansing rituals.*" She said:

> The ladies came to the house, the house with the white picket fence which was next door to our store. The ladies got me ready, making me very clean by scrubbing me from head to toe with brushes and water. Brushes which were a little bigger than toothbrushes and water that smelled like Javex or like smelly things used inside of cars [MO: Distortion of women and girl child relationships].
>
> The ladies washed inside my ears, cleaned and put stinging stuff inside my nose using a cotton-tipped little stick and took stuff from a little bottle and put the stuff into my eyes. They used a little squeezy thing. It stings my eyes and makes water come out of them. I had to close my eyes but I wasn't supposed to. I was supposed to do it right and keep my eyes open [MO: Chemical torture in her eyes]. When this stuff was put into my eyes it was like looking through a wet window.
>
> The ladies used brushes on the insides too. They brushed my mom, my home, and my dog house. The ladies gave me red Kool-Aid because it was part of the preparation because they tell me it will

make the water red after the consummation ceremony [MO: Make the water red was coded language to distort the truth that Sara would suffer vaginal and/or anal bleeding when raped].

When the ladies finished scrubbing me I had to stand in the bathroom by the tub to dry off. It's cold standing there naked. Afterwards the ladies dry my mom, home, and dog house. They have to make sure I'm not wet anywhere so they use a big towel thing in my mom and it makes me feel choked. Sometimes they use their fingers to put yellow slippery stuff in my dog house [MO: Sexualized torture with the application of Vaseline or lubricant to her anus]. All the scrubbing made me feel raw but I feel clean because this is how you get purified. That is what I learned in the insider schooling. Then the ladies put my clothes on, a little white dress with white socks and black and white shoes. A man from the USA base gave the shoes to me.

One of the ladies took me to our store next to our house. It was daytime. I waited in the store with my dad until the man came.

Following the organized group gathering and the torture-raping of Sara by the man, women inflicted the final group torture victimization of Sara. It ended this way:

The ladies come into the cabin, they have to clean me, to scrub my home and my mom with the brushes, little ones, bigger than toothbrushes and put more cream in my home to take care of my home. They put hot cloths in my home because it's hurting and they have to make it better.

My head is so heavy; they have to lift my head up when they pour water and Kool-Aid down my throat [MO: Chemical torture of drugging]. I'm like the sink and like a tap that won't stop because when they pour the water and the Kool-Aid down my mom it just goes right down. The water smells like peppermint and like the water used in the preparation. Nobody talks.

The little cabin is like the dark brown and black house in the storybook in the family school. With little steps, a little roof in front where you can sit and not get wet. Inside the windows are black, I can't see out of them. The books also tell me about the consummation ceremony [MO: Intentional psychological distortions using coded language of "consumption ceremony"].

I stay in the little cabin until I am able to walk again. Then the man picks me up and takes me home during the dark time. The man talks to my mom but I go lie down because I have to be quiet. I be sad and water come in my eyes and on my face. I got in trouble [MO: Terrorization—instilled terror and silence because what Sara meant when she said "water come in my eyes and on my face" was that she started to cry and "trouble" meant she was beaten].

These like-minded group MO patterns of torture-trafficking victimizations are comparable to ritual dramas. Ritual dramas fundamentally serve to provide gratification for those involved (Leach & Fried, 1984). In this group's victimization of Sara, there was the man who torture-raped her, but there were also the other adults who participated voyeuristically. To increase their gratification, ritual-dramas can also include music, chanting, dance, mime, costumes, and evilism themes. This can explain why Sara and other women frequently spoke of the group perpetrators as being in circles, chanting, and speaking what sounded like gibberish. Specific music and songs were used by individual torturers; this became obvious in some of Sara's drawings. Lee repeatedly liked the song "Tie a Yellow Ribbon Round the Old Oak Tree."

By applying organizational theory to these group crime scenes, and referring to Richard Draft who indicates that rituals create relational bonding with like-minded others, as well as reinforce a sense of group identity (1995), we observe that adult torturer-traffickers do bond. They began moulding Sara's sense of bonding and identity as being "one with satan" to keep her emotionally attached to "the family." Her emotional bonding was a complex paradox of insider superiority as the "chosen one," that normalized her captivity, oppression, and repetitive torture victimizations while destroying her sense of being human.

When Sara was re-remembering this torture group violation, she was in a dual state of awareness. She would explain the ordeal as if she was back to feeling like the seven-year-old little girl when the torture ordeals were committed. This explains why her language sounded young. We recorded her memory in written form as she spoke. Linda wrote out Sara's verbalization as she re-remembered her ordeals while Jeanne sat with Sara on the floor to comfort her, saying, "Sara, you will be okay." When emotional terror memory came, Jeanne said to her, "Sara, you are safe, this ordeal happened years ago, when you were just a beautiful little girl. You are now a woman and no longer there. You will be okay." These statements grounded Sara so she did not become consumed by the memory she was recalling. Sara told us these statements helped her believe we heard her, understood her distress, were staying present with her, and not abandoning her; she was not left alone in her memory. Sara's re-remembering ordeals such as these took hours of support and stamina.

Jeanne and Linda's Reflection on the Power of Caring

Often, we reflect that staying present with Sara through her recalling of a torture ordeal is similar to staying present with a woman in labour. If the labour goes on for 12 hours then nurses stay present to validate her emotions and physical labour. The same applies to working in an intensive care unit; the nurse stays present to be aware of the status of the critically ill person. Our experience working in these areas of healing care grounded us to stay present with Sara.

There are other ways we understood Sara's flashbacking responses. Caring about her when she expressed having to "get it out" we considered normal and essential healing. Her responses were comparable to the experiences of Vietnam veterans who speak of "living in a split time zone" (Shatan, 1997). We stayed present with Sara to assure her that the feelings of being in a split time zone of past and present were normal, and we would assist her in staying reality-connected.

Another perspective understands the healing power of validation (Jones, 1995). Staying present with Sara as she travelled through her memories permitted us to validate her, as she could see we were writing what she was telling us. This validated that we were listening and believing her.

Nursing evidence comes from experience (Paterson, 2003). Understanding how our caring was assisting Sara provided us with developing knowledge and scientific evidence as Capra had mentioned. We know our caring was outside the services a woman who has survived non-State torture can access in Canada. The Centre for Victims of Torture (CCVT) in Toronto offers services to immigrant individuals who have suffered torture. The Centre is not funded to offer services to women who have survived torture inflicted by private individuals in Canada.

THE IMPACT ON SARA AS AN ADULT WOMAN

Reflecting on her memories, Sara spoke of how the torturers' evil actions of conditioning continued to impact her functionality as an adult woman.

> When I was older, August the 29 was the day I was to be sacrificed. It was the destiny of the Chosen One, the day I should feel honoured to be sacrificed for satan. Every year there is a big ceremony. First there is preparation, the purification ritual, have to get cleaned, about a week before the ceremony, then, there is the big ceremony. August 29, I have to practice being sacrificed to satan. The family would have the ceremony out in the woods. I would be taken there but it

was never my time. They would say, "It's not your time" depending on the full moon or other things, always next year, always another time. As an adult I knew I had to return to "the family" for the sex stuff, preparation rituals, ceremonies and or sacrifices. I would get a phone call saying it was "time to come home." I always felt so tired and dizzy when I got these messages and I would just do. I was like a zombie.

I feel so terrified when I have flashbacks about being taken to the sacrificial ceremony, placed in the circle of fire. I find my-Self lying stiff and flat on my bed with the flames all around me. It's horrifying. I can't move, dizzy, and terror. It's so hard when I'm in the flashback to not believe it's really happening, to not believe that I'm burning alive. It was especially terrifying the first time I had this flashback.

Sara's statement that on "*August 29 I have to practice being sacrificed to satan*" clarified the motivation of why she called "Flight into Freedom" the night of August 25. It explains why she said she was going to die in four days' time. August 29 was almost upon her. It explains her statement, "*It's all planned…my death…for the 29th…before I have to go back to work.*" She was terrified, and in an emotional state that satisfied the torturers' pleasure as listed under attitudes in the Depravity Standards items. Enduring years of being set up and manipulated into thinking she was going to be "*sacrificed,*" and then each year being told it was not the year, meant Sara feared 1993 was the year she would die. Because of the decades of evilism conditioning, Sara did not comprehend that "being sacrificed," if carried out, would be an organized crime of murder. This illustrates how "the family's" use of coded language of "sacrifice" kept Sara psychologically terrified and captive. Inflicting terror satisfied the torturers' pleasure as listed in the Depravity Standards under attitudes.

Conditioning Sara to believe she would have to die by suicide if she told on "the family" began as a toddler when she was taught death ditties, sharing two of these as:

DEATH SONG CHANT

We are one

We are one we are one

I will not forsake my family

I will not forsake my family

Die

Die

Die

DEATH STORY

I will never tell on my family

I love my family

My family is me

We are one

To tell is to die a horrible death

I can never escape this—my destiny

I am one with my family destiny whatever will

be, will be (go to sleep).

Sara explained that as a child she had to learn the "Death Story" by repeating it aloud to her parents. It was also, she said, to be repeated silently every night. Sara believes it was chanted as a lullaby when she was an infant. It was a bedtime story, especially used during "birthday ceremonies." These death ditties were tools of psychological torture that served to entrap Sara in ongoing emotional terror, to remain silent and remain in a state of constant captivity as the "perfect victim."

When Sara was a preschooler, she spoke of being forced to sit in a hallway and taught how to cut her wrists, explaining:

> From the time I was a very tiny little girl I was taught that sacrifice was the ultimate gift to the family, to satan. I didn't understand self-sacrifice to be suicide so I lived all my life with an intimate connection this was a good thing.

The complexity of Sara's conditioning that she had to die was deeply distorted when mixed with "the family's" necrophilic or pseudo-necrophilic MO. When Sara was poly-drugged into a state of being unable to move her body—lifeless—she was then torture-raped. There were brutal torture ordeals that left her, to this day, with a belief that, at times, "the family" was involved in actual killings and necrophilic acts. We have heard other women similarly disclose this possibility. This raises the question: Are these family-based and like-minded torturers not only serial torturers and traffickers but killers? A question we will discuss in Chapter 12, Part 3.

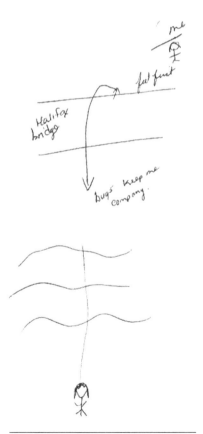

Fig. 26: Suicide-femicide conditioning of Sara

SUICIDE-FEMICIDE CONDITIONING AND RESEARCH

Sara explained that suicidal-conditioning was reinforced when she was an adult by women perpetrators. She depicted the process of how the women pressured her to die by suicide in figure 26. She described:

> When I sought professional counselling, the counsellor took me into a women's group which was like the family. They also taught me "how-to" do self-sacrifice. They would take me to practice how to jump off the bridge. I was told to visualize how it would be as I sank under water and how peaceful I would feel and I was counselled how to sit in the bathtub to cut my wrists and visualize how my blood and all my pain would run out of me, or I was counselled how to run my car into the water and how good that would feel. All the pain would go away, always the programming "go to the water, go to the water, all will be okay if I just go to the water." The battle to fight this programming urge of self-sacrifice was relentless.

At our April 30, 1996 meeting, Sara's verbatim description was:

> I was supposed to get up at 3 a.m. and go to the bridge, lock the car up, and go to the top of the rail. Wear purple skirt. Purple shoes, purple earrings, play tape, and float like an angel at the bridge. Open your arms, look down at the nice water because I like water, jump into the water and be pure.

Sara went on to say she was forced to practice how to jump off the Halifax Bridge by "being made to stand up on the chair at the master's home [the female therapist] and at her office." We have named this form of victimization suicidal-femicidal conditioning (Sarson & MacDonald, 2018c).

Research: Non-State Torture Suicidal-Femicide Criminal Victimization Questionnaire

In 2018 we placed our non-State torture suicidal-femicide criminal victimization questionnaire on our website (Persons Against Non-State Torture, n.d., d). We did so mindful that women who read our published article on suicidal-femicidal conditioning might need to tell their story.

Seldom are we contacted by men. We respect that femicide—the specific killing of women and girls (Canadian Femicide Observatory for Justice and Accountability, n.d.)—would not fit for men, suicidal-homicide would. However, of the immediate 14 respondents, one was a man, 13 were women. Four were Canadian, eight were from the US, and two were from the UK. We learned that:

- Ten respondents were directly told to kill them-Selves

- Eight respondents were taught how to kill them-Selves

- These 18 responses mean some individuals were both told and taught to kill them-Selves

- Some respondents were told to kill them-Selves
  by multi-perpetrators:

  - Eight said professionals told them to kill them-Selves

  - Fathers, mothers, other relatives, family friends, human traffickers, and pimps were identified as having told respondents to kill them-Selves

- Primary methods on how to kill them-Selves included: cutting their veins or their throat, or stabbing them-Selves, followed by a vehicle crash or other "accidents" with guns, jumping from dangerous heights, drowning, burning, and drug overdosing. Other deadly methods used by the perpetrators were triggering phone calls and sending a letter.

Counselling a person to kill them-Self is a criminal offence in Canada. If non-State torture is not criminalized, the perpetrators' MO of conditioning a woman or girl to appear to have killed her-Self will not be seen as a femicidal crime.

HOPE'S INSIDER SCHOOLING AND EVILISM CONDITIONING

We would learn Sara's insider schooling was not a unique MO. Hope, when participating in our kitchen-table research project, also briefly described being insider-schooled. Sara and Hope were subjected to insider schooling in two different Canadian provinces by different families.

Evil actions of the non-State torturers' MO of insider schooling present the darkest side of the family-based, intentional destruction of a girl child. The insider-schooling torture ordeals illustrate the unlimited degrees of torture a child can be subjected to—a reality that must be acknowledged and unsilenced. It is an insight into crimes against their humanity. Hope's schooling victimization, like Sara's, must be read as adults' intentional, purposeful, organized non-State torture crime against a girl child—against Hope. Hope disclosed that:

> Insider schooling happened in everyday family living; other schooling was specifically directed on teaching me "the family" rituals, ceremonies, and how to cope with pornography and prostitution. I was told, "What goes on in the family stays in the family." I heard over and over "you get what you deserve," making me feel it was all my fault. Fear of the consequences was made more real when told "you tell, you die." If I felt fear it was my fault for being weak.

> My mother was one of my trainers. They taught me about the superiority of "the family" and about the weakness of outsiders. I was taught about loyalty and obedience to "the family." I was taught about secrecy, about just doing. I was taught to read and write backwards using my left hand. As I passed each test my power grew, at least that was their dogma.

> Triangular shapes were silencing traps. I was taught how to keep silent by automatically surrounding my-Self with the three sides of a triangular shape. I was taught to see triangles everywhere. The symbol of the "ε" also meant traitor, it was also touted as a way to keep the demons within. Nothing was sacred from being used with

trickery; everything was a mind-spirit trap. "The family" flourished on deceiving children, creating chaos, creating the nothing-makes-sense feelings, massive confusion, and just doing.

From a very young age I was taught that I had the marking of the number "4" on my forehead and on the palms of my hands. I saw what I was told to see. Why wouldn't I? Later in my life I came face to face with myself in the mirror and de-programmed myself of these deceptive thoughts.

"Natasha," which is rooted to the name satan spelled backwards, was a name given to me. Before a ceremony started I had been given some type of pills and stripped naked before being robed. As the ceremony progressed I got diarrhea, I think that's what the pills were meant to do, the feces was smeared all over my body as they pissed on, shit on, humiliated, demoralized, de-spiritualized me. I was made to think I was "the Chosen One." The ceremonies I was taken to all happened inside of buildings: my grandfather's hay loft, barns, inside houses, and inside a church. Every site meant either I was a witness to the horrific event, a victim used within the horrific event, or a victim forced to participate in the event which "the family" called their rituals and ceremonies like a "marriage to the beast" ceremony. "The family" taught me that committing suicide became a purification ceremony. There were cleansing rituals that went along with preparation rituals. These rituals meant I was scrubbed with a wire brush from head to toe, inside and out. Scrubbing continued until it brought blood. "The family" said adulthood starts at age seven years. By the way, outsiders also have their rituals and ceremonies.

Hope and Sara's telling of the torturer-traffickers' MO of "insider schooling" are very similar. There are variations in that the bizarre creativity is individualistic, thus endless in how they enact their dehumanizing brutalities. The differences are that Hope had processed her memories long before we spoke to her. Sara was revealing her memories for the first time.

It was deeply intense to stay present with Sara and other women as they struggled to overcome their terror and horror, to disclose the acts of human evil they survived. Expressions of human evil have a bone-chilling physical feeling, even when spoken of as memory. This has been painful work for the women, and Linda and me, because of the social and legal refusal to accept that non-State torture victimizations exist. This silencing upsets me.

Waking in the morning I frequently lie in bed absorbed in the enormity of such injustice. One morning I found my-Self thinking about the 2010 Chilean mining accident and the 33 men trapped so deep underground (Rashid et al., 2013). Reading about their rescue after being trapped for 69 days is a story of wonder. Three separate drilling rig teams, the Chilean government, the US NASA space agency, and corporations from around the world, all cooperated in drilling a tunnel through the earth and building a capsule to extend a caring "hand" to rescue the men.

As I lay in bed that morning, after writing this chapter, I imaged the tunnel that made it possible to welcome the men back into their communities. Doing this work to help rescue Sara and other women is like trying to drill through social denial bedrock that fails to hear their calls for help. An escape tunnel for their journey to society's surface gets plastered with blocks thrown down the tunnel over and over again. Their rescue cries remain unheard. A caring capsule is still not present for them, as it was not for us.

Then I think Sara and the other women have been trapped "underground" for decades—not 69 days—but decades. How can this be just? How can it be that adult torturers are permitted to keep hunting and brutalizing children, their own or those of others? Why is a safe tunnel not built for them to walk safely and freely on this planet's surface? It is a painful, heinous, and grievous injustice I considered as I lay in bed thinking about another effort, another way to build a tunnel for women to reach a caring surface. I am hoping there is courage out there to hear what Linda and I, Sara, and the other women in this book are voicing. They are women unsilencing their lived herstories. A welcoming tunnel must open for all the women and little girls who have survived the evil actions of non-State torturers; and of course, this applies to little boys and men so harmed.

CHAPTER 9
MOVING ON
_____

November 7, 1994

Sara phoned expressing being "afraid of things I don't even know yet, of abandonment, of not being good enough, of being a monster." She had suddenly realized she was in her apartment; her clothes were wet, so she rationalized she must have been outdoors because it had been raining. This was the second similar event of the week. Both times, Sara said, she could not remember going out. Sara appeared to have had dissociative responses to triggers she could not explain, at the same time saying, "people really do live like this." This statement suggested Sara was attempting to develop the realization that the torture brutalities she had relationally normalized were actually violent ordeals.

Looking back to September, Sara said she had lived in an "*other world*." We related to Sara's description, given the journey we were on with her. We needed to understand Sara's "other world" of the family-based criminal co-cultural world of serial non-State torturer-traffickers.

In 1995, literature from the Registered Nurses' Association of Nova Scotia defined culture as a way of life that:

1. Involved a family structure with relational practices, habits, and behaviours that included personal and group rituals, dress, and food, for example;

2. Encompassed, for instance, beliefs, values, attitudes, perceptions, spirituality, expectations; and

3. Included the meaning of language, verbal and non-verbal interactions, gender communication norms, and illustrated personal space or boundaries.

Sara's co-cultural "other world" fit into these defining elements of culture. However, what was neglected is acknowledging the culture or co-culture of organized criminal groups. Yet nurses come in contact with individuals who are violent, and who commit crimes. We nurse those who have been victimized, as well as support them in their healing of traumatization that is a consequence of their victimization. If professional associations fail to recognize the co-culture of family-based criminal groups, this places severe risks on those being harmed, especially for those serially victimized, as Sara was. For us, it kept us working underground, and in isolation, because there was no place in the health care system for Sara to fit without being pathologized—a blame-the-victim perspective and practice.

As revealed during the kitchen-table research conversations, these everyday-looking families had a deep and seemingly invisible organized pattern of criminality, with a network connected to like-minded others. In Canada, and other countries, their invisibility was and continues to be directly related to persistent social and systemic denials of non-State torture crimes by wrongfully misnaming them as an assault. This denial provides impunity for the torturers.

It was mind-bendingly difficult to decode the destruction of Sara as a consequence of "the family" co-culture of human evil actions. Sara's parents were similar to the parents described by Carrie, Hope, Kate, and Phoenix's friends. All these perpetrating parents were involved in their communities, taking roles as a municipal councillor, a firefighter, a member of community organizations, and church members. They participated in Home and School Association activities and volunteered in school programs.

Alex, introduced in the previous chapter, lived on her father's farm. She took the bus to and from school; her father was the school bus driver and the student driver training instructor. Alex also said her father and his like-minded male-torturers were deacons of their Mennonite church; her father was a Sunday school teacher. Alex said "*I was powerless*" against the positional power her father held in their community.

Family-based non-State torturer-traffickers were skilled at manipulating society in order to camouflage the torture-trafficking brutalities they inflicted on their selected daughters and other children. When one of Sara's parents was dying, we asked Sara to ask her parent if she/he would speak with us. We did this because Sara insisted on having a connection with her dying parent. This was one of the situations where we all had to agree to disagree. We observed that this contact kept Sara somewhat immersed in the family indoctrination. Our opinion was that this harmed Sara's recovery. Sara disagreed. To make the best of this situation we thought maybe her parent would take the opportunity to give insider evidence that would help protect Sara and assist us to gain further clarity of the co-culture. This did not happen.

November 21, 1994

Sara drew figure 27.

This drawing further explained part of Sara's March 10, 1993, flipchart journaling seen in figure 7. On the top left-hand corner of this flipchart sheet, Sara had written about being tortured and "taken in the woods." Furthermore, her flashback of "red and it hurts" represented Sara's increasing awareness of trying to make sense of what happened to her in the woods. Sara was finally able to explain what happened, as illustrated in figure 27. Clarifying this drawing, Sara said she was taken into the woods by Lee and his wife, who then forcedly aborted her.

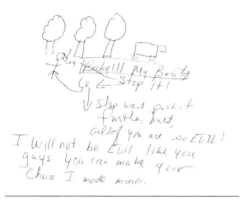

Fig. 27: Forced abortion in the woods

Referring back to August 1993, Sara had written these words that she could not explain and we did not understand:

baby, Woods, Lee, blood, hurt, strap, abort, hit you with branches and they stung…weren't supposed to have Lee's baby. Did not want Jeanne & Linda to know afraid you would believe Sara was bad. Beat with branches not to tell and welts all over your body. Bleeding badly from the abortion. Trying to stay still. Worse memory ever. Staying really still. I am really angry at me because I hurt someone.

Our observational experience was it took Sara multiple attempts and ways for her to gain informed, understandable, and meaningful awareness about ordeals she had suffered. Between August 1993 and November 21, 1994, when Sara drew figure 27, there had been various indicators suggestive of this specific abortion in the woods ordeal. But it took this amount of time for Sara to integrate its violent meaning and explain it clearly for her-Self. This was her recovery work. This pattern of gradually re-remembering and comprehending would be repeated for years as Sara recovered.

Jeanne's Reflections

It was 2 a.m. when Sara called. There were many calls that November 21 night. Sara left no messages. Night calls came at any time and very many when Sara was struggling not to be overrun with terror, trying to stay safe. On the edge of desperation Sara continued to call my home number, which was listed in the telephone book. This caused my husband stress. To his credit, he stayed with the process of my being up sometimes for hours in the middle of the night, and then getting ready for work in the early morning. These desperate calls would last for many years although Sara did try to respect the boundaries I asked her to uphold; it was close to seven years before Sara settled.

"Double Torture"

Relational connections for women who have survived acts of non-State torture and who are integrating their torture victimizations are both painful and healing. Women's bodies often re-remember and feel the torture-pain their bodies dissociated in order for them to survive. Sara had reflective words of wisdom about the pain of re-remembering. She created the following list to express how she experienced the healing of her dissociative survival responses. She said it was like being tortured all over again. She called it *"double torture"* involving:

- flashbacking
- re-enacting
- immobilizing
- running
- remembering
- witnessing
- talking
- crying
- integrating
- feeling

- knowing

- being

Sara had asked for a home visit support. She wanted to fully integrate her forced abortion recovery. Her apartment was the most comfortable place to do this release and integration healing work. This took the form of a testimonial. Sara recalled:

> They told me in the truck what was going to happen. They told me I was pregnant. Lee got me pregnant. The "chosen one" is not supposed to get pregnant...They slapped me and told me to shut up. Took me into the woods...Their eyes were creepy. I knew they were mad. Unpredictable. Hit you...in the face and other parts of your body. I didn't want to let go of her [baby]...They said, "You little bitch and you little bastard." Everybody called me, even in my house, "bastard."

Sara needed to lie in her bed, covered and warm. Women frequently feel chilled and shiver when re-remembering a shocking torture-victimization memory. As Sara was talking she started breathing quickly, moaning, and began to cry out very quietly. She put her hands over her ears, trying not to hear Lee and his wife's voices, and all their yelling. Sara said she was also yelling. Hearing the voices of Lee and his wife was verbal memory. Other women, including the women who participated in the kitchen-table research, also mentioned this. Carrie said, "their laughter still haunts me. I can still hear their laughter ringing inside my head, inside my ears."

Continuing, Sara explained:

> It's like a movie. I was scared...They told me I was bad because I was a bitch and a bastard. Because I was supposed to be the chosen one...I didn't know what to do...I ran. It was dark and wet and cold. I tried to hide. You can't get away. They knocked me down. They lit

a fire and dance around you and say stuff. When Lee did something to me. They put the fire close to you. It hurts down there. Across my legs—and blood. It hurts now. They hurt me bad that night. She sat on my arms. Lee did the legs. He spread them open. I just gave up and cried while they were at it. All the cuts and bruises. I was bad… they beat me up. They didn't want to; they had to because I ran away. I was bad. I had a bad seed in me. I didn't know what it meant. I didn't get away. I didn't save [the baby]…It's my fault—I gave up. I just let them do it—I shouldn't have let them. I didn't want to do it. I don't want to eat it. They cut it and stuck it in my mouth. I get sick. I'm too tired. I just lay there and don't help her. I didn't save her. They laughed. They call me bad body santana.

I was between 13 or 15, and all by myself.

This is how Sara's multiple layers of re-remembering and healing happened. Each time she developed more clarity and comprehension of what being born into "the family" meant. That Sara was forced to consume pieces of the aborted tissue is a MO of family-based torturer-traffickers that Alex shared in Chapter 7. Also, now we understood why one of the requests Sara asked of us on September 6, 1993, was "no dancing around her." Sara had been humiliated by being "danced" around by Lee and his wife during the forced abortion in the woods ordeal. This was another dehumanizing MO that caused deep psychological wounds of humiliation. The profound harm caused by humiliation can be more long-lasting than physical torture (Vorbrüggen & Baer, 2007). This fact goes back to our model of Self. The knowledge that emotional pain can stick to a person like glue and resurface repeatedly, regenerating deep emotions of humiliation, shame, and worthlessness were emotional feelings Sara re-experienced with flashbacking integration recovery.

When a woman releases and integrates a specific torture-victimization memory, emotional feelings such as terror and horror also tag along. These can be paralyzing emotions that invade the here and now. Releasing deep memories took hours. With Sara, these were the times when we did home visits so we could leave her in her apartment before we drove back home, often in the early morning hours. These were exhausting hours for Sara and us. However, providing care to women such as Sara, who struggle to let go of actions of human evil that they suffered, is a precious gift.

REPRODUCTIVE HARMS RESEARCH

Because women were telling us horrifying reproductive torture ordeals, in March 2007, we conducted a short-lived 10 question reproductive-harm research questionnaire via the internet. We framed the wording to be familiar to women who might respond. Fifty women answered the 10 questions. This is what they shared:

Question 1: What country are you from? Canadian (20%), US (52%), Europe (12%), Australia (8%), New Zealand (4%), Israel (2%), and other (2%).

Question 2: Did you decide not to have a child because you thought it would be impossible to keep a child safe? Yes (36%), no (54%), and non-applicable (10%).

Question 3: Have you ever experienced a forced pregnancy by ritual abuse-torture perpetrators? Yes (72%), no (28%), non-applicable (0%).

Question 4: Have you experienced forced abortions by ritual abuse-torture perpetrators? Yes (68%), no (32%), non-applicable (0%).

Question 5: Have you experienced a live delivery when still enslaved by ritual abuse-torture perpetrators? Yes (51%), no (47%), non-applicable (2%).

Question 6: Did rapes occur during or after an abortion or delivery? Yes (59%), no (29%), non-applicable (12%).

Question 7: If a pregnancy or pregnancies occurred was the infant(s) killed/sacrificed? Yes (60%), no (18%), non-applicable (22%).

Question 8: If a pregnancy or pregnancies occurred was the infant(s) cannibalized? Yes (54%), no (29%), non-applicable (17%).

Question 9: If a pregnancy or pregnancies occurred did the infant(s) disappear? Yes (42%), no (34%), non-applicable (24%);

Question 10: If a pregnancy or pregnancies occurred was the infant(s) kept within the family? Yes (10%), no (68%), non-applicable (22%).

In 2021, we still hear from women who as children were forcedly impregnated when tortured and trafficked. They suffered forced abortions or were left alone to deliver the baby who then disappeared.

CLOSURE

In 1996, we assisted Sara to gain a disability pension. She could no longer manage her professional obligations. This was a loss and grief for Sara. She and we had hoped she would be able to eventually return to her profession. Sara never did. Thirty-six years of family-based co-culture victimizations altered her life forever.

Our intention in writing this book is to unsilence the voices of women who tell their stories of surviving non-State torture, of surviving this crime inflicted against their humanity and to unsilence our developing knowledge about non-State torture victimization-traumatization care. For some women, their victimization began in infancy, for many in childhood, and for others, the torture continued into their adulthood or occurred solely when they were adults. We have wonderment in these incredible women, at their capacity to never repeat the torture they suffered. They often voice this capacity by remarking "I'm never being like them."

July 2, 1997

Sara wrote this reflective-integrative statement which described her increasing awareness and the healing integration of nature. She detailed her ability to see beauty. The outdoor interventions were changing her worldview, as described in figure 28.

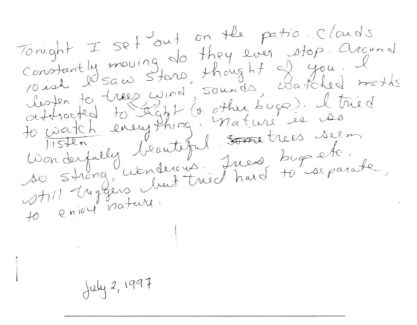

Fig. 28: Sara's reflective integrated statement

Sara was reflecting on the question we asked her to think about: What is different about her today? Sara drew this accompanying image of how she was experiencing her differences, illuminated in figure 29.

Fig. 29: Sara's "What is different about me today?"

We have taken selected paragraphs from her six pages of responding notes. She wrote:

> It's different here in reality with my eyes in front of my head a lot more than ever before…the biggest thing is I'm really here, seeing for the first time. It's very unfamiliar. These are new feelings, not common feelings for me, don't want to push getting to know Sara, needs some time to get used to…There is no mist in front of my eyes, just depth, height, I don't just see a thing I see all of reality.

> I have a huge urge to connect with nature. I see the trees and know what I miss on one day I will see on the next day.

> I used to talk to my-Self all the time in "the family," inside my head trying to understand what was happening to me. When people did bad stuff to me my Self-talk would be: Why me? It was very lonely and silent in "the family." I've just realized this for the first time how silent it was. But, I was always listening, 24 hours of the day, every day. It wasn't silent inside my head; it was busy all the time. It was

so hard talking inside my head because I'd get all mixed up. It makes more sense to me now when I can talk to others, when I can talk out loud.

You know, it hurt very deep inside when I had to say, "Yes, I like it," when I didn't like it, when they were putting their penises inside of me everywhere, when I had to say, "I like it," when "Mommy Franklin" was hurting me. This was so hard because it made me feel so bad. It took everything away from me. It was so hard when I had to say, "No, it's not hard enough," and they'd push their penises so hard into me it was like ripping my insides. I said what I had to say, what they wanted me to say. It was like it wasn't even me talking; it was like they took everything away from me. It hurt me very deep inside. When people touch me and pretend it's an accident I know now it's not an accident.

Today, I still have concerns and am not quite secure in believing it's all over, the getting it out and the terrible hurt of healing. I still feel like maybe evil is lurking on the sidelines. Yesterday, I didn't have a headache and today I just had one or two scraping sounds, like chalk scraping on the blackboard. I don't take everything so personal so I'm not jumping to Self-sacrifice, Self-hatred. Hope is more attainable.

I feel very different with more confidence. I realize I can look at people, I can see them, I can hear them and I don't have to agree with what they are saying and I don't have to go out of my way to get people to like me…I know I don't have to do everything at once, there's probably a lot of processing about reality and I know the processing won't kill me. One of the hard things is I don't understand a lot of people's sentences so I feel there is so much to learn so quickly. It's different talking to you [Linda and Jeanne]. I have more vocabulary, more deep questions, I understand you on a different level. It feels more even, instead of having you way up there and me way down there.

We, too, were making serious changes in how we were to proceed.

Linda's Closure

It was 2000 and "Flight into Freedom" was ending. I did not make my decision lightly. I had many mixed emotions—anger, sadness, guilt, and a sense of loss about ending my work with "Flight into Freedom." This private nursing practice with Jeanne had been such an important part of my life. But I had come to an impasse. I had to find a way to cope with all the stress I was living. It did not matter which way I went about it with Sara, she kept resisting my caring. She kept finding ways to triangulate and put roadblocks in my way to continue to support her in her healing and work with Jeanne. And I was dealing with such heavy concerns about my youngest daughter's resistive behaviours towards me, complicated with conflicting parenting approaches between my husband and my-Self.

In addition, I was still working as a care coordinator for home care. I was beginning to feel overwhelmed. Something had to give. I knew I had gone as far as I could with caring about Sara. Yet I felt badly that Jeanne was left to support her on her own. However, I made the ethical choice to walk away from "Flight into Freedom" and to stay with my daughter, hoping and believing she would take hold of her life in a healthy way. My responsibility for my family was crucial. I also knew I had to care for my-Self. When I look back on my decision I know I made the right one at the time. Alas, I had control only over my own actions and have had to live with the consequences of the actions of others. I still contributed to supporting Jeanne with Sara by listening to her concerns about the demands of the work. In 2018, Sara and I reconnected, and I am supporting Sara in her activism and through social media.

Jeanne's Next Steps

Because I had been the person who answered Sara's first telephone call in August 1993, I was the one with whom Sara predominately sought connection. Sara pursued me when she was desperate for connection, whether I was at Neptune Theatre, away from home visiting other family members, or during a holiday. Holidays were more terrifying for Sara because they offered convenience and safety for the torturers to inflict more torture, terror, and horror. Sara's desperation meant she would call my home number. Consequently, my family became intimately involved, a situation I had to deal with repeatedly.

Our two sons were university students in their early 20s and living at home. When I was not home and Sara called our home phone number, they, or my husband, would answer the phone. This meant they became impacted by Sara's desperation. My husband, a police officer, felt fearful I would be physically hurt by the perpetrators. He thought I did not understand what I was dealing with. One son expended emotional energy trying to support Sara during her telephone calls to our home; the other went into wanting to beat up the perpetrators. This meant I had to keep challenging Sara and set a boundary that she was not to engage in conversations with them. I informed her that I had told my family they were not to speak with her. This angered and upset Sara. She found talking to my family comforting. However, it was adding stress to my family. It meant I had to explain to them some of what Linda, Sara, and I were dealing with. This meant I had to tell Sara I needed to sufficiently explain to my family some of our work and the risks that confronted all of us, therefore making full confidentiality impossible. This, too, upset Sara.

I had to say to Sara that it was impossible for me to answer all her telephone calls. I had to set time limits because in the very early days the telephone calls were endless, full of desperation, long, and exhausting for her and for me. The calls interrupted everyday activities such as meal times, other responsibilities for aging family members, and fun time with family. Every aspect of my life was compromised. I had to explain to Sara

I needed to trust her to not kill her-Self, knowing that Linda and I cared, but I also had to Self-care. I explained if I did not Self-care and care for my family, I would not be able to continue coping with perpetual crises "the family" and others persistently attempted to inflict on Sara. If I could not Self-care this would mean I would have to end my support for her. Such truth-telling was essential. Sara needed to hear reality spoken truthfully because she had been lied to all her life. Truth-telling would be essential to Sara's recovery of trust. She would, in time, seek my truth regardless of whether or not she liked to hear my decision-making opinions.

My family only complained periodically. They were more concerned about my well-being. There were no discussions about why Linda and I had been supporting Sara and paying all the costs. Sara had no financial means to do so as her professional wages, as she told us, were taken by her father. She was deeply in debt as her credit cards were also used by "the family." Keeping her poor meant she could not afford to pay for support— to pay us.

Ending "Flight into Freedom" was the most reasonable decision Linda and I could make. We knew and valued supporting Sara; however, we also realized there were other women and girls who had been, would be, or were being tortured and trafficked within the context of family-based systems. We could not ignore that intergenerational family-based non-State torture and human trafficking existed. I had taken a year off work to focus on writing, to try to get published, and to create educational fact sheets in an effort to break the silence that dismissed or misnamed and invisibilized non-State torture as a crime of assault. Linda and I were called "crazy" for speaking out; we were told there were people spreading discrediting rumours about us, saying that we were just nurses and did not know what we were doing. We needed to fight back. I never returned to my public health nursing career.

Following the closure of "Flight into Freedom," I continued to voluntarily support Sara. There would continue to be days my telephone would ring 30 or more times. There would be days Sara went into flashbacks and re-enactments. There were always days when she was learning how to keep rebuilding her relationship with/to/for her-Self. There were days I constantly challenged Sara and told her how frustrated I was when she stubbornly did her own thing and got into difficulties. I would then be the one she reached out to for support. Sara had to learn what healthy emotions were. I did not hold back when expressing my emotional frustration. Sara had healed sufficiently by this time to cope with my emotional expressions because she understood caring demanded this honesty. She was also enjoying my laughter; in the early years it was far too risky and triggering for Sara to hear Linda and me laugh.

The hard and painful work did not end. I no longer did home visits. I continued to care about and support Sara, meeting in public places. Telephone caring connections were ongoing, as recorded examples shared below.

October 27, 2005

9:10 p.m. painful telephone conversation:

> Jeanne, I'm hurting like hell…I'm scared I'm going to hurt my Self… it's torture, after torture, after torture body memories…it feels like something is falling out of me…it burns…I didn't have a chance to make it through life—now I don't know if I will make it.

December 2, 2015

A phone conversation:

> My trafficking continued in school. In the morning before I left home I was ordered to walk home and not take the bus. I was given

a code name and when a car pulled up beside me and the driver said the code name I got in the car.

This December memory was new. This often happened. Suddenly a piece of Sara's past-victimization ordeals popped into her awareness. Another painful reality needed processing. Added to these new memories and her body memories, Sara needed to recover from surgical procedures. Little attention was paid by the health care staff to her disclosures of having survived non-State torture. During one procedure she asked that no family be admitted to her hospital room. When she awoke, she says, she was surrounded by family members.

2019

Supporting Sara has never ended. In 2019, Sara realized she had kept an intimate relationship with suicidality because, she said, it was her "*best buddy.*" She had refused to give it up; it had been for all her years the only "safe" relationship she had with/to/for her-Self. It "disappeared" suddenly. This surprised her. Sara also finally let go of wanting a family. She grieved this loss. She feels she could never have a relationship with a man because of the 30-plus years of non-State torture and trafficking dehumanizing ordeals she suffered. She says such a relationship would be too terrifying.

In 2019, Sara said she was almost healed. She never wanted her sleep invaded by a nightmare again and she wanted her body talk memories to end forever. Will this ever happen? We do not know. Each woman's recovery is different. How women heal depends on so many variables: how soon they are believed, the degree of care needed and available, how long they were victimized, the degree of psychological distortions and worldview corruptions they endured, the support they had, or conversely the rejection they experienced, the social inclusion and integration that embraced them, the law, policing, and politics of the country where they live. These are broad conditions that accompany their own skills and temperament when confronting so many variables. As for Sara, it is always thrilling each time she makes big leaps forward. Sara has increasingly become a quiet activist, with a driving need to be included in society by having non-State torture victimization recognized and criminalized as a specific crime. Until this legal remedy occurs, it sends a message that society is not listening to her. It says she does not belong.

CHAPTER 10
A TURNING POINT

Sara disclosed that when she telephoned us a perpetrator was sometimes present listening to our conversations. A persistent question Sara asked was: *What would we do if she disappeared?* Our response was always the same: We would call the police. We surmise this was a way the perpetrators kept tabs on us. No doubt this was also undermining our caring about Sara. Perhaps by compelling Sara to telephone us night and day, these demands would make us give up supporting her, thus "the family" would recapture Sara. Or maybe they wanted to know what we would do if Sara did "disappear." There were many risks we were initially totally unaware of—this was one. Another was the suicide note Sara revealed she was forced to write, and in it blame us.

We understood Sara's Self-blaming response, given she had been conditioned to take the blame for all the violent acts every perpetrator inflicted on her—she deserved it—it was her fault. We also understood Sara had not yet been able to distinguish and let go of harmful relationships. Being violated was the only relational and familiar connection she knew. Even with much discussion, Sara was not willing to let go of "the family" connections because, she said, "*I want a family.*"

January 1995 was a critical turning point. Sara had to decide the direction of her life. We informed Sara that we could not continue supporting her, given the perpetual and often life-threatening crises Sara's ongoing connection with "the family" and other perpetrators created for her and, consequently, for us. For our own safety and well-being, we had to place this ultimatum before Sara.

With the unparalleled work of supporting Sara "underground," being effective in our daily paid work, being part of our family's relational lives, managing our "Flight into Freedom" commitments, and evaluating the financial impact of our pro-bono support of Sara, the perpetual crises had to cease. This was the only way forward.

Jeanne's Reaction

By now I was noting my body's response to all these demands of caring and stress. My bladder was responding to this stress, causing me to be up using the bathroom in the middle of the night. Otherwise, I was still sleeping soundly.

Linda's Reaction

My son mentioned I was having too many beers at night. This made me realize I needed to cope differently—like stop stuffing my emotions by drinking too much alcohol. Instead, I had to settle my emotional responses. I had to adopt a long-term view whereby conviction and jail time of non-State torturers was possible. Experiencing body ache was my biggest response to stress and still is.

One of the other stressors for me was trying to keep all the notes and evidence of Jeanne's and my social, political, and professional activism organized. The overflow from my office gradually became my "wall of chaos" as shown in figure 30. For a number of years, these boxes and piles of paper sat on the floor and shelves lining the wall of my dining room. I hid it occasionally by covering it with blankets, not that they hid anything! The effort counted. I am sure this wall of chaos caused stress for my family too.

As Jeanne and I viewed the photo while writing this book, it took our breath away. It made our stomachs turn. It was a photo that spoke of traumatizing experiences—memories came rushing back. We were working so hard to stay

Fig. 30: Wall of chaos

present with Sara, with our families, trying to keep our multitude of social justice efforts organized, and not throw away important files. Neither of us has a clear memory of how long it took for this wall of chaos to eventually disappear. As my internal chaos decreased, I filed the essentials, recycled the rest, and the wall of chaos gradually vanished never to reappear!

AN ULTIMATUM

In January 1995, we had to make a serious boundary-setting decision regarding our relationship with Sara. We informed Sara if she continued to make contact with "the family" and with other perpetrators we could no longer offer her support. By this time Sara had sufficient insight to understand the reasons why we needed to place this ultimatum to her. Our files recorded how this intervention unfolded. Sara responded: "Jeanne, are you saying if I have a contact with my family you will not see/help me anymore?" Then she proceeded to write: *No choice, need Jeanne & Linda's help, feels family need, feels forced, sees choices as—see family no more J & L—do not see family more help from J & L.*

This is how Sara listed the consequences:

See the family	Fight Big time trouble
Belong to a family	Perhaps death of soul or all of me
Perhaps get hurt	Not see the family
Conflict/tug of war	Feel sad
My values versus theirs	Feel lonely
Probably not get hurt	All alone
Feel sad	NOT BELONGING

We needed to be as sure as possible that Sara understood our position. Obviously, there were torturers who wanted to regain control and captivity of Sara and the pleasures derived from her life-long endurance of withstanding tortures of all forms. As Sara said, all she knew was "*torture touch*." However, Sara had to comprehend that her chronic victimizations caused her suffering which triggered her into perpetual crises. She then sought our support—day and night. This continuously over-taxed our time and energies—and hers. If this pattern continued, crises would never end and we would never succeed. This situation had to end. Sara had to make her decision. All we could do was be clear, truthful, serious, insisting on safe boundaries, and explain our limitations.

Sara made her decision.

June 14, 1995, Sara Made Her Choice

Five months after making her choice to disconnect with "the family" Sara left a telephone message. She had gone all by her-Self to visit "*our tree.*" She described walking in the park where we introduced Sara to nature. She said it was raining. "I'm getting wet and the rain seems like tear drops." Sara was expressing the healing success of our working on altering her relationship with nature—the woods, trees, and being able to feel the rain.

CHAPTER II

UNSILENCING: SPEAKING THE TRUTH

―――――

2004: TAKING THE ART AND VOICES OF SURVIVORS TO THE UN

It came true! Dana Raphael, the woman who was at the 2003 US conference where we presented, did as she said she would. She made "Our Dream" to present at the UN come true.

With Dana's invitation, we spent two weeks in March 2004, attending the 48th session of the Commission on the Status of Women (CSW), at the UN Headquarters in New York City. That was the year we learned that private individuals or groups who commit human rights violations are referred to as non-State actors. This knowledge led us to rename the term non-political torture that we had been using to non-State torture. We then categorized ritual abuse-torture (RAT) and spousal torture as forms of non-State torture. We reminisce about this CSW event. Reflecting on our intensity to seek out every morsel of knowledge and advice possible, this became another life-altering event. This nurtured our future human-rights defender activism of unsilencing the truth about non-State torture victimizations.

Spending two weeks at the UN CSW used up our paid-work holiday time. Paying for all our expenses meant finding inexpensive accommodation; we ended up renting a room in a woman's apartment. One of us slept on a small couch, the other on a mattress on the floor.

Dana Raphael planned the non-governmental organization (NGO) panel for March 8, International Women's Day. She titled it "The Many Faces of Torture." In preparation for our presentation, we reached out, via our website, to the global community. We invited persons who identified as having endured ritual abuse-torture to submit their testimonials—poems, stories, photos, paintings, letters, and drawings—for us to take to this UN CSW panel-presentation. We thought we might receive seven submissions; at least this is what we hoped for. Instead, 400 pages of survivors' testimonials arrived from 61 persons from six countries—Canada, the US, Costa Rica, England, Germany, and Scotland (Sarson & MacDonald, 2008). Their submissions were accompanied by consents for us to show their testimonials, to place these on our website, and/or share for educational purposes. We titled the display *Voices of Survivors* and mounted their testimonials into 10 portfolio binders.

Our presentation was entitled *Ritual Abuse-Torture: A Research Discussion Presentation Identifying Human Rights Violations*. We will never forget the man who asked whether we believed in human evil. Attendees took time to look through the *Voices of Survivors* display. When testimonies are respected this can free an adult from believing the torturers' imprisoning lie: If you tell, no one will ever believe you.

Voices of Survivors

From the *Voices of Survivors* display, we shared four examples of testimonial art. From Sara, from Shelle and Jeanette from two different US states, and Karen from Germany. They identified as "RAT survivors."

Shelle. Her submission entitled "Tortured: Needles in my breast" is displayed in figure 31. Shelle shared this reflective comment:

Fig. 31: "Tortured: Needles in my breast"

I'm so glad I was not stuck in fear and was able to send you pieces of "my voice." In some way I feel a sense of healing with this, a voice of being heard. It is a powerful thing, the voice, when it braves to speak and is no longer limited to a whisper.

Karen. Her submission was called "Child of Darkness" illustrated in figure 32. She wrote:

Fig. 32: "Child of Darkness"

Can you imagine what happens to the soul of a person who has to see and has to go through all those things that happen when they are the victim of ritual abuse-torture?

You feel helpless, alone, without any hope left. There is nothing to hold onto. The inner core is captured in fear all by itself. I think my drawing speaks for itself and does not need many words.

Jeanette. Her submission was "Cat-of-Nine-Tails" illustrated in figure 33. She explained:

Fig. 33: "Cat-of-Nine-Tails

Born into a RAT family/group, I was tortured, including raped hundreds of times from 1954–1978 by my father and other[s]. Acts of torture perpetrated and organized by my father and others against my person for the purpose of inflicting terror and pain; to express power and to gain control of my thinking processes, my senses—my sense-of-self. I was whipped with a cat-of-nine-tails, hung upside down with large and hemp ropes, and threatened with a hot welding rod. I was raped, chained to the wall and raped, and photographed. Bestiality was forced unto me and photographs taken. Paregoric, LSD, and other unknown drugs were forced into my body.

I survived ordeals of RAT that took place not only in the family garage and basement but organized in the homes of others, in a Mormon church, and in the out-of-doors on a large rock. Transported—driven and flown by small aircraft—and trafficked within and outside of my home state.

Sara. She shared her experiential memories of how guns were used as a tool to terrify her, as shown in figure 34. Her testimonial submission reads:

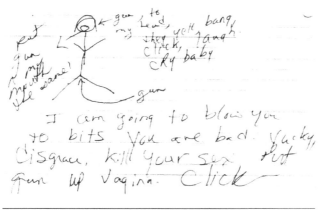

Fig. 34: "Terror"

Terror	At my temple
LIFE-THREATENING	The HARDNESS OF THE METAL
Terror	In my mouth
In my ears	In my vagina
Click	At my temple
The CLICKING SOUNDS	Life-threatening memories IN
In my mouth	MY BRAIN of the clicking of their guns.
In my vagina	

Unsilenced Testimonies

The 400 submissions that formed the *Voices of Survivors* were *unsilenced testimonials*. The phrase *unsilenced testimonials* is adapted from terms Meredith Mantooth captured in her thesis (2012). *"Unsilencing,"* she says, came from Michel-Rolph Trouillot's 1995 book, *Silencing the Past: Power and the Production of History* which explained that drawings gave voice to the silenced aspects of people's lives. From John Beverly's 2004 book *Testimonio: On the Politics of Truth* came the Spanish word *"testimonio,"* meaning testimony in English, explaining that written or graphic testimonies give voice to voicelessness, and reveal historical lived experiences which typically are a consequence of violence and oppression. This was absolutely true, as expressed in the *Voices of Survivors'* testimonials which were predominately herstorical versus historical.

Mantooth referred to the value of unsilencing testimonies because of the 700 drawings international observers collected. They gave crayons, pencils, and paper to children living in refugee camps in Honduras and Mexico in the 1980s. Children were asked to illustrate their homes before fleeing, then upon their arrival at the refugee camps. Sixty-three drawings turned into a 1986–1987 across-Canada *Disrupted Lives* exhibition. The children's art was remarkably effective at relaying their experiences to others. In our opinion, the same holds true for those who submitted their unsilencing testimonies for the *Voices of Survivors* display. Their unsilencing testimonies were illustrations and expressions of their personal victimization ordeals. Their lives were without question "disrupted."

THE UN: A PLACE FOR UNSILENCING TESTIMONIES

Our 2004 dream to present at the UN continued. We have presented on NGO panels, not only at the UN CSW sessions in New York City but also at sessions at the UN in Geneva and Vienna. We never lose our focus.

Non-State torture must be named nationally and globally as a specific criminal human rights violation. That no one shall be subjected to torture is a fundamental human right of all peoples, as stated in Article 5 of the *Universal Declaration of Human Rights*. However, as previously explained, this human right has generally not named non-State torture victimizations as a specific form of violence perpetrated against women and girls. We continuously pushback at structured patriarchal misogyny and discrimination; it denies women and men are equal persons and must have the equal human right not to be subjected to torture, regardless of who the torturers are.

Emotionally Moving Moments

During the UN CSW 2007 session, with support from other women's NGOs, we successfully achieved having torture included in the UN CSW outcome document as a form of violence inflicted against the girl child (UN Commission on the Status of Women, 2007). Although not specifically termed non-State torture, torture is named along with other forms of violence and sexualized exploitation of the girl child. UN CSW sessions concluded two weeks of work by delivering important outcome documents. The 2007 outcome document refers to the girl child because the main theme during this CSW session was the elimination of all forms of discrimination and violence against the girl child.

This CSW outcome document becomes a tool we and others can use to pushback at the misopedia—the hatred of children—in patriarchy. Misopedia gives rise to many forms of violence of the girl child including sexualized exploitation in prostitution and crime scene pornographic victimizations. This outcome document serves as a supportive healing tool. We can show women who suffered non-State torture victimization that torture is recognized in the document as a violation of human rights. It can help women realize that patriarchal misopedic and misogynistic violence exists globally. It may break down their sense of being the "only" one and therefore understanding it is absolutely not their fault.

Another emotionally moving moment occurred at the end of one of our non-State torture UN CSW presentations. A Black African woman told us not to stop talking about non-State torture. She said she had not realized women in other countries suffered such a human right violation; she always thought it was only Black African women who did.

In 2007, we successfully advocated for Jeanette Westbrook, and a Canadian woman, to speak to Yakin Ertük, the UN Special Rapporteur on Violence against Women, its causes and consequences. This gave them the opportunity to submit their confidential testimonials of non-State torture victimization. Although it was decided their victimizations were too old to process, submitting their testimonials did offer a form of justice. They both remarked how this helped to change their lives. Having their stories heard and recorded at this global level was a form of unsilencing their voices. This is the undeniable strength that unsilencing testimonials provide. The UN CSW offers a pushback forum for us to unsilence our developing non-State torture knowledge, and to support women to unsilence their testimonies.

Jeanette Westbrook is the woman who came to the airport to check us out because we were unknown Canadian presenters at the US conference. When asked what our presentation meant, she said prior to our presentation she did not have sufficient *"verbiage"* to explain the non-State torture victimizations she suffered. Nor did she have the right words to make her victimizations understandable to others. Once gaining the language, she said, she *"felt calmer"* and this *"freed"* her to tell her story in a way she never had before. In 2004, Jeanette participated in the "The Many Faces of Torture" panel. Since then she has told her story many times on subsequent UN CSW NGO panels.

Elizabeth Gordon

We supported Elizabeth Gordon to join us in the NGO presentation *Non-State Torture & Violence Against Women & Girls* given at the 2015 UN CSW session (Persons Against Non-State Torture, 2015*)*. Elizabeth unsilenced her testimonial of being born into a non-State torture family, and of being tortured and trafficked by her parents and their friends. A collection of her testimonial art is in "torture parties" figure 35.

Fig. 35: "torture parties"

Elizabeth explains:

This slide has drawings of different ordeals from when I was a young child.

The "parties" drawing is from an ordeal when I was six. An "uncle" was a trafficker and a torturer. He and his so-called "friends" rented out children to different men around the city for a few hours and collected them afterward. I was drugged with fizzy drinks.

The buyers were men who got their fun from the sexualised torture of children. On this day I was trafficked, transported in a taxi or black car to a man who had a large house and grounds. I had been taken to this man's house before. I was taken into the basement. The man had two big metal dog cages and "exercise equipment" including two chains hanging from the ceiling, wooden bars on the wall, ropes, and a rack. There were other men there too. They were having a party, drinking and laughing. Their perverted fun was the sexualised torture and rape of children. I was subjected to forced nakedness. I was caged. I was hung up on the wooden bars and raped by all the men. I was beaten with the whip and tied to the rack on the floor while being raped again.

The little drawing "caged" is from an ordeal when I was four years old, though caging was what the men did often. It was outside at night in a field at the back of a house. The men forced me naked into a cage in a trench or dug out pit in the ground. It was dark, freezing cold and there were insects crawling all around. It was the end of a night of torture rapes by a group of men who said, "Dump her in the cage and leave her there."

The "camera man" drawing tells of so many ordeals by many different men from when I was two years old who violated me in ordeals including taking child crime scene photos and films. These men were pedophile perpetrators of non-State torture child rapes and they took child crime-scene photos to sell to their like-minded friends in their organised crime networks.

Being taken to "parties" is the MO tactic of using coded language by non-State torturer-traffickers. Conditioning a child not to reveal what they are suffering can be hidden by "educating" them to use distorting coded language. For instance, if Elizabeth was asked where she was and responded saying, "I was taken to a party," the probability is her response would be misunderstood by everyday listeners. They would not suspect she was taken or transported to a non-State torture group gathering. This MO of using coded language is effective in manipulating and maintaining the torturer-traffickers' invisibility.

Providing safe opportunities for women to speak out are emotionally moving moments and healing interventions. Speaking out in public and receiving public acknowledgement, such as at the UN sessions, may sometimes be more effective than trying to seek legal justice. This is the reason we share our speaking time when we give presentations. Being silenced burdens a woman with the heaviness of social oppression. We respect that we too need to be unsilenced in doing this work! This is part of the "talking cure." In April 1996, when we spoke with Judith Herman, author of *Trauma and Recovery* (1992), her advice was that research said speaking out can be healing. This reinforced what we already knew; we had never been silent about the violent experiences in our childhood lives—we were not going to be silenced about disclosing non-State torture victimizations. We appreciated Judith's encouragement and support of our work, by telling us to keep building a healthy foundation and "people will come."

Emotionally moving moments happen every time we speak about non-State torture; it is a horror story we do not apologize for sharing (Sarson & MacDonald, 2019a). To apologize would mean we or women victimized are doing something wrong—we and they are not. This is an uncomfortable story. It needs to be uncomfortable. There is no other response when hearing the truth spoken. We take every opportunity to speak out because we wonder who would pick up after us if we stopped doing this work. The most common response of individuals is to say, "I'm glad you are doing the work because I couldn't." As honest as this statement is, it does leave us wondering how to pass on what we know and what Sara and other women have taught us about supporting and caring about them.

Doing this work has always been about taking ethical, right, and caring actions. From the moment we met Sara this fact never left us: *How can it be that in Canada, intentionally or otherwise, government after government, politician after politician, women, and men dismiss the reality that*

Canadian citizens, beginning with babies, are tortured by private individuals or groups? Additionally, the intentional and wilful resistance of the structural and governmental levels that ignore women's need for legal naming of non-State torture tells us there is a lack of political empathy for women and girls who have survived such victimizations. This is political cruelty. So it is always an emotionally moving moment when we and the women in this book are unsilenced.

Alex, who we introduced in Chapter 7, said (Sarson & MacDonald, 2018a):

> When society minimizes [NST]…it is taken personally…and feels like it is…me…they are looking down on…reinforcing the feeling of how the [torturers] minimized my worth when they tortured me… Not having the law care enough…reinforces what the [torturers] said, "No one will believe you. What makes you think you are so special that someone would even want to save you or care about you."

UN Milestones

In 2004, "The Many Faces of Torture" panel was our first UN milestone. There were others between 2004 and 2018. But in 2018, the chapter we co-authored with Jackie Jones was included in the book *Gender Perspectives on Torture: Law and Practice*. This book was launched on March 20, 2018, during the 62nd session of the CSW. Its launch was supported by UN Permanent Embassy representatives of Denmark, Chile, and Norway. Participating in the launch and panel discussion was also a milestone. Our personal and remarkable conversation with Juan Méndez, a prior UN Special Rapporteur on torture, whose work launched this book, was insightful and heart-warming. He identified that the global community needs to address violence perpetrated against women and girls that amounts to torture by non-State actors. He was proud to support our work.

It has been one of our goals, from the first months of Sara's disclosures, to break the silence with published articles. We knew how difficult it was for us back in 1993 when we could not find literature on caring for a person who had suffered non-State torture victimization. We wanted to change this—and we have. We were doing so at the book launch. Jeanne was on the panel and had the opportunity to discuss our chapter entitled "How Non-State Torture is Gendered and Invisibilized: Canada's Non-Compliance with the Committee Against Torture's Recommendations."

Another milestone transpired in 2019. We spoke on a UN CSW panel entitled *CSW 2019: Violence and Torture Against Women & Girls in Trafficking & Prostitution: Educating Service Providers.* This was a landmark because since 2004 we were generally alone in speaking out about family-based non-State torture; in 2019 eight panellists spoke of non-State torture. Women spoke of the non-State torture committed against them when exploited as women by traffickers, pimps, and buyers. And they spoke of when they were little girls, even preschoolers, tortured and trafficked by family and non-family members. Megan Walker, Executive Director of the London Abused Women's Centre, Canada, to whom we had given a two-day training workshop in 2015, shared that the Centre had added non-State torture to its intake form. They are now recording data from women's Self-identifying non-State torture victimization stories. To our knowledge, this is the first Centre in Canada to do so. To us, this panel represented the beginning of a social movement. It was a milestone in that we and the women we support, and who have supported us with their completion of our participatory research questionnaires, are no longer alone. We have non-State torture questionnaire responses not only from women in Canada, but from the US, the UK, Western Europe, and Australia, but also from women in the Philippines and from Indigenous and Black women who reported being subjected to non-State torture suffered in human trafficking, in prostitution, and or in pornographic victimizations. Activists from African countries and Papua New Guinea, shared their experiences about working with women who were subjected to non-State torture ordeals, but because of the demands of their work, the activists did not have the energy to ask the women to complete the questionnaires.

UNSILENCING OPPRESSION AND VIOLENCE BY PROFESSIONALS

Never to be forgotten is the night we met Sara and she quietly began disclosing the names of some of the torturers. It was not information we had asked for. It was a testimonial she needed to speak. Listening, shock waves rippled through our minds. Sara was naming persons one or both of us knew. They were persons we sat in rooms with, persons we had professional connections with, persons who had shared hotel rooms, persons whose home we had visited and left uncomfortable because of the female children's behaviours, persons who touched members of our families in some way. They were women and men; they had positions of power and authority; they were using and abusing their positions to do direct harming and/ or to be corrupt and cover up violations. They were persons who breached the public trust their positional power socially granted them. Sara had no knowledge we knew any of the persons she named.

Jeanne's Ethical Dilemma

Sara named a perpetrating individual who came in contact with my partner at his workplace. This individual was considered trustworthy by him and his coworkers. I did not want my partner to be a potential pawn for the perpetrators to use to create more havoc in my life, nor in Linda's and my work with Sara. I made the decision to tell him the man Sara had named was Lee. He was the man Sara had identified as "satan."

After I did this I disclosed to Sara I had not kept this piece of her information confidential. I explained my rationale. Sara got angry at me. I was not prepared to risk more crises. It was 1995 and we were constantly struggling to find ways for Sara to stay alive, to function as safely as possible in an unbelievable and almost incomprehensible situation, and to try to heal. There was no one else to draw on for help. Sara had to decide what she wanted to do. I understood this was another stressful dilemma for her. Sara often got angry, saying she would never be back. Leaving our office banging doors and staying angry for a few weeks before returning—Sara has never left. She has remained in contact with me since 1993.

Women's Victimizations

Published literature and mainstream news media tell of professionals who assault (Penfold, 1998), abuse (Grant, 2019), and murder (*Associated Press*, 2006). Because torture by non-State actors is not specifically named and criminalized in Canada, and in many nations, professionals who torture women and girls can escape detection. Or, if caught in Canada, they will not be criminally charged with torture. Escaping detection is also made easier because women who survived family-based torture may still have dissociative responses. This can make them extremely vulnerable to revictimization by perpetrating professionals. Conditioned to believe it was their fault, their feelings of shame and guilt can burden them with a fear of telling. Sara, Carrie, Hope, and Lynn provide testimonials that reveal being subjected to violations inflicted by professionals.

Sara's Testimonial

As to alleged professional perpetrators, Sara drew figure 36. It depicts one of the violent ordeals she encountered within a health care institution. She explained that the female therapist tied her to a chair during her last appointment of the day. The therapist, Sara said, forced her to watch "sex" pornographic videos and a video on multiple personality disorder (MPD). Terrified, Sara declared she had to listen to the therapist's threat that viewing the video would make her become multiple. The therapist, Sara reported, told her she would then be able to have her medicated and institutionalized. These were terrifying ordeals because Sara felt so emotionally and cognitively overwhelmed. She feared she would go crazy, or be forced to die by suicide. Sara, like other women, thought no one would believe her. She tried to inform the institution but no disciplinary action was taken.

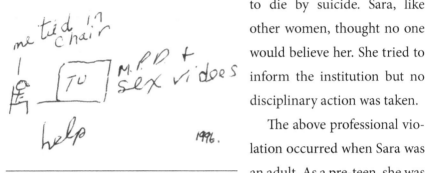

Fig. 36: Professional victimization

The above professional violation occurred when Sara was an adult. As a pre-teen, she was seriously neglected by a male doctor. He was called to make a home visit. The sexualized violence Sara had suffered was so brutal, she began vaginally hemorrhaging after being group torture-raped during a visit to members of her biological family. He instructed the family to keep her quiet and resting and she would be okay. He left. He abandoned Sara.

Carrie's Testimonial

Carrie was in her 50s when she participated in our kitchen-table research project. During her participation, she shared that at age 19 she attempted to die by suicide, following her terrifying "exorcism" ordeal. She explained this "*break-down*":

> Landed me in hospital. The doctors labelled me schizophrenic. It was during this hospitalization I started talking about the devil

coming to get me. I remember having horrific nightmares and being so terrorized by the images in my nightmares that, at times, I found my-Self crawling across the floor on my hands and knees trying to escape the horrifying images. The nurses and doctors didn't listen to me. They didn't try to understand my experiences. Instead I was placed on a locked ward. I was told I was crazy and treated with drugs. I became addicted to drugs until 1978 when I stopped at age 38. I know drugs didn't help me heal. Drugs kept me from remembering, from feeling and from working through my suffering. With drugs there is no body-mind-spirit connection.

While I was in hospital I was raped by a psychiatric intern, in a wooden supply hospital elevator, with a male patient looking on. The rape happened when I was trying to get back to the ward. I'd been left behind by the staff following a dance I'd gone to. Feeling scared and confused because I was alone, I accepted the intern's offer of a ride in the elevator; that's when he raped me. While I was being raped by this intern I remember thinking I shouldn't have gotten into the elevator…this is my fault…it's my fault for getting left behind. I also remember thinking the rape was my fault because I was too scared to walk through the tunnel to get back to the ward; I remember thinking I'm not doing anything to stop him. I remember the red slacks I was wearing.

Tears ran down my face. I knew I couldn't report the intern for raping me. Who would believe me? Even though I felt…overwhelmingly so…that I was responsible for what happened I also knew I had to get out of this hospital if I was going to survive. But, before I could get out I had to go before three doctors, three doctors who didn't even know me. I had to prove to them I was not crazy. I got out!

During later times of overwhelming suffering and struggling I was also labelled with multiple personality. This wasn't and isn't true. It's plain to see I have been given many labels by professionals. These labels have been extremely hurtful and harmful to me beginning during my school years. Teachers and the educational system labelled me "retarded and stupid." While it is true I couldn't do my schoolwork it wasn't because I wasn't capable. It was because I was a child growing up and trying to cope with being a victim of ritualized torture. I couldn't do my school work because I was using all my energy and skills to try and stay alive!

There were other very harmful experiences. For example, at the age of 12 years I was infected with a venereal disease. My father took me to the doctor, a member of my father's group, and he did an internal exam. Can you imagine how I felt…the confusion…the terror…the entrapment! The tone of his touch…the tone of his language…my father's language! I still remember this doctor saying to my father, "She's a very promiscuous girl." I didn't even know what the word meant but the tone of their voices was absolutely demoralizing to the core of my being.

My father took me to the public health nurse to be treated for this venereal disease. She didn't ask me one question, not a single question about how I contracted a venereal disease. She should've asked questions because I was just 12 years old. I felt she looked at me with contempt. I'll always remember the tone in her voice, it made me feel so, so ashamed. I didn't understand what was happening. I didn't know what a venereal disease was! I didn't say a word, I couldn't. My father was with me. I remember feeling so terrified. Why didn't the public health nurse ask me some questions? She had to know what had happened to me, I just know it.

Hope's Testimonial

Also involved in our kitchen-table research project, Hope began by telling how she "tried to make sense of a relationship I had with a counsellor."

Every time I tried to discuss this relationship with others I'd be shut down and shut up. I just had to get some of my feelings and thoughts out; I needed to talk about my devastation, my two months of hospitalization with time spent in the quiet room getting my sense of overwhelmingness under control. I had to talk about what it was like returning home, still overcome with trauma, lying there in my bed, curled up into a ball for several months, a towel rolled up between my legs to catch my urine because I couldn't propel my-Self to even go to the bathroom.

It's my opinion I did a great deal of my own healing work, I bought books, read what I could, did research, yet my efforts went unacknowledged and unrecognized while this counsellor was given and took all the credit. It was as if she was the one who knew what was best for me. This invalidation hurt me terribly, cutting into my already deeply wounded Self-esteem, crunching it down even further than it already was. Failing to recognize my efforts, any person's efforts, is simply unfair and disrespectful. From this experience I learned it wasn't healthy to feel my survival depended on her, or on any person for that matter, so in order not to be stuck in the harm of this past counsellor-client relationship it was necessary for me to speak out and be listened to.

Unexpectedly, I experienced real crying—with tears—for the first time, and I mean real tears for the first time! After I had released what I needed to say I was able to move on, just as I expected. This experience is an example of my wisdom—my knowledge and my knowing—of what was necessary for me. And, these benefits I reaped in my talking and in being heard during two kitchen-table research meetings.

In closing, Hope said, "If my breaking the silence about ritual abuse-torture and evil gives others a better chance of getting out of their isolation, fear, terror, pain, and suffering, then I'll be happy."

Lynn's Testimonial

Beginning in 2000, we voluntarily spent two afternoons a month for over two years meeting with Lynn to support her in her healing. Our time with Lynn was different in a variety of ways than with the other women who participated in our kitchen-table research project. Firstly, the non-State torture and sexualized exploitation Lynn suffered was committed by her husband, his three male friends, and the countless men who "bought" her. Secondly, she said she had never been abused or tortured as a child. Thirdly, she escaped after four and a half years of captivity and fled to live with her mother. Fourthly, Lynn said "with no other options in sight I decided to participate in the kitchen-table research project, refusing to be pathologized and labelled crazy or mentally ill."

Lynn described that the professional violations she suffered were by police and a priest. She began her telling, describing how she was a captive in the windowless room and often handcuffed to an iron radiator.

> When I heard whispering out in the hallway it meant Ben and the goons were negotiating with perpetrator-clients so I'd brace my-Self because I never knew what would happen.

> One day I saw policemen in the hallway—my heart raced—I was being rescued! Then more shock, shattered hope, and devastation; my trust in humanity was utterly destroyed. The cops weren't there to rescue me; they were my next perpetrator-clients. In one fell swoop all hope of being rescued disintegrated into an overwhelming sense of hopelessness, helplessness, powerlessness, and despair.

> The policemen became regulars, coming in pairs, six plus four—10 in total—from two different police forces. Young, good-looking, dark haired, moustached, married, some came in uniform, others in plain clothes, taking turns, using the buddy system—buddies who liked to watch, buddies who acted as controllers watching the time, buddies letting Ben know they wouldn't be back the next day because they were off duty. Buddies! Policemen raping me with their police shirts on, numbers on badges with sharp points stuck into the cold flesh of my chest; policemen terrorizing me with their power, their bodies, their words, uniforms, badges, and with their guns. Their

voices spewed threats and intimidations; my life-threatening risks expanded overwhelmingly. They were Ben's protectors, not mine!

Violent oral rapes followed by cold, hard, long guns stuck deep into my throat. Three clicks: click...click...click pierced my left ear as it picked up the threatening death sounds of a gun clicking...More terror as their ice-cold voices punctured me, "Stay still bitch or I'll kill you!" Guns sticking out of open holsters were placed on the floor next to the bed for me to see—more terror. Buddy stood against the wall in brown pants with his camel beige jacket pulled aside to expose his gun—more terror!

The policemen were on duty when victimizing Lynn. According to Canadian law, they would be considered State torturers and charged under section 269.1 of the *Criminal Code of Canada*. Under this section a State torturer is listed to mean an "official" such as "a peace officer" and if found "guilty of an indictable offence...[is] liable to imprisonment for a term not exceeding fourteen years" (Government of Canada, 2020). This is a reality we have encountered repeatedly. The torturers are frequently both State and non-State actors. For instance, perpetrating acts of torture when in their "official" State capacity, and then again when removed from their "official" capacity, becoming non-State torturers. It is necessary to question whether torturers who are, for example, high-positioned elected politicians, are ever in any other capacity than that of being a State official—a State torturer?

Following her escape, Lynn sought support from the Roman Catholic priest who married her and her husband. This is her description of what occurred:

I went to visit the parish priest. For two hours I explained my horror—the terror, the torture, the repeated rapes, and the policemen as perpetrator-clients. His advice numbed me. "Go back; you broke your Catholic commandments; it couldn't have been that bad;

you gave your body to another man, you are a prostitute." The priest had given me holy reason to blame my-Self and another reason to think I harboured evil within.

Added to these destructive violations were present-day painful experiences. Lynn disclosed having survived non-State torture to two physicians. One gave no acknowledgement of even hearing her statement. The other immediately left the room, leaving her on the examining table, saying as he left, "Oh, you are one of those people." He never returned.

Like other women who never tell, Lynn was silenced because "Over the past 20 years, whenever I took an occasional baby step out into the world to test whether people would listen to me, I got knocked down."

SEXUALIZED HARMS BY OTHERS QUESTIONNAIRE

On our website, we have the participatory questionnaire called sexualized harms by others (Persons Against Non-State Torture, n.d., b). Individuals can voluntarily complete it and 33 people did. Twenty-eight identified as female, four as male, and one as other.

They told us they were harmed by professionals in Canada, the US, the UK, Western Europe, Australia, Asia, and Israel. The sex of the perpetrators were:

- Sixteen (48.5%) identified the perpetrators as both male and female;
- Fourteen (42.4%) stated the perpetrators were male;
- One respondent identified the perpetrator to be female (3%);
- Two respondents said the perpetrators were male, female, and transgendered (6.1%).

The sexualized criminal violations were reported to have occurred in large institutional settings, a mental health department and hospital, private offices, religious office spaces, hotels, motels, a lodge, homes, and home offices, in workplaces, out-of-doors, and in a student residence.

The perpetrators crossed all sectors of society. They were nurses, doctors, psychiatrists, psychologists, social workers, dentists, judges, lawyers, police and military officers, clergy, nuns, mental health and feminist counsellors, politicians, mentors, and educators.

The forms of violence inflicted were identified as:

- Pressured into nakedness
- Sexualized manipulation of their body
- Raped vaginally, orally, anally, with objects and an animal (dog)
- Set-up and trafficked to like-minded others
- Forced into pornography
- Forced drugging by mouth, injection, or inhaled
- And 18 individuals (55 %) identified that victimization involved acts consistent with non-State torture violations

Some respondents extracted them-Selves from the victimizing situation following one violation while others it took up to five years or more. All reported some form of harassment or being stalked, including being followed when walking, on a bus or train, and into religious and community settings. Others reported being followed by a car and some individuals had the terrifying situation of being forced off the road while driving. Perpetrators used threatening notes which respondents said were left on their car or they received threatening emails or telephone calls. Some of these events were similar to Sara's experiences. She had not completed the questionnaire.

Methods used to extract them-Selves from the professional perpetrators included:

- By my own determination

- Supported by a safe professional or a safe friend, spouse, or partner

- Moving away to another housing complex, to another community

- Changing contact information, for example, telephone and email

- Reporting to police and professional associations which resulted in no action taken, or conversely, reported to the police and a professional association action was taken.

- Rescued by other staff who witnessed it and I lived with them.

- Attempted suicide by motorcycle; almost died, when I got taken back a staff person found me crying and about to overdose so drove me straight to his friend's house in another town.

- Ran several states away, and once I arrived I moved in with helpful group of people that kept me safe…[The perpetrators] had me under their control for 18 years. They were everywhere…ring trafficking. Even when I would move, they were there. It was very difficult to escape their reach.

A must for promoting women's safety requires using clear, correct terminology. The women we support did not know they suffered sexualized crimes perpetrated by professionals until these violations were clearly discussed. One experience occurred when we were supporting a woman who described a professional's actions. He had been raping her. She did not have this insight. Unless we speak clearly and name the violations, call it victimization and crime, this reality can escape women who have been non-State tortured as children.

A HEALING NECESSITY: SOCIAL ACKNOWLEDGEMENT

On April 8, 2019, Elizabeth Gordon conveyed the impact that a lack of acknowledgement about non-State torture has when she cannot name and speak freely of the non-State torture she survived (Sarson & MacDonald, 2020a). She wrote:

> Sometimes I feel so isolated…like being in a place and no one talks my language…and I have to keep relating in their language even though it is not my language. It's a social isolation…difficult to describe.

Carrie, when shown our ritual abuse-torture model at our last kitchen-table research meeting with her, asked what healthy caring meant. Healthy caring is the final outer ring of this model. Answering Carrie's question has many relational layers. Healthy caring is, for instance, living in a society that nurtures social inclusion, non-discrimination, non-violence, and respect for human dignity, and human rights equality. This means social acknowledgement of persons who have suffered a non-State torture crime. On a person-to-person or interpersonal level, this means the women of this book need the people they relate to within society to be respectful and non-discriminatory. Intrapersonal caring is learning healthy Self-care, by having the opportunity to heal, to become relationally aware of who they are in their relationship with/to/for Self.

Further to Carrie's question about healthy caring, this caring must not be the sole responsibility of the helper and the person seeking support as in our isolated relationship with Sara. Individuals with socio-political positions must also be held accountable for their part in the healing process. This means developing socio-political, structural responses that support a woman's access to societal validation, inclusion, and truth-telling denunciation. This means having and enforcing a law that names and criminalizes torture when committed by non-State actors. It also means developing policies and practices that are non-State torture informed, and with the ability to protect and investigate. Would an investigator know that a torturer may use a hot light bulb as a tool for raping? If they were investigating, would they consider a light bulb might hold DNA evidence? This is torture-informed investigative knowledge.

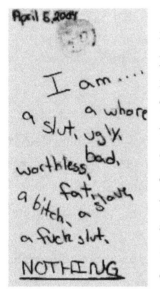

Discriminatory patriarchal and misogynistic policies and practices housed in socio-political structures magnify the complexity of non-State torture caring and recovery work. These policies and practices reinforce the torturers' message that socio-political structures do not care. In turn, strengthening the torturers' dehumanizing misogynistic messages that the women or girls were worthless, a "nobody," and a "nothing," as Sophie reveals in figure 37. Sophie was a youth when she contacted us via email. She described how she was told by the system's practitioners that she was lying when

Fig. 37: "Nothing"

she tried to tell of the torture victimization inflicted by her aunt and uncle and other non-State torturers.

Non-State torture victimization is a crime committed against the humanity of women and girls. Social, political, and legal injustices that deny non-State torture victimization can cause emotional pain that simmers over a lifetime, adding to the pain already suffered, and compounding the pain re-experienced during integrative recovery. A country's politicians and political structures could help ease the suffering by simply acknowledging, naming, and ensuring the law on torture covers all crimes of torture regardless of who the torturers are—non-State or State actors. Women who have survived non-State torture experience revictimization, social exclusion, discrimination, and stigmatization when politicians and political structures block their truth-telling.

Jeanne's Reflections

As a child growing up with a violent father I came to understand injustice is painful. I watched my father bribe the Roman Catholic priest. He came to the house to tell my mother she needed to stay with my father. The priest was not concerned about the risks and dangers my father's violence placed on us. He was happy to tell my mother she had an obligation to stay, shove the twenty-dollar bill my father gave him into his pocket, and leave.

I also learned, as a five-year-old, the emotional power of experiencing justice, even though it was informal, and not formal justice. It is a memory I have cherished my whole life. Even today it influences my activist determination. All women and girls who have survived non-State torture victimizations must have the law written in a manner that acknowledges their human right not to be subjected to torture by non-State actors.

Strange as it may seem, the experience of knowing what receiving informal justice felt like came as a consequence of being sexually assaulted when I was five by male and female sibling teenagers. My mother had fled my father. We were living at my grandmother's in Hectanooga. One day, walking from school to my grandmother's, I was sexually assaulted by the teenagers. I have no detailed memory of what happened. The only memory I have is visual. It is one of seeing a hand on my naked abdomen. Nothing more.

When I reached my grandmother's house my mother met me at the door. This, too, is a visual memory. She often spoke of how torn my clothes were, how scratched up and bleeding I was. She said I must have tried to get away from them by running through thorny bushes. Without hesitating, she calmly took me by the hand and we walked the mile to the house of the teenagers. My mother knocked on their door. Their mother answered. My mother showed me to her in the same condition as I had arrived at my grandmother's house. The teenagers' mother told her son and daughter to get a strapping board. As my mother and I walked away I heard the teenagers wailing as their mother beat them. At that moment in time, I knew what justice felt like. There was no blame placed on me, so there were no inter or intrapersonal issues to distract me from taking in the full emotional feelings of having received justice.

Additionally, this experience taught me to respect that women may only have fragmented bits and pieces of memory about an overwhelming victimization experience or ordeal. We distinguish between the words *experience* and *ordeal* because ordeal generally has the potential to be horrific, severe, or life-threatening, whereas experience may not. Surviving all acts of non-State torture are ordeals. I was not tortured. I have never forgotten the emotional justice I felt that day as my mother and I walked away realizing the youth were held to account. I do not know if my memory would be different if my mother had acted differently. My mother became the teller of my sexualized assault testimonial. I am the teller of my justice memory testimonial! The women in our book are the tellers of their testimonials.

CHAPTER 12

NST VICTIMIZATION-TRAUMATIZATION INFORMED CARE: PART I

_____

OUR STARTING POINTS OF CARING

This was our **Starting Point of Caring**. Even though Sara did not know she was born as a single whole human being—we knew she was.

This was our **Starting Point of Caring**. Even though Elizabeth, who shared her testimonials in this book, and Jan, a woman in her 70s, who contacted us for support via email, did not perceive they were persons covered with skin—we knew they were (Sarson & MacDonald, 2014).

This was our **Starting Point of Caring**. Even though Sara and other women did not perceive they had human rights—we knew they did. However, this knowing had to be greater than "our" knowing. The greater knowing meant introducing them to the *Universal Declaration of Human Rights*. The *Declaration* states they have the right to be born free as equal human beings; it expresses that they have the human right not to be subjected to torture. This was global confirmation. The world decreed this in 1948. Although this is still not the human rights reality for women and girls in 2021, it does not invalidate what the *Declaration* meant for them to have.

This was our **Starting Point of Caring**. Even though Sara and other women we supported did not know or perceive they were persons whose human rights were violated by their families and like-minded group tor-turers—we knew they were.

This was our Starting Point of Caring. Even though Sara and other women did not know, perceive, or emotionally feel they were persons whose torture victimization was not their fault and they were not to blame—we knew. They would come to learn that total responsibility for committing the crime of torture belonged to the torturers.

This was our Starting Point of Caring. Sara and other women would need time to comprehend their relationship with/to/for Self—we knew this to be true. They would need time to understand that they developed survival responses and these were uniquely normal. They would need to know that developing non-State torture survival responses meant they were not disordered and did not have a disorder. They needed to know that once exited—that is, having escaped from the torturers—healing their post-traumatic stress responses was a focus of recovery.

This Remains our Starting Point of Caring. Women's victimization herstories and their survival responses must be heard, discussed, under-stood, and respected in order to promote integrative recovery and healing. Our starting point in 1993 was the development of non-State torture victimization-traumatization informed care. From this point forward in our book we will generally refer to non-State torture by the acronym *NST*, and *NST victimization-traumatization informed care*. Once a woman has exited, we have named her survival responses *post-traumatic stress responses,* using the acronym *PTSR* not PTSD (post-traumatic stress disor-der) (Sarson & MacDonald, 2019a, d). The women we have supported are not disordered and must not be so labelled.

Sara's recovery, and that of other women, involves healing the destruc-tion inflicted by non-State torturers. They aim to destroy Sara's and other women's relationships with/to/for Self; to attempt to destroy their sense of knowing they were unique human beings. In Sara's healing, for example, the statement we intentionally said in 1993, and still convey when discussing the NST crime she survived is, "Sara, you are a person." Respectfully and repeatedly verbalizing "you are a person" contributed to Sara's and other women's healing. This statement assisted Sara to reclaim her personhood, to reclaim her intimate relationship *with/to/for her-Self*. By learning to perceive her-Self as a person in her relationship *with* her-Self, she comes *to* own her statement, "I am a person." She does so *for* her-Self in order *to* begin to identify "Who I am."

Stephanie Fohring's 2018 article "What's in a Word? Victims on 'Victim,'" recounts how persons who were criminally victimized described that they did not want to be labelled "victim." The societal responses they encountered stigmatized, victim-blamed, and fostered their social exclusion. Sara needed to hear she was a person. Just as we and society need to remember Sara and all women so violated are first and foremost persons whose human rights were repeatedly violated. Their identity must be "I am a person."

NST: AN INFRINGEMENT OF HUMAN RIGHTS

A failure to take seriously a woman's or girl's NST victimization disclosures not only leads to secondary revictimization, but this disregard can also silence, abandon, and isolate her. This may or can produce the environment whereby the torturers continue to serially torture and traffic her. This was Sara's situational environment. Being socially silenced, abandoned, and isolated is painful. Researchers concluded that social exclusion causes emotional pain comparable to physical pain (Eisenberger et al., 2003). Women and girls have survived heinous NST pain; society must not knowingly inflict societal anguish onto them. It makes their recovery more complex when society fails both to acknowledge them and negate their legal right to denounce the non-State torturers.

We have Questionnaire 1 on our website which we distribute, when possible, prior to any presentation we give (Persons Against Non-State Torture, n.d., a). It asks if respondents differentiate assault from torture and why. We have gathered 734 responses and over 90 percent categorized torture as distinct from assault or abuse. They explain that torture is more destructive, severe, and sadistic; it causes more pain and suffering, is dehumanizing, and deadly. There were a few women who stated they chose being tortured over being assaulted or abused because they knew what torture was; they did not know what abuse was. Some respondents also shared their own stories when answering this question. For example, one woman wrote:

> The extent of violence against me goes beyond conventional narratives of "abuse" into systematic destruction of my self and physical, sexual, and emotional violence that has severely impacted my ability to participate in the world decades later. Moreover, the stigma I experience because of what was done to me is extensive.

This woman's statement reflects what we just shared from Stephanie Fohring's article. Respondents to our Combating Discrimination and Stigmatization Questionnaire, which follows in the next section, similarly reflect experiences of being stigmatized.

The global human rights standard written in Article 7 of the *Universal Declaration of Human Rights* says all persons—women and girls—"are equal before the law and are entitled without discrimination to protection of the law." Therefore, governments and politicians must take action to assist in the development of social-legal inclusiveness. They need to take responsibility for contributing to women's NST social recovery and healing by assessing the laws in their country, and asking (Sarson & MacDonald, 2016b):

1. Is there a law in our country that criminalizes torture when perpetrated by non-State actors? If not, as a government it is necessary to name and criminalize NST as a crime of torture.

2. If there is a law that covers NST crimes, is our country applying it in a non-discriminatory manner? That is, is it being legally named as a torture crime when women and girls have suffered NST victimizations? If not, our government needs to initiate non-discriminatory legal policies and practices.

Laws that specifically name forms of violence perpetrated against women and girls can have an impact on their safety. According to research findings of Richards and Haglund, when a country has, for example, a *specific* marital rape law in place (2018):

- There is a 7.3 percent increase in the probability of routine enforcement of gender violence laws;

- Significant reductions in societal discrimination regarding violence against women and girls increase the probability of selective-to-routine enforcement of marital rape law by 7.7 percent;

- Rape prevalence drops approximately 26 percent compared to countries with fewer legal protections.

Based on the findings of Richards and Haglund, a law that specifically criminalizes torture perpetrated by non-State actors could impact the safety of women and girls.

A 2016 UN report by the Department of Economic and Social Affairs stated that when a specific group is statistically invisible they are at the highest risk of being socially unrecognized and thus socially excluded.

This report goes on to validate that discrimination exposes a person to stigmatization. This can lead a person to internalize a sense of shame, to have low Self-esteem, increased levels of fear, compromised mental and physical health, and increased stress. These responses all contribute to limiting women's agency—their ability of day-to-day coping. When a country does not have a law acknowledging NST, the persons so tortured are statistically erased. To promote their social inclusion requires creating a law that acknowledges and names NST. Creating NST law means discriminatory laws and policies are removed and institutional transparency initiated. This would prevent women's experiences of institutional betrayal of trust (Smith & Freyd, 2014), and eliminate abuses of power and corruption that invisibilize them as persons who have endured the specific human right violation of NST.

COMBATING DISCRIMINATION AND STIGMATIZATION QUESTIONNAIRE

In September 2009, we placed a participatory research questionnaire on combating discrimination and stigmatization on our website (Persons Against Non-State Torture, n.d., c). It asked respondents if at any time in their lives they experienced discrimination or stigmatization as a result of disclosing NST. We have received 136 responses of which:

- Ninety percent were female persons; eight percent were male persons, and two percent identified as other or transgendered persons;
- Seventy-nine (58%) individuals were from the US; twenty-three (17%) were from Canada; twenty-two (16%) were from Europe; and the remaining responses were from Australia, Africa, New Zealand, Israel, and an unidentified country.
- The forms of NST identified included:

- Twenty-one persons (15%) said they had been tortured as a child or youth;
- Eight persons (6%) identified spousal torture;
- Twenty-one (15%) said they had been tortured in childhood and adulthood;
- Two (2%) were tortured when trafficked;
- Eighty-four (62%) individuals identified suffering ritual abuse-torture which generally involved human trafficking to like-minded individuals or groups.

- Asked if they were unjustly labelled or treated as unworthy after telling a non-offender about the NST they endured, of the 120 who responded in the affirmative:
  - Twenty-one (18%) said they had always been treated in this manner;
  - Thirty-five (29%) said most of the time they had been; and
  - Sixty-four (53%) individuals said sometimes they had been treated in this manner.

- Asked if the risk of experiencing discrimination or stigma prevented them from disclosing, the majority, 107 (81%) of the 133 persons who responded said this risk kept them from disclosing. Most times they were fearful so withheld disclosing, or considered the risks before telling.

- Deepening the previous question, we asked how often discrimination or stigmatization was experienced when they disclosed. The majority, 86 (65%) of the 132 who answered this question, said they experienced discrimination and stigmatization from telling for years because they:
  - had difficulties finding appropriate support and help;
  - were not believed; and

- had been unable to access justice.
- Asked what types of discriminatory or stigmatizing behaviours they encountered, the most prevalent explanations included being ignored, dismissed, given negative labels, treated as if they were crazy, and automatically medicated within the health care system.
- When asked a relational question, the majority said they experienced discriminatory and stigmatizing responses in their friendships, with their partners or spouses, and with care providers such as doctors, nurses, social workers, and clergy. Such responses were also encountered in their daily lives—within educational institutions and workplaces.
- The majority of the respondents thought eliminating discriminatory and stigmatizing social responses could be achieved by addressing the:
    - failure to respect them as persons;
    - lack of education and understanding about NST and its effects, including exploring harmful rumours and lies about NST crimes;
    - personal biases and disbeliefs that human beings would inflict NST;
    - personal fears of realizing humans are capable of inflicting acts of human evil; and
    - distortions created by the media when reporting NST crimes.

The majority of respondents were women. When women learn that discriminatory patriarchal social constructs stigmatize women and girls simply because they are women and girls, this education contributes to their healing.

PATRIARCHY, MISOGYNY, AND HUMAN RIGHTS VIOLATIONS

Healing from NST required educational discussions with Sara and other women. This included sharing insights on how being born a female person in a global patriarchal society automatically placed them and all women and girls at risk.

Social Formation Model

Our feminist discussions involved sharing a social formation model, illustrated in figure 38 (Sarson & MacDonald, 2018a, b).

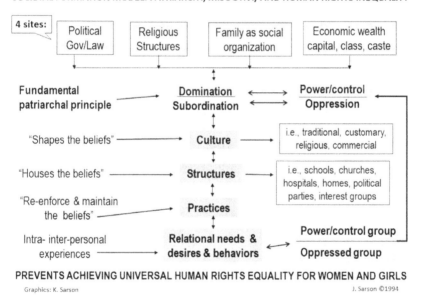

SOCIETAL FORMATION MODEL: PATRIARCHY, MISOGYNY, AND HUMAN RIGHTS INEQUALITY

Fig. 38: Social Formation Model

The model is an innovative expansion of the 1981 writings of educators Herbert Gintis and Samuel Bowles. This social formation model organizes how patriarchal societal power is held and maintained. Four main organizing sites are identified as (1) government, politics, and law; (2) the control exerted by religious organizations; (3) the positional power given to family structures as relational organizations; and (4) power of economic wealth and capital. These four sites create the fundamental patriarchal principle of male dominance over female subordination. This exerts male power and control over female oppression. Patriarchal domination and female subordination then shape culture, influencing its structures, practices, and relational needs and desires including inter and intrapersonal relationships as illustrated in the model. Briefly discussed in the following paragraphs are the main organizing sites.

Government, Politics, and Law

Legal equality and justice for women are undermined when national legal systems are discriminatory, (UN Women et al., 2019). This reinforces the reason torture committed by non-State actors needs to be named and criminalized as torture, if women and girls so victimized are to gain non-discriminatory legal equality and have access to truth-telling justice (Sarson & MacDonald, 2016b, 2019e). To be effective such a law needs to be implemented to reinforce attitudes that promote women's and girls' equality before the law, with equal protection of the law. Legally naming NST as a crime means developing knowledge about the survival responses of women and girls, plus having the investigative skill to comprehend the MO of non-State torturers as explained in our previous chapters.

When government institutions refuse to name and criminalize NST, discriminatory practices are shaped, thereby institutionalizing legal inequality for women and girls who have survived NST crimes. Cathy Parnitzke Smith and Jennifer J. Freyd coined the term "institutional betrayal" (2014). In their article, they validate that many forms of oppressive and suppressive harms and injustices occur within institutional practices. When political and other structural institutions are uninformed, do not listen, or have uncaring practices, institutional betrayal occurs. Individuals depend on being able to trust the practices of political and other structural institutions, to uphold their safety and well-being following a victimizing and traumatizing crime. A violation of this trust is institutional betrayal. Smith and Freyd's article mentions that institutional betrayal can contribute to increased dissociation and anxiety, including detrimental health and relational consequences. Compounding these are further threats to mental and physical health, such as internalized shame, low Self-esteem, increased emotional fear, and stress caused when socially unrecognized, thus socially excluded (Department of Economic and Social Affairs, 2016). It becomes shocking when these responses are added to women's NST survival responses. They all emphasize the severe limits placed on women's day-to-day coping. It is transparent why government, politics, and law must take responsibility to contribute to women's and girls' NST victimization-traumatization recovery.

Religious Organizations

The previously mentioned report on justice for women discusses the way societies organize the secular and religious rituals of marriage and divorce (UN Women et al., 2019). Globally, many countries' religious norms refute the equality of women and girls regarding marriage and divorce. As an example, women in Algeria and Djibouti must provide reasons or conform to specific conditions to gain a divorce; men are exempt. Globally, only 52 percent of married women or those in a union make their own decisions about sexual relations, contraceptive use, and health care (UN Women, n.d.)—all issues which religious perspectives impact. Thus, the intra and interpersonal relationships within and between women and men are influenced by religiously instilled norms based on the fundamental patriarchal principle of male domination and female subordination.

Family as a Relational Organization

Male dominance privileges men's positional power within the family structure. Recognizing the world as a global patriarchal community, in 18 countries husbands have legal authority to prevent their wives from working, and 49 countries lack laws to protect women from domestic violence (UN Women, 2018). More than one billion women lack legal protection against sexualized domestic violence (Tavares & Wodon, 2018). The World Health Organization's 2017 report reveals one in three of the world's women, including Canadian women, experience physical or sexualized assaults perpetrated by an intimate partner. However, this data, taken from global reports, does not identify that women and girls suffer NST perpetrated in the domestic private sphere. Therefore, the NST of female spouses and daughters remains invisible. In a report on families in Bhutan, men and boys eat before women and girls (Boudet et al., 2012), which is an illustration of male domination and female subordination practices. Similarly, during her participation in our kitchen-table research, Hope said the misogynistic norm in the NST family she was born into was that her father and male siblings ate before her.

Economic Wealth and Capital

UN Women, the UN organization dedicated to accelerating women's and girls' equality, states women's work pay is 23 percent less than men's income, and up to 30 percent of income inequality is due to women's inequality in their household (2018). Some women who survived NST crimes have been able to recover and participate in work lives but they too will suffer work pay inequality. Others have not recovered and are confronted with the reality of poverty.

Subordination and Oppression. Insights about global patriarchal subordination and oppression illuminate for women and girls the non-State torturers' misogynistic and misopedic tortures. Learning herstorical feminist information can be helpful and healing. For instance, hearing the words of the women who opened the 1993 World Conference on Human Rights, in Vienna, Austria, say, "being female…makes many women vulnerable to routine forms of torture, terrorism, slavery, and abuse that have gone unchecked for too long" and that such violence is perpetrated within family relationships, mainly by fathers, husbands, and boyfriends (Bunch & Reilly, 1999, p.18). Women's feelings that NST victimization was their fault can be eased. Herstorical evidence can help women who were alone in the NST victimization they suffered, to realize that socially they are not alone in the world's violent patriarchal discriminatory society. This destructive relational impact was expressed by a woman who wrote to us on July 23, 2019. She affirmed that:

> Being convinced of no entitlement to be alive, no equality or belonging and not a soul to care if you live or die. You really are not human if nobody wants you or cares or protects or values you. Having no sense of entitlement even to exist…causes extreme non-assertiveness but that is not mental illness.

It is important for the women to understand that subordination and oppression of women and girls drive beliefs, values, and attitudes within the patriarchal culture. These are housed and operationalized in structural policies and practices which are handed down into relationships, including into their relationship with/to/for Self. Undoing patriarchy means women and men must come to know each other as of the same species, thus as equal human persons, so the fundamental patriarchal principle of male domination and female subordination will no longer exist. This means all forms of misogyny and violence against women and girls must end. This includes directly addressing the NST of women and girls so that social discrimination, stigmatization, and exclusion, which complicate their suffering, end.

We repeat: healing is not only an individual responsibility. Society must not be exempt from its responsibility to realize all of society contributes to either the harming or the healing of others—contributes to the social pain or to the healing of women and girls who have survived NST victimizations.

NST VICTIMIZATION-TRAUMATIZATION INFORMED CARE: PART 2

EXPLAINED: A RELATIONSHIP WITH/TO/FOR SELF

Personhood, womanhood, human rights, feminism, and a relationship with/to/for Self were elements in the starting points for our work and support of Sara and other women who were NST violated. These starting points are included in our nursing whole-person care and the helping relationship teachings.

Barbara Narrow's 1979 definition of nurse teachings is "the process of helping a person to learn those things that will enable [her]…to live a…fuller life, and help [her]…learn how to reach [her]…optimal level of physical and mental health." Sara and all the women in this book and those they represent deserve support to achieve this goal.

When Sara sought our support, she asked at our September 6, 1993 meeting for assistance to develop a healthy relationship with her-Self. We explained our practice of working together to achieve goals. However, we also informed Sara we had a non-mental illness perspective, as we were not qualified to work with mental illness. We also explained to Sara our belief that a baby is born as a single human being. For us, this meant she was solely one person. These were positive statements for Sara. She was adamant she was not mentally ill and was "*not going to have multi-personalities*."

Our framework also came up during our kitchen-table research project. Hope said she had "multi-personalities." We explained we would only address her as one person when listening to her share her story. She agreed. We spent two years in meetings with Hope without difficulties. In July of

2002, she said, "A thought that keeps me grounded is that every time I allow myself to share some of the things inside of me I discover I am not unlike many other people, I am not a terrible person."

Relationship with/to/for Self Model

At our September 14, 1993 meeting with Sara, we introduced her to our relationship with/to/for Self model. We re-illustrate and explain further the relationship with/to/for Self model in this chapter, as figure 39.

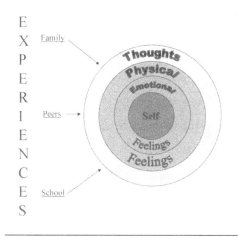

E
X
P
E
R
I
E
N
C
E
S

Fig. 39: Relationship with/to/for Self Model

For experiential teaching purposes, to help Sara and others visualize this conceptual experience; we have the circular model reproduced on a large plastic sheet. When placed flat on the floor it becomes a visual educational tool about the development of the relationship with/to/ for Self. This model framework has shaped our practice, including with children (Sarson & MacDonald, 2016a). Approximately 90 percent of 1000 evaluations from ten-year-olds in relationship education classes, said learning they had a relationship with them-Self was the most important aspect they learned. The program was cancelled due to cutbacks in public health programs.

Explaining the Model

First comes explaining the concepts of the model, as we did with Sara in Chapter 4. We presented to Sara a hypothetical experience of a woman walking on stage to give a speech; she stubs her toe and falls in front of a large audience. She might then have negative "Thoughts" about her ability to present her speech. Stubbing her toe meant painful "Physical Feelings" and her "Emotional Feelings," probably involved embarrassment. Recalling this experience years later, her stubbed toe pain is gone, but the painful emotional embarrassment may easily return. This is an example of how emotional feelings can stick like glue to shape one's conceptual relationship with/to/for Self and in relation to others such as peers, school, and family.

Applying the Model

Self. Experiential learning about one's relationship with/to/for Self begins by imagining being seated in the innermost circle named "Self." From this position one begins to examine the impact of the outer three rings.

Thoughts. This ring asks a person to think about identifying and developing her own thoughts, beliefs, values, attitudes, perceptions, and worldviews. These can change, sometimes instantly, given new insights. It may require a specific experience to transform perception, or it may take much longer before a person will or can let go of old ways of knowing.

The care we provided for Sara is shared throughout this book. We constantly introduced Sara to the interventions of clarifying and separating her own thoughts, beliefs, values, attitudes, perceptions, and worldviews from those of "the family." For instance, we asked Sara to separate her thoughts from those of her father and Lee, as illustrated in our November 1 meeting, in figure 6 on thoughts and beliefs. Outdoor interventions where Sara gradually experienced learning to hug a tree changed her thoughts and perceptions about the woods. She came to know the woods were not dangerous; it was the torturers who used the woods as weapons who were the danger. Sara needed the experience of seeing "Franklin the Turtle" cut in two before she could challenge her conditioned perception of psychological captivity. Value shifts occurred instantly when we asked Sara if teaching preschool children to head-bang was appropriate. She immediately realized her belief was a result of "the family" conditioning. Sara let go of suicidality spontaneously after 26 years. It remains a puzzle to Sara that one day she recognized she had let go of her "best buddy." Maybe it was because Sara had healed sufficiently to trust being alone with her-Self? All these transformations altered Sara's thoughts, beliefs, values, attitudes, perceptions, and worldviews, thus her relationship with/to/for Self.

Not only was Sara challenged to transform—we were as equally challenged. Our worldview changed forever. We had to accept that NST is perpetrated within families. This was a new belief and perception about the forms of family or domestic violence inflicted against a daughter or spouse. We had to grapple with our perspectives about human evil actions, and how close to home those were who inflict such actions. Indeed, they were individuals we knew.

We experienced firsthand political resistance. Our perception of Canada was altered when Canada failed to amend its *Criminal Code* so that NST would be identified, and the women so violated would no longer be invisible.

Accompanying this was institutional betrayal, knowing we could not trust the health care system to care about Sara or other women so we worked underground to be safe. Confronting societal systemic discrimination challenged our thinking about access to equal care and justice.

Another shock about injustice came when we learned that people tortured by the State are entitled to acknowledgement and torture-informed care in Canada. But women tortured by non-State actors in Canada are not entitled to justice for the crime of NST they endured or to NST victimization-traumatization informed care.

Our developing thoughts and knowledge about caring expanded our insights. We realized NST perpetrated within a family system adds unique forms of victimizations that must be considered. Forms of NST victimizations generally not endured in State torture happen when a child is born into or an adult marries or partners into a NST relationship, such as (Sarson & MacDonald, 2009b):

- *Relational Torture*. This includes the destructive distortion of the parent-guardian-child bond. Beginning in infancy, a child is forced to bond with, thus normalize, the dehumanization and captivity perpetrated by the very people society has deemed responsible to care for and nurture them.

- *Acculturational Torture*. Being taught not to relate to the "outsider world," as Sara was, creates a distorted worldview. Consequently, when exiting from a NST family there can be a lack of understanding of ways of behaving, of the meaning of language, of the ability to exercise free speech, and personal decision-making. Attempting to fit into mainstream "outsider" society demands social adjustments, adding stress, disorientation, confusion, anxiety, and even panic.

A woman described, to us, the impact of her acculturational torture when first exiting (Sarson & MacDonald, 2009b):

> When I first arrived at [my friend's] flat, I had no idea that I was allowed to use the toilet at night so I went in the bed. I had no idea of how to sleep at night, I had never learned how to. Re-enacting the rapes and beatings that happened at night I constantly had panic attacks. I would then hit my body all over, over and over again and freeze in a trancelike terror state. I couldn't stop shaking and rocked backwards and forwards. The first day I was asked what I'd like for supper I burst out crying when sausages were suggested. No one had ever asked me what I'd like to eat. I'd never known I could choose anything. It was also a trigger, a terrifying reminder of forced oral rapes. I was completely traumatized and dehumanized.

Our new developing knowledge pushes us to keep exposing the need for NST victimization-traumatization informed care. If the health care system does not learn about NST and its impact on women's lives, mistreatment will occur.

Physical Feelings. This is the next circle named in the model. Having experienced surgeries Sara can relate to present-day pain. She realizes that this pain fades away and does not return if mentioned. However, there is exceptional knowledge that arises with cellular NST memory pain. This pain can return when re-remembering a NST ordeal. This demanded new awareness development for Sara and other women. They needed to learn the skill of differentiating present-day pain from cellular NST memory pain. This skill was important. Instead of responding with "What's wrong with me?" Sara and other women are able to answer their question by differentiating present-day physical pain versus when having NST cellular memory pain. NST cellular memory pain will be discussed later, in Part 3 of this chapter.

Emotional Feelings. This is named next on the model. Imagine the hundreds and thousands of messages non-State torturers threw at Sara, and other women, when they were girls and or adults. The verbal torture messages told them that they were "nothing, worthless, stupid, ugly, bad, fucking shit, fat, or sluts." Lynn said she was called "piece of meat." Imagine all these messages hitting women and girls, leaving them emotionally feeling non-human or an "*it*," as Sara said. This verbal torture combined with the physical and sexualized tortures contribute to the destruction of the woman's or girl's relationship with/to/for Self. This is the intentionality, the purposefulness of non-State torturers—it feeds their pleasure for their destruction of other human beings—of Sara and the women and girls they torture. As explained earlier, emotions stick like glue; these can give rise to Self-hatred, loss of trust in Self, damaged Self-esteem, Self-worth, and other negative emotions that "attack" a woman's relationship with/to/ for Self.

As with physical feelings, Sara, for instance, was also forced to believe she had no emotional feelings, that she was not supposed to care, or if she was scared there was something wrong with her. Much like being forced to believe physical torture did not hurt, emotional feelings also were not to exist. Similar to physical feelings, Sara and other women needed to learn the skill of differentiating NST emotional memories from present-day emotional feelings.

Doing the opposite of what the torturers did was a fundamental intervention principle. Our positive letters written to Sara, for her to take home and read, was a planned intervention to challenge the emotional destruction hurled at her since childhood. Reading aloud to Sara from positive stories was another caring intervention, focused on making a healing dent in all the emotional devastation she suffered.

It must be understood that all these circular layers of the model work together to influence behaviours; without identifying that a woman has survived NST her behaviours can be severely misunderstood. Carrie, who participated in our kitchen-table research project, described that she was given many mental illness labels. All were wrong. Her mistreatments led to years of drug addiction.

This was the model we shared with Sara in our September 14, 1993, meeting. She found it so powerful she became very quiet and then said, "Is it possible that I'm hidden under the pain of suffering?"

A Survival Response: A Fractured Relationship with/to/for Self Model

Imagine a person is still a whole person; however, their body, mind, and spirit have become grievously overwhelmed by severe torture-pain and near-death suffering. A shattering of the relationship with/to/for Self occurs spontaneously, as demonstrated in figure 40.

Women may describe the shattering as a fracturing, a distancing, or a dissociative response. They frequently describe this survival response as feeling and imagining they were shattered into thousands of pieces. Sara often spoke of this feeling as glass smashed into millions of pieces. With every NST ordeal suffered, a serial shattering response occurs, whereby each NST ordeal is held separate from other ordeals.

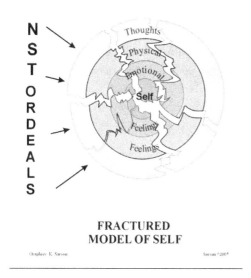

**FRACTURED
MODEL OF SELF**

Fig. 40: A Survival Response: Fractured Model of Self

Women also describe their fracturing as so extensive they may not perceive they have a whole physical body or skin. For Jan, the woman mentioned in the previous chapter, her shattering survival response left her perceiving she was without skin (Sarson & MacDonald, 2014). She said: "It's miraculous that the human mind and body can recover from NST. I'm awed that I have been on this journey for 22 years and interested to see what living in my own skin will be like." The distancing dissociative survival responses are unique to each woman. As shown by Sara's drawing in Chapter 8, she drew each part of her body detached—her hand from her wrist, her wrist from her arm, her arm from her torso.

When sharing her story during our kitchen-table research, Hope drew her perception of her physical body, illustrated in figure 41. The tangled threads represented her brain. She drew breasts, partial legs, and two circular body shapes without arms.

For Lynn, when held captive, tortured, and trafficked by her husband and his three friends, and the buyers, she described her physical shattering of Self-perception in this way:

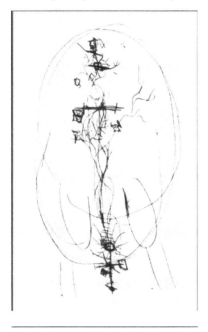

Fig. 41: Hope's drawing of her physicality

Following my escape, and over time, experiencing my relationship with myself came mostly from my sense I existed solely as a head, not as a head connected to a body but just as a head.

Lynn described growing up in a non-violent family. The NST victimization she suffered occurred when she was in her mid-20s. We shared with Lynn that other women's sense of physicality is also shattered by the acts of non-State torturers. She responded with, "I didn't realize other people who had been tortured by family members also speak of experiencing them self as a head. This helps me feel more normal."

Lynn's statement "this helps me feel more normal" is critical to a woman's recovery. When shared, women's drawings or verbalized testimonials explaining their survival responses help other women be okay as they work to heal their relationship with/to/for Self. Identifying the adaptation survival responses creates a belief a woman is not crazy or mentally disordered. The survival-shattering response does not change their physicality from being a single physical human being.

Another interpretation of the "spaces" visualized in the shattered model of Self is that each act of the overwhelming life-threatening NST ordeal is kept separate, which, in effect, works to keep a woman alive. Elizabeth Gordon describes how each of her unprocessed NST, trafficking, and captivity victimization ordeals were separated and stored in individual "black boxes." She goes on to say of her healing that "relief and freedom came when I trusted opening a black box to release the memory" (Sarson et al., 2019c).

Each woman's integrative healing process is unique; it has to fit for her. For Elizabeth it included art, drawing picture-memories before verbally describing and connecting to her NST memory. For Sara, it was "getting it out," with free-flowing writing on flipchart paper. Sometimes months and even years passed before she could explain the meaning of what she had written. For other women, it was gradually emailing us a few sentences at a time until we could capture their whole story and write it out to forward it to them to work through with their support carer. For others it was just saying it as it happened, to be heard and validated. Women often tell us, "I know you know."

Mistreatment

Jeanne's Reflective Experience

As a child, around the age of eight, I remember my mother went for help because she was feeling "depressed." The psychiatric (mis)treatment she was given to fix her emotional depressiveness was insulin shock (mis) therapy. No one said the violence she was surviving was the cause of her emotional depressiveness-distress response. I remember her talking about how fearful this one insulin shock (mis)treatment was. This had a lasting impact on me. As a nurse, I refuse to dismiss the misogyny inherent in psychiatric treatments that pathologize women and girls who have survived violence, often serial violence. Instead of confronting the tragic impacts of pandemic relational violence perpetrated against women and girls, the so-called caring system unjustly pathologizes them.

Temi Firsten

Going back a few decades to 1988, Temi Firsten, who worked in Canadian psychiatric institutions, confirmed that misogyny existed in psychiatric treatments (1991). She conducted research asking why women's experiences of violence were not considered a root cause of women's suffering; for example, women's expressions of anxiety, depressiveness, hostility, suicidality, and Self-destructive acts. Seldom were women asked about violence. If women volunteered disclosures of violence they still faced being misdiagnosed with disorders. Treatment interventions could be ineffective and harmful. Even when hospitalized, women suffered physical or sexualized assaults perpetrated by male co-patients. This too was negated. This brings to mind the rape Carrie suffered on the elevator in a psychiatric hospital and how she felt it would be risky to disclose her victimization, so she did not.

Firsten commented that she saw staff interventions that treated alleged perpetrators as reliable informants. This risk has prevailed for the women speaking in this book. Women tell us that as children, if they acted out, their torturing parent(s) would tell teachers it was because they had psychiatric problems, and had not taken their medications. It is a gross professional failure to ignore the perpetrators who inflict violence against women and girls. Ignoring this serves the perpetrators. Being seen as "reliable informants" supports the oppressive and violent tool of discreditation that perpetrators use to subordinate the voices of the girls and women they torture. This places the girls and women who are NST victimized in states of ongoing psychological (mis)treatments, institutional captivity, and life-threatening suicidal risks.

Sara was adamant that being labelled with a mental disorder was a psychological tactic and threat used by her family and by alleged professional perpetrators. Sara informed us:

> Not only was I raised never to tell on the family, the family also told me no one would believe me if I did tell. They told me I'd be considered crazy, I'd be sent to the mental hospital, and be so drugged I wouldn't be able to talk…I'd be dead. So dead I'd spend my life rocking back and forth as I wove baskets all day. To make their threats real, my parents used to drive me by the mental hospital and tell me that's where I'd be locked up.

For women and girls who have suffered NST victimizations, learning what the normal survival responses and behaviours can be is critical to their healing. This includes understanding women may present filled with chaos, as illustrated in Sara's early "getting it out" raw journaling. These journaling sheets are shared to show what can evolve if caring freedom is permitted. The urgent question that must be considered is: *How does society think a woman or girl "should" react or respond when she has been subjected to NST severe pain and suffering ordeals? How do any of us think we would react if suffering the NST ordeals women have shared?* The unsilencing of Sara's story, and that of other women, must be comprehended as adults' organized torture crimes perpetrated against all ages of women and girl children. Given there was no NST victimization and healing knowledge available when Sara sought our support, this is what we had to learn—how to become NST victimization-traumatization informed and to care. We next focus on sharing more of our acquired knowledge.

DISSOLVING CAPTIVITY AND VICTIMIZATION ACCESSIBILITY

In this section, we explain our observations of supporting Sara's process of healing her dissociative responses which trapped her in a vulnerable state of conditioned-captivity and serial revictimization. Although Sara was a "captive adult" for decades she remained visible in the mainstream community both as a child and adult; her captivity was unrecognized, invisible, or ignored. Sara is not alone. Other women also describe stages of being a "captive adult"—visible but invisible. We share our documentation of Sara's gradual dissolving of her conditioned-captivity and dissociation, which eventually ended her serial revictimization.

How women recover may vary, depending on their age when they escaped. During our kitchen-table meetings, Carrie said the NST victimization and trafficking ended when she was about 12. She suffered several pregnancies and miscarriages at this age. Perhaps the torturers feared exposure if Carrie had carried a pregnancy to term. Therefore, Carrie's pregnancies may have been their motivation to end their serial NST victimization of her. Although Carrie's childhood NST victimization ended, she remained emotionally terrified into adulthood.

Hope married young, to a non-perpetrator. This provided an escape for her. However, when she had children she took them to her "family." This was before she re-remembered and comprehended the NST and human trafficking ordeals she had suffered. Once she began re-remembering, she worked to keep her children safe. She wanted society to be forewarned about intergenerational risks if NST victimizations are invisibilized. Other persons—women and men—contacted us to share their experiences of intergenerational risks. This concern of risks was a question in our reproductive research. We asked women if they decided not to have a child because they thought it would be impossible to keep a child safe. Of the 50 women who responded to this question 18 (36%) said they decided not to have a child for this reason. Another woman consequently chose an abortion.

Terror was and is the absolute fear that something *"bad"* was going to occur if Sara did not comply with the demands of the torturer-traffickers. This generally describes emotional terror responses (Hanle, 1989). The torturer-traffickers do not want to be exposed; they are constantly exerting terror tactics to keep the girl or woman powerless and silent. Inflicting terror is also a pleasure for them. Lynn explained that her husband seldom covered her eyes when he was torturing her because "He wanted the pleasure of seeing the terror his torturing created." He would say to her, "I enjoy seeing the terror in your eyes, bitch."

Women explain that a terrorizing MO of the torturers was killing pets or other small animals. For Alex, this life-threatening terrorization ordeal occurred when she was six (Lane & Holodak, 2016):

> My dad took me to a farm that had baby rabbits. I picked up the cutest one and hugged it. My dad took the rabbit from me and broke its neck. It happened so fast and the look he gave me was clear—this could happen to me as well.

Alex (Jones et al, 2018) and Carrie, as children, were horrified when the torturers beheaded chickens that jumped around headless, splattering blood everywhere. The message was this would happen to them if they did not do as demanded. Terror arises because of who the perpetrators are and the message they deliver. We think that after each NST ordeal, Sara and the other women this book represents lived every day in a state of *relational terrorism.*

Relational terrorism that Alex suffered can "travel" with a woman after she has escaped or exited. It is made more frightening when, at societal-political levels, perpetrators of NST and their MOs are not identified to exist. The outcome is that the NST victimization and terror women survived is denied as a form of violence perpetrated against them. Such denial promotes the belief that there is no safe social place for them, which then maintains their hypervigilance response. We have been contacted by a lawyer defending a woman who fled Canada for this very reason; there was no safe place in Canada. Alex also fled Canada to be safe from her father. NST must be acknowledged to firmly establish women's safety.

Horrification

Schmemann explained that being horrified can give rise to speechlessness (2000). Based on women's stories their horrification responses left them unable to verbalize or describe the horrifying NST ordeal suffered. This is why, sometimes, women can only draw the ordeals they suffered. This is the reason Sara, at times, could only draw; once drawn, she could then begin to develop language to explain her drawing.

Not only can horrification give rise to speechlessness, but also stuttering, and muteness. Sara, for example, had episodes of suddenly becoming speechless and stuttering, years after exiting. We considered this was her brain letting go of horrification cellular memories. Her speechlessness and stuttering went away suddenly, just as they had appeared. Each episode lasted several weeks. Over the years Sara had three episodes of the release of horrification response memories.

Horrification memories can give rise to physical coldness, shivering, tremors, and seizure-like responses. We suggest seizure responses can be compounded by the release of the body cellular memories of electric shock torture seizures. Sara did experience seizures during her release of electric shock memories.

Women's horrification ordeals vary. One woman described how, as a child she witnessed a murder. She saw her sibling pushed off a cliff. She explained it was declared an accidental fall. She said she became mute in school for about a year.

When processing such NST memory ordeals, women can re-experience seeing, hearing, tasting, smelling, and re-feeling these heinous ordeals inflicted with dehumanizing disregard by the torturers. Family-based torturers have pleasure creating terror and horror. When women work to integrate their NST victimization memories, the emotions they endured at the time tag along. This means Sara needed caring support to realize she could overcome her past emotional terror and horror, and integrate her victimization memories. This was necessary so Sara could dissolve the conditioned accessibility that made her vulnerable to chronic serial revic-timizations by "the family."

Sara's Conditioned Accessibility

When Sara first sought our support she was still a captive adult. Being accessible meant "the family" and like-minded torturers chronically vic-timized her. As an adult, Sara would get a telephone call stating "come home." This triggered a dissociative response. She would get dressed, sometimes instructed what to wear, and go wherever directed, including to NST group torture gatherings.

Insights into her dissociative revictimizations came when we began getting mainly middle-of-the-night telephone calls. She would be pan-icked, saying she must have gone out but could not remember what hap-pened. Other women tell us they too received triggering telephone calls, triggering dissociation, and they did as directed. When counsellors contact us for support, they also describe that the women they are helping are still dissociative and still victimized. For example, a counsellor explained that a woman she was supporting had been away and returned with money she could not remember how she got. Exploitative accessibility such as this can go on for years until a woman has healed her dissociative responses—remembering to remember.

Creating teachable remembering-to-remember insights began by piecing together with Sara her awareness of her emotional and biological responses to the "come home" messages. First came Sara's learning that on hearing the phrase "come home" she experienced a sense of heightened tension but also emotional excitement, and a sense of relational belongingness. Sara next realized she had a physical "rush" feeling, followed by a sense of physical numbing. We assume that in preparation for the NST ordeals, Sara had an adrenalin rush. At the same time, a release of her body's endorphins, dopamine, and serotonin hormones clicked in, creating an anticipatory relational response. This included emotional excitement and belongingness when reconnecting with "the family," and at the same time feeling a numbing *"no pain"* response in preparation for the torture ordeal. It appeared these physiological responses and sensations all began before Sara arrived at the victimization gathering. This hormonal mixture response or swing may be physiological and psychological conditioning—a consequence of years of NST conditioning that began from birth (Sarson & MacDonald, 2009b). We suggest Sara's "no pain" response helped keep the torture pain at a dissociated level.

Sara explained she did not feel she had left the revictimization ordeals until she inflicted Self-pain. After being tortured this meant that she had to inflict pain—head-banging filled this need. This conditioned Self-harming was first explained in Chapter 4 at the December 13 meeting, when as a toddler her father told her head-banging bruises made her pretty. Until Sara could comprehend her massive conditioning she remained vulnerable to responding in countless Self-harmful conditioned ways. Working with Sara was like travelling through a minefield to assist her to dissolve her conditioned accessibility.

Dissolving Conditioned Accessibility

Every advance was a struggle. Moving from adult captivity to integrating, exiting, and healing is not a linear process through the non-State torturers' psychological minefield. However, our charting notes helped make dissolving Sara's accessibility process understandable and gave us a safe direction.

Dissolving conditioned accessibility was a gradual back-and-forth process for Sara. "The family's" totalitarian relational-conditioning and control had shaped Sara's perceptions. Her conditioned beliefs placed, as explained in earlier chapters, a distorted value of superiority on "the family." This conditioned Sara's conviction that as outsiders, we were inferior. This distortion impacted how Sara absorbed our outsider information. It felt like we were constantly hitting up against a titanium wall, up against an underlying resistance that limited and prolonged Sara's ability to safely exit and heal. Confirmation of her resistance came when Sara informed us that outsider information did not relate to her. We were helping and caring but "the family" conditioning was continuously in the way. Because Sara's resistance and unawareness were ever-present, this meant she could only integrate information at her own rate of speed. She could not comprehend alternative perspectives if introduced too soon. Until Sara understood NST victimizations were acts of violence she would be chronically accessed and victimized by "the family." Persistence was critical.

In addition, by mid-1995, Sara explained the torturers had threatened to harm us if she did not comply with their demands. This also made her vulnerable to emotional blackmail and revictimization.

Our observations of Sara's process of exiting "the family" required: (a) she prevent being chronically accessible and victimized which was maintained by her dissociative responses, and (b) gradually heal her dissociative responses to integrate the understanding that NST human evil actions of "the family" were organized crime. This occurred during the back-and-forth work achieved by Sara:

1. **Sara's accessibility to being victimized related to her disconnection-dissociation conditioned response.** This response meant she "forgot" she had "attended" the NST violent family and group gatherings or "parties" where she was victimized.

2. **Sara's accessibility to being victimized related to her disconnection-dissociation conditioned response which was gradually decreasing.** Sara began to slowly recall the NST victimization ordeals she suffered. However, being harmed was her normal, so Sara had limited comprehension of how being victimized was causing her suffering. Additionally, Sara was relationally bonded to "the family." They were the only intimate and familiar relationships she knew. This relational bonding meant Sara was reluctant to let go of these relationships; consequently, she suffered ongoing victimizations.

3. **Sara's accessibility to being victimized continued, related to her disconnection-dissociation conditioned response but with shorter timeframe recall.** Sara could recall the victimizations and with increased comprehension of her suffering. This signalled that Sara was integrating. She was realizing she had been harmed and the type of NST harms she had endured. Sara began feeling emotionally terrified. She decided to try and stop being victimized by attempting to break her response and her behaviours of automatically answering the phone, or the security buzzer that unlocked the entrance door to her apartment building. This buzzer gave perpetrators access to her because she opened the door to whoever knocked. Sara also put a sliding lock on the inside of her door and a peek-hole in the door.

She then had to practice using these safety interventions and remind her-Self she had a right to say "no" to those who were victimizing her.

4. **Sara's accessibility to being victimized continued but with a decreasing disconnection-dissociation conditioned response followed by a quick recall of being victimized.** This alerted us that Sara was developing an increased comprehension and integration of her reality. She was processing the NST ordeals more quickly and understanding how horrific these ordeals were. Sara became more and more determined to develop ways to exit safely. She succeeded at not answering the security buzzer. She also began using a phone answering machine to avoid hearing the perpetrators' voices. This began decreasing her risks of hearing programmed triggering words such as "come home." Being successful offered her the motivation to continue her efforts, although she was not always successful.

5. **Sara's accessibility to being victimized continued but with a decreasing disconnection-dissociation conditioned response.** Sara's comprehension and integration of her victimization ordeals were progressing. She managed to exit out of the violent NST family gatherings; however, she was still struggling to totally Self-protect. Although she was quicker to process and understand boundary violations, Sara kept having difficulties, for example, saying no when "the family" demanded she gives her salary to them. She did ultimately succeed. As Sara's comprehension increased, her work on diminishing her dissociative response improved.

6. **Sara's accessibility to being victimized continued with recall, and with increasing comprehension and integration, but still with a limited ability to fully Self-protect.** For example, when a family member returned home after having been away, Sara took a risk to

connect with the individual. She described suffering physical and sexualized violence. Although terrified, she delayed disclosing the victimization to us. Sara remained vulnerable because she still could not let go of "*I want a family.*"

7. **Sara now limited her accessibility to being victimized. She had immediate recall with increasing comprehension and integration with an increased ability to Self-protect.** Sara heard a coded programming word and became highly triggered; she made the connection about the meaning of the word. She then chose to process the experiential memory that the word triggered. This indicated she was gathering an increased Self-awareness in her developing relationship with/to/for her-Self.

8. **Sara was consistently working on being non-accessible and breaking the NST human trafficking victimizations.** She was achieving ongoing daily comprehension and integration skill development. Sara now had an ever-growing Self-awareness of her relationship with/to/for her-Self and with/to others. She had differentiated and separated from "the family" although it would be years before she emotionally totally let go, and stopped insisting she wanted a family. Sara also explained she generally did not dissociate anymore. She wrote a celebratory message knowing and stating "*I did it!*"

Observing Sara's process of moving from conditioned accessibility into dissolving accessibility was emotionally painful and slow. Our support of her and our knowing she was being victimized, combined with her lack of understanding of her reality, was draining. Sara would come to our meetings battered, not visually bruised, but with muscles so sore she was visibly in pain. She would explain she had been beaten because she would not stop coming to meet with us. This was also the emotional pain we felt. She was being beaten, but we and Sara knew if we withdrew our support she probably would die by Self-directed suicide.

It was like walking through a minefield to undo "the family" conditioning. Being in "the family" created a sense of emotional belongingness for Sara, forging relational attachments and group bonding emotional feelings she had been forced to believe were positive—that she was special. But the positives were destructive negatives that fostered Sara's vulnerabilities of Self-harming distortions. There was always a no-win 'damned if you do and damned if you don't' dangerous life-threatening suicidal environment that dripped on us everywhere we turned in this minefield.

As Sara kept dissolving her dissociative responses and building safety, she also needed to build safe Self-care practices in her apartment. For a number of years, this meant Sara slept in her closet. A caring intervention was to encourage Sara to Self-care by putting bedding on the closet floor. This intervention was doing the opposite of what the torturers did, which was to leave her naked, cold, and without bedding on a hard floor.

Sara did not comprehend outsider relational risks. When she tried to stop isolating her-Self and build new relationships these, too, in the earliest years, were with individuals who assaulted her physically and sexually. Others took advantage of her financially. Even though Sara had no money, she had a credit card. She used her card to buy items for people so they would like her. This financial debt added to the crises. Sara's need for relationship connections was understandable. What was difficult was the intentional harm outsiders were inflicting—they recognized Sara as a vulnerable person and callously took harmful advantage of her.

SARA'S REFLECTIONS ON HER CHILDHOOD NST CONDITIONING

All Sara had known since birth was totalitarian relational conditioning and control that shaped every aspect of her development. When we met her, we gradually came to understand she was living in an atmosphere of relational terrorism and horrification. She never knew when she would be tortured, trafficked, exploited in other ways, or her life "sacrificed." We had to accept this was her relational norm until she began to understand the reality of what she was enduring and had endured. The deadly depths of the conditioned distortions inflicted by "the family" and others were never-ending.

Sara began recalling detailed childhood memories, including a day after being massively torture-raped by her father and mother in their home. Sara ended her recall with this statement:

> I'm three. Someday I'll be four. It's dark in my room, I'm scared, nobody there but me. I have to make me better. I have to hit me. I banged my head and body on the wall. My daddy showed me colours [bruises] on me and tells me this is pretty. Makes me better for the next time. I'll be a better princess. I go to sleep after. When I wake up I have a hurt in my head but that's good. My daddy tells me when I was two.

When Sara re-remembered and told of certain ordeals, she expressed these at the age she was at the time when the NST ordeal occurred. The above excerpt was spoken from such a place in time when Sara was three. These memories were extraordinarily detailed, gut-wrenching, painful to hear, and often included horrification that accompanies acts of human evil. It appeared certain life-altering NST ordeals were specifically encoded, as was this memory. Other ordeals reached a "level" of being the norm; our persistent observations suggest these were not encoded in the same detailed way when Sara recounted them. This was not a response unique to Sara.

Sara said she learned to mimic the outsiders at a very young age. When starting school she would copy other children's work when they were tasked with drawing their family. She said she knew not to expose "the family." She learned how to memorize her role as a professional and said she had been very effective at her work.

Society's lack of information about NST human trafficking families places victimized women and children at life-altering risk. Prolonged accessibility and chronic victimizations occur when a girl or woman internalizes what the torturers said, that no one would believe them if they told. This forces them to believe there is no way out—that they can never escape. Undoing this manipulative tactic of torturers is a responsibility of society. This means ensuring there is a way out by delivering informed protection. When women or girls come into outsider society the culture needs to care, and be open to contributing to their healing, because the acculturational adjustment is huge. For 28 years Sara has said repeatedly that *"caring is the key."* Social caring demands prevention as the only sensible solution—NST must be unsilenced!

NST VICTIMIZATION-TRAUMATIZATION INFORMED CARE: PART 3

INTEGRATING, HEALING, AND EXITING

The following further discusses our observations, our developing NST knowledge, and our interventions that began with caring about Sara. These were reinforced when we supported other women who survived NST human trafficking victimizations.

Remembering

From birth, growth and development rely on absorbing and continuously remembering multitudes of experiences. Memory imprinting is required for ongoing learning. Forced dissociation is the opposite of learning to remember; it is about being forced into forgetting.

From listening to women we have concluded that torturers intend to inflict torture-pain to the degree they cause dissociative responses in the

girls or women they torture. We assume torturers watch for their dissociative responses, but for very different reasons than we did with Sara. We
noted when Sara's eyes appeared to be going into the back of her head; this
was a pre-indicator that her awareness was shifting into a dissociative state.
We would ask: Sara, where are your eyes? She would then become aware
that her eyes were going into the back of her head because this produced
a physical feeling. Sara became aware of this feeling—this was her new
learning signal to remember and benefit from remembering to end dissociating. The torturers wanted Sara to dissociate—to achieve their pleasure
of torturing her, but also presumably to force Sara to forget, thus preventing their exposure. This MO was not unique. For Elizabeth Gordon, the
family-based torturers forcedly conditioned her, she said, to "remember
to forget."

When meeting with us during the kitchen-table research project, Hope
remembered one specific NST ordeal that overwhelmed her. She learned
this caused her to dissociate and experience a fracturing of Self:

> I had been given some type of pills...I got diarrhea; I think that's
> what the pills were meant to do. The feces were smeared all over
> my body as they pissed and shit on me. Humiliated, demoralized,
> de-spiritualized. There was a box standing on end with an old, faded
> mirror propped inside. This faded mirror created a distorted image
> of me as I was forced to look into it while being told, "Look what you
> did to her." The "her" was me. But the box with the faded mirror was
> a technique "the family" used to force me into splitting, disconnect-
> ing, and dissociating from the horror. Then I was forced to stab a
> bag of straw with a knife, forced to keep stabbing but inside was my
> pet rabbit. That's better than a baby I thought. Do you see how the
> disconnection, dissociation works? And, it started so early.

Hope wrote us to say that she realized the two years spent sharing such
details of her story was a surprisingly positive experience for her because

we had clarified with her that we could only work with her as being one person, as this was our practice. She also shared an integration moment that was the opposite of being dissociated:

> Integrating my sense-of-self is some of my most unfamiliar feeling work because after our second kitchen-table meeting I did have an experience of integration while driving in my car. It was weird. This, a single person experience was very terrifying when, all of a sudden, I realized I was speaking and listening to only me versus having multiple conversations. Was I shocked!

Like Hope, other women tell us they remembered being forcedly conditioned into perceiving them-Selves as different people or personalities in different ordeals. When women ask us if they are different persons we speak of the physical reality, that they, like us, have one body, one brain and mind, one heart, and one personhood. We explain that torturers aim to destroy their relationship with/to/for Self; therefore, to guide healing and rehabilitation requires regaining their relationship with/to/for Self.

This explanation is also necessary for women needing to develop their perception and sense of having physicality. Women frequently inquire if the inside of their bodies would be the same as ours. Our answer of "yes" is sometimes difficult for women to perceive. But this is the anatomical truth. The simplest way to word our practice guidelines is to focus on doing the opposite of the torturers. This refers to truth-telling (Sarson & MacDonald, 2011). This is the opposite of the lies and distortions torturers inflict. Doing the opposite requires finding caring ways for a woman to begin to trust in her-Self, to rebuild her relationship with/to/for her-Self. Women need to be helped to remember they are persons, and the NST ordeals inflicted on them never define who they are as persons. Rather, they need to remember that the NST ordeals define solely what the torturers did to them.

Belief Clarification

Our experiences and repeated observations indicate that when a woman is challenging her internalized distorted beliefs, she can have various physical responses, such as headaches, dizziness, nausea, shivering, sleepiness, and she may verbalize she does not feel well (Sarson & MacDonald, 2011). Sara also had other sensations in her brain. She felt and could hear sounds she described as *"electric zaps"* occurring. There were also times Sara described that her brain felt watery. During intense shifting of beliefs, she had brain-pain that moved often from the frontal region to the sides of her head, and sometimes deep into the back of her head, referred to as the occipital lobe. These physical responses were generally felt immediately. Headaches, however, could last for hours or even a few days. Over-the-counter medication generally did not produce much relief. These sensations basically ended as Sara dismantled the non-State torturers' distortions, and built her own thoughts, beliefs, and perceptions in relation to/with/for her-Self. Other women expressed similar responses.

It appears neurogenesis may be occurring during belief clarification, as the brain rewires itself, creating new connective neural pathways because of brain neuroplasticity (Begley, 2007). Researchers Amy Banks and Judith Jordan also proposed that the human brain is hardwired for relational connection (2007), suggesting a safe and trusting relationship is essential for risking belief-shift healing. Sara says trusting the work of belief clarification occurred because *"caring was the key."*

Sleep promotes healing. Sleep is important when physical responses and the physiological process of neuroplasticity are occurring. We also promote exercise, such as walking in safe areas when physically possible. It is helpful to promote mind and body fitness when doing this difficult, complex healing work.

Although headaches occur when a serious transformation of beliefs happens, we also observe headaches can be an aftermath of the release of full story memories. We must consider these headaches to be a consequence of brain neurogenesis, in response to gaining insights into what the torturers did. Such shifting of insights, we contemplate, alter distancing-dissociative neuropathways, and give rise to new pathways that result in women's expressions of having brain-pain in the form of headaches. Also, there must be an impact on the amygdala in the brain, with the release of intense dissociated emotions when emotional and belief awareness is gained. Given that the primary role of the amygdala involves processing memory, working with emotional responses, and decision-making, we surmise that this release of emotions creates these unfamiliar brain-pain physical feelings, which can be frightening for women to experience. Research studies are continuously elaborating on the role of the amygdala (Bonnet et al., 2015), but studies can never be done when a woman or girl is being tortured. Whatever the impact of the NST ordeals voiced by the women in this book, we take strong exception to the thinking and labelling of women and their responses as "disordered." It can never be ethically or intellectually accurate to label as disorders whatever survival adaptations women developed—they have *survival responses* to the atrocities committed against their humanity—they are not disordered and do not have disorders. These are our explanatory observations and suggested understandings.

Cellular Memory

When women's NST memories resurface, they can and do re-experience and re-feel the torture-pain as if the torture-pain is happening in the here and now. When there is a release of torture cellular memory, women need support to cope with how re-remembering can take over the here and now.

It can be very frightening to be alone, especially when not understanding what is happening. Once women understand what is happening, this can reduce their fears.

Women can feel like the person—the child—they were at the age when the NST human trafficking victimization occurred. It is like time travel backward into the NST victimization ordeal. Or, as Chaim Shatan said, about working with Vietnam veterans, reliving their ordeals was like living in a split time zone—at the same time feeling they are both in Vietnam and their hometown. This is similar to how a woman can feel, captive in the life-threatening NST ordeal but also struggling to stay in the here and now. This is terrorizing, mixed with the fear they are going crazy if they do not know what is occurring. Knowledgeable support is essential.

Based on our supporting experiences, not only do women feel like the age they were when captive and NST victimized, but their body releases the NST physical, emotional, and spiritual pain they withstood. They re-see their victimization. They re-see the torturers and re-smell them. They may re-hear some of the torturers' humiliating words and laughter. Their body can feel as if they are being re-cut, re-burned, re-whipped, re-beaten, re-hung, re-spread-eagled, and re-torture-raped. They re-feel their captivity—there was no escape then—it feels like no escape in the here and now. Their physical cellular and mental memory became unsilenced as they re-remember and integrate the knowledge of the torture they survived.

Without understanding this integrated knowledge, women may have cellular memories and not understand why they are feeling as they do. They may keep asking, "What is wrong with me?" Lynn, who was held captive, tortured, and exploited for four and a half years by her husband, his three male friends, and the buyers, described many Self-discovery cellular body memories during our time of supporting her healing. For years Lynn had experienced cellular memories which she had never understood, describing this one:

For years and years my mouth never felt clean. It didn't matter how much I brushed my mouth and my teeth, I always had a salty or bloody taste in my mouth. Even the toothpaste and mouthwashes tasted salty. Once I made the connection the saltiness and dirtiness tastes were sensory taste memories from all the oral rapes… my mouth feels cleaner! I'm even craving a lime Popsicle. I think I could eat one without being triggered by its penis-like shape and the memories. I'd forgotten how I used to love lime Popsicles. Amazing!

Model of Cellular Memory—"Body Talk"

Based on our observations, every part of a woman's body that was tortured can hold cellular or "body talk" memories (Sarson & MacDonald, 2011), as illustrated in figure 42. For example, women may have sensations indicative of

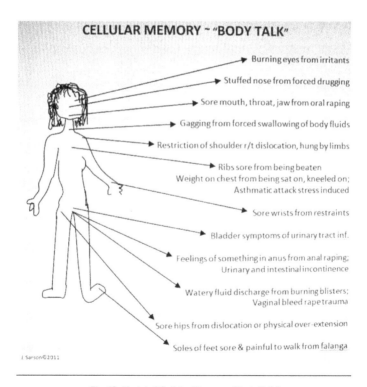

Fig. 42: Model of Cellular Memory—"Body Talk"

a bladder infection but laboratory results are negative. It can be her body is re-remembering the bladder infections she had when victimized. Sara had re-occurring cellular memory pain in the soles of her feet from them being beaten. This is known as *falanga;* it is a common form of classic torture (Larsen et al., 2018). In the early years, every part of Sara's body was releasing her victimization cellular body memories—needing to "get it out." Once her memories were released and worked through, Sara spoke of feeling lighter. Capra's scientific criteria for model-making sought subjective experiences; many women have voiced to us their cellular memory "body talk" responses.

As Sara experienced her flashback memories, she needed support to understand what happened to her, what was done to her, how it felt not only physically but emotionally, and spiritually. Her body talk cellular pain and suffering gradually eased and faded but was never forgotten. When her body talk memories jump in unexpectedly, Sara becomes fed up with these present-day invasions and wants them to end. Regrettably, we have no answer about how her body deems to heal after over 30 years of torture-traffickers victimizations. Healing is unique for each woman.

As Sara processed the NST victimizations suffered, she became increasingly relationally connected with and understanding of her-Self. Sara spoke about how recovering was and is painful and difficult work. At times the pain seemed never to end. Recovery included experiencing a form of vicarious trauma when seeing, hearing, smelling, feeling, and knowing the truthful reality of the NST and the trafficking she was subjected to, and by whom. This is Sara's reflective statement:

> I can't believe what I'm seeing…understanding…I shut out reality. I did not see things for what they were. Was I in zombiehood? I had so much loss. It makes me sad and angry, sometimes overwhelmed. It hurts as the reality comes clearer and clearer. What I don't under-stand about the process is I think I have the reality but then another

layer of clarity comes. Reality gets more intense at night. Just when I think the worst is over, my broken heart, collapsing, I can't do this anymore. Agony…painful rage…just when I think the worst is over.

Reality is so unimaginable but so personal. Reliving wasn't as bad as remembering. It's the knowledge, the images, the feelings, the pain of reality, it gets worst.

Along with Sara's vicarious trauma responses came a knowing of her losses and emotional feelings of grief. Sara made this loss and grief list in 2005:

I lost my childhood,

I never had a partner,

I never had a chance to have children,

I was not allowed to have friends, only in "the family,"

I never had fun,

I never laughed,

I never saw beauty, only black and white,

I suffered, forced abortions,

I lost my life,

The ugliness that was done to me, so horrific, so much pain,

I hate this fucking world. I am so angry.

Acknowledging Sara's losses gave reasons for the many interventions we engaged in with Sara. There were opportunities for her to capture beauty and freedom and to gain her own agency. We went outdoors for Sara to see, for the first time, the many colours of the changing autumn leaves, to have the sensation of feeling rain, to hug a tree; these were awe experiences. We also grocery shopped with her. We sat and licked ice cream cones so she could pick whatever flavour she wanted. When the Christmas season came, we toured the town to see the colourful lights. It was no longer Sara's "role" to be NST victimized at Christmas. Sara learned she was no longer "the present."

Sara was developing her reflective knowledge. These processes of healing also involved massive educational learning for her to answer the question, "Who am I?" It required growing a critical reflective consciousness, to move not only out of victimization but also out of oppression. Learning personal Self-awareness and critical problem-solving for personal growth is about moving out of oppression (Frieire, 1993). This is what our interventions were aimed at. For Sara and other women, learning to become independent thinkers is to develop Self-reliance. It is about becoming free. This is the relational knowledge of gaining a relationship with/to/for Self. Sara and other women NST victimized need support to come to know they are persons, entitled to human rights equality. However, as Sara says, "*It was a hell of a journey.*"

NST Memory is Coming: The Bell Curve Response

A general bell curve response can be explained if, for example, a woman considers how she feels when becoming ill, perhaps with a flu bug. The bell curve of becoming ill might at first begin by feeling fatigued, maybe with a slight cough and sore throat. As her illness progresses the bell curve of symptoms peaks as her temperature rises. She has chills, her throat becomes inflamed, and she feels nauseated with full-body aches. Once this acute stage passes she begins to slide down the recouping side of the bell curve. There is a gradual lessening of her symptoms and eventually, all the misery is gone.

Repeated observations suggest that when a woman's NST memory is beginning to surface or re-remembered she can experience a bell curve of responses. We created this visual bell curve response to illustrate how a woman may respond when re-remembering an ordeal or be highly triggered around specific holiday dates when her victimizations increased. This model is in figure 43.

Re-remembering a NST human trafficking ordeal presents somewhat like the bell curve of becoming ill, then recouping. For Sara, it could start with a "what's wrong with me?" sensation, proceeding to feeling emotionally down, then escalating into emotional and physical responses such as anxiety, nausea, dread, fear, and terror, but not knowing what these meant. By getting it out, she broke through the survival dissociation to re-remember the NST human trafficking ordeal. Then Sara would retell the NST and trafficking ordeals the torturers subjected her to. Sometimes this took hours and hours. Also, Sara said, with a sense of panic, that she had to *"get it out,"* which was a battle through terror, horror, and cellular torture pain memory. This was the acute stage on the bell curve.

Having released her memory meant Sara began sliding down the aftermath recouping side of the bell curve. Her physical feelings of pressure were gone once her memory was out. In the very early days of caring, Sara's immediate response was to not remember the NST ordeal. We address this specific response in the next section.

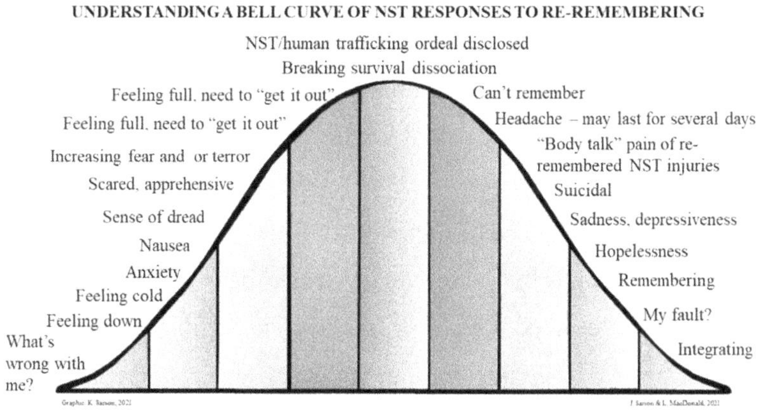

UNDERSTANDING A BELL CURVE OF NST RESPONSES TO RE-REMEMBERING

NST/human trafficking ordeal disclosed
Breaking survival dissociation

Feeling full, need to "get it out"
Feeling full, need to "get it out"
Increasing fear and or terror
Scared, apprehensive
Sense of dread
Nausea
Anxiety
Feeling cold
Feeling down
What's wrong with me?

Can't remember
Headache – may last for several days
"Body talk" pain of re-remembered NST injuries
Suicidal
Sadness, depressiveness
Hopelessness
Remembering
My fault?
Integrating

Graphic K. Barson, 2021   J. Sarson & L. MacDonald, 2021

Fig. 43: The Bell Curve Figure: Responses to Re-Remembering Model

Based on our observations, Sara's emotional and physical responses on the downward side of the bell curve represented how Sara felt after being victimized. Sara had a list of aftermath consequences to consider, understand, and heal from. Healing was difficult because it meant more insights that could trigger suicidal feelings, vicarious trauma responses such as sadness, depressiveness, hopelessness, remembering, and questioning such as, "Was this my fault?"

In the earliest years, this bell curve effect also occurred before an approaching holiday. Sara would have an anticipatory bell curve response prior to being "*rented out*," as she named being tortured and trafficked. Prior to a NST ordeal Sara would telephone, wondering what was wrong with her. She would be experiencing many of the sensations listed on the upward side of the bell curve. Because of her survival dissociative response and her conditioned unawareness, Sara did not understand the meaning of her sensations. The significance only became increasingly clear to Sara as she began dissolving her dissociation by integrating her reality.

Recouping after being tortured and trafficked meant different body talk than the anticipatory rise into terror. After a complete NST memory is released, our thinking is that the painful cellular, body talk memory Sara and other women re-suffer represents how they felt in the past after they had survived being NST victimized. Even though women tell us they cannot remember how they suffered after NST victimization, their body in the here and now releases much cellular body talk memory. Women, including Sara, experienced feeling physically battered: bruises can appear; their faces can feel swollen; they can suffer low back and abdominal pain from being torture-raped; they may have watery vaginal fluid when their vagina was burned; they may have inflamed, sore skin and tissue wounds from being burned and cut, and joint pain from being tied down, hung, or having their hips over-extended. Women feel bereft, even beyond bereft.

They feel abandoned, alone, not cared about, discarded, trapped, coated with sadness, depressiveness, and hopelessness, even though the torturers told them as children they did not have emotions. For Sara, if she did think she had emotions this was a sign of weakness and terrorizing. Still, in 2021, at times experiencing strong emotions can be disconcerting or even scary, especially rage and anger.

After the Release of the NST Memory: "I Can't Remember"

Sara's memories came spontaneously. Our observation suggested this happened when her mind and body were capable of handling re-remembering her lived reality. Following the release of memory, Sara could not recall her just-disclosed memory. This was Sara's persistent pattern in the early years. Working together, we supported Sara, writing the memory she was releasing. When she came out of her state of recalling the memory, we did not discuss her recalled memory; instead, we spent time supporting her to become present in the here and now. Often, she would telephone the following day to say she could not remember the memory she had released. Our practice was not to tell her. We encouraged her to be patient, and her memory would slowly return. This is exactly what occurred, time and time again. In the early years of healing, her recall of the NST ordeals would slowly emerge over a period of weeks. Gradually, recall times shrank into days, eventually into an immediate recall. We remain adamant that a woman needs to own her victimization memories, to know, without a doubt, it is her mind and her voice that recalls whatever details she encoded at the time she was NST victimized. Only once did Sara ask to see our written notes of her released memory. She returned the notes and never asked again. She trusted her-Self and her recall.

Major bell curve memory recalls came in full-story detail. There are, however, bits and pieces, or remnants of memory that Sara cannot make sense of. These may come as flashes of physical images or may be emotional feeling memories; sadly, her body can and does spontaneously re-enact past cellular responses. For example, in November 2019, she was washing her dishes and suddenly had the sensation she was being raped—a most distressing, lingering NST victimization intrusion into her present-day life.

Women's healing may be enhanced by healthy alternative interventions. Acupuncture, massage, physiotherapy, boxing exercises, yoga, meditation, specific group work, community connections, walking, swimming, and other safe, non-Self-harming interventions are all acts of Self-caring.

Chemical Torture: Drugging Responses

Sara and other women know they were drugged. Multi-forms of drug-ging—pills, liquids, injections, nasal inhalants, or delivery by mask are persistent MOs of non-State torturers. Drugging made the women, when children, powerless and often unable to move. We spent several long evenings with Sara during her recall of different drugging memories; she endured muscular paralysis and at another time a sense of blindness response. These body talk responses were terrifying for her and uncom-fortable for us. Our nursing backgrounds were essential in supporting Sara to work through her responses, which lasted long minutes, but felt like hours. Healing poly-drugging responses is a required intervention.

A woman may exit a NST organized criminal family system, still re-enacting her drugging cellular body talk responses, not understanding what is happening to her. Based on our observations, a woman can have episodes of drowsiness, slurred speech, drooping eyelids, or eyelids sud-denly feeling heavy and closed (Sarson & MacDonald, 2011). She may feel she has no muscle control, lose her balance, or seem to be staggering as if drunk. Chemical drugging memories may cause nasal congestion and a burning sensation in her eyes. She may suddenly fall over feeling dizzy when sitting down in what others may perceive as a "fit." A loss of speech and stuttering can occur. As previously mentioned, years after Sara's exiting and recovery she had episodes of loss of speech and stuttering. These cellular memory episodes appeared suddenly and disappeared just as suddenly. However, they did last several weeks. We consider this to be Sara's body releasing stored memory responses of past NST chemical drugging and horrification ordeals. Since horrification can produce such a response, we consider this to be a reasonable explanation of Sara's mute and stuttering episodes.

Based on our practice, healing drugging responses can occur when a woman understands she is having a drugging re-enactment memory response. This helps answer the question: "What is wrong with me?" There is nothing wrong with her. She is having cellular body talk memory release. Understanding this diminishes her fear, which in turn decreases her stress.

For us, interventions begin with naming the drugging cellular body talk memories, then working with a woman to learn how to stay present in the here and now. For example, we intervene by calling her by her name, encouraging her to identify her environment by naming objects she sees in the room, the colour of the walls, and when she is seated, we encourage her to watch her feet move so she knows she is in her body. We avoid asking her to look at her hands because in past NST ordeals she was forced to use her hands to touch people or objects in manners that were victimizing. As well, during the NST ordeals she may have had blood on her hands (Sarson & MacDonald, 2011). As she becomes stronger at overcoming the drugging chemical body talk memory responses, she can heal the drugged powerlessness the torturers created when inflicting their chemical tortures. The more she wins, the greater her skills become at gaining back her relationship with/ to/for her-Self, which the torturers tried to destroy. These drugging cellular memory responses can decrease, and potentially totally disappear.

Drugging Questionnaire

In our online questionnaire which focused on identifying the harms inflicted in NST victimizations, drugging was listed as one of the potential harms. Four drugging modalities were listed: alcohol, pills, injections, and inhalants by mask. Of the 60 questionnaires completed, 25 respondents identified drugging with alcohol; 39 identified drugging involving pills; 33 said injections; and 15 said masks were used. Many respondents listed suffering multi-forms of drugging. Fifty-seven respondents were female; the remaining respondents identified as male and other. Canada, the US, the UK, Europe, and Australia were the respondents' countries of origin.

Validation of the transnational reality of NST victimization and traumatization comes not only from the completed questionnaires but also from the voices of those who shared additional comments. A woman wrote the following significant comment on her questionnaire:

> I'm glad to see the work you are doing…No one could help get me out of the home until at 17 my father screwed up and stabbed me with a knife to kill me but I lived and then was placed in a foster home.

> I have been in therapy since then (40 now)…I function normally on the surface, but suffer daily with horrible "pictures" that come unbidden without triggers, I can't sleep much as I can get stuck in nightmares, I used to cut for 25 years but promised my doc I would quit and did, have anorexia since I was little. I did not bond with my mother or other adults, and lived mostly locked up in isolation separated even from my siblings, so am socially a mess, if I could just find some way to slow down or stop the pictures and nightmares I would be grateful…I have tried suicide many times but am such a failure, I never even succeed at that. I am not worth the air I breathe (waste)…I am not currently trying to off myself, as I do have several things to "live for," but myself is NOT one of them. I can't have friends because I am too weird and scary and they all run for hills if they get to know me a little bit…What is wrong with our species?

Safety

Dissolving Sara's disconnection-dissociation accessibility responses was complex because she was still in a state of active captivity, being tortured and exploited when she first sought our support. As previously explained, dissolving her disconnection-dissociation response was essential if she was ever to be safe. During the early years, this response caused Sara to experience episodes of losing time and finding her-Self driving late at night, not remembering why.

For another woman, she too was unable to understand what or why she had episodes of confusion, a loss of time, or finding her-Self wandering the streets not knowing where she was or how she got there. Although she was no longer being tortured and trafficked, she had not integrated the NST and trafficking victimizations.

Not being able to remember who the torturers are or were, and what the torturers did and can continue to do to them is dangerous. Non-integration of NST trafficking victimizations places women at dangerous risks. Women's integration of their victimizations and associated risks are essential healing requirements of our practice. Otherwise, it also places those who are caring at risk. We learned this when Sara exposed the bombshell that she had been forced by women torturers to write a letter stating we were responsible for her suicide had she died by suicide.

NST SUICIDALITY AND FEMICIDE

NST is a human rights crime against the humanity of women and girls. Capra's scientific model-making criteria asked for subjective experiences; tragically, we hear from women who have suffered the unconscionable neglect of social denial that creates suicidal responses. This subjective experience must no longer be permissible culturally, governmentally, politically, and institutionally. The development of NST victimization-traumatization informed care and healing is the responsibility of all sectors of society. Legal prevention begins with naming and criminalizing NST as a torture crime.

We reflect on Sara's first telephone call in August 1993, when she said she was going to die by suicide in four days. Her state of being was, in fact, motivated by three major thematic issues identified in the suicidality model in figure 44. These were:

Fig. 44: Model of Thematic Issues of Suicidality

Self-directed suicide was based on a belief that this is the only way out, therefore the only action in a woman's control.

Sacrificial suicide refers to the torturers' MO of enforcing an ideology of human evil infiltrated with religious-based distortions and coded language. Torturers conditioned Sara to normalize the belief she would be "sacrificed" to "satan" for "the family." "Sacrifice" was a coded word to cover-up that suicide was a way to die for "the family." Likewise, "satan" was a coded word used to refer to male torturers, oral rape, or an erect penis.

Non-sacrificial suicide relates to conditioning Sara to die by suicide if she ever told on "the family." This was a MO of the torturers to ensure their organized crimes were not exposed.

This model, like all our model-making, took years of intense observations, digesting all the victimizations Sara described to us and to her-Self. These suicidal victimization thematic descriptions shaped our knowledge about the MO tactics of the family-based non-State torturers. Not only were these described by Sara but also by women who participated in our kitchen-table research, and later by other women. This suicidality model helped us plan healing interventions.

Sacrificial Suicide

Sara was in a life-threatening crisis when she called that August 1993 night. We did not know back then that Sara was unknowingly responding to the evil actions of the "the family's" NST schooling of "sacrificial" and "non-sacrificial" suicidal conditioning. It took several years for us, and for Sara, to clarify this MO. In August 1993, Sara's conditioning was that August was the month she believed she would be "sacrificed" at "the family" group torture gathering. Sara's psychological conditioning of fear and terror became triggered every August. Her terror occurred because every year when Sara went to the August torturing group gathering, she never knew if she would be "sacrificed." This never-knowing was a yearly emotional blackmail tactic and another MO of "the family."

Sacrificial suicide conditioning was instilled by "the family" by framing their organized criminal group gatherings as ritualized ceremonies such as "marriage to satan," described in the section on acts of human evil. These ritualized group gatherings are ritualized dramas; they instil a sense of group belongingness, comfort, and help to stabilize relationships with like-minded others, giving support to their NST organized crimes. Our perspective is that these ritualized group gatherings shape their co-culture and fulfill their pleasure of inflicting acts of human evil. They creatively use whatever tools at their disposal. We were told that books were kept by the torturers. Women were unaware of what was in them; except they feared them. Other information has been that they read scientific books to learn how to maximize psychological captivity. In the group process, they learn from others' evil creativity. Torturers use costumes, face masks, and made-up ditties, as Sara explained in Chapter 8. Other women report similar practices.

In 2006, a woman described that when she was a child, at a group torture gathering or, as she said, at a "sham ritual," one of the adult perpetrators standing beside her whispered to her, "This is how we trick the fools." She understood this to mean that creating ritualized shams was a way to distort "outsiders'" perceptions about NST groups if their existence was exposed.

Non-Sacrificial Suicide

Non-sacrificial suicide conditioning was saturated with Sara being "taught," since toddlerhood, how to die by suicide if she ever told the "outsiders" about "the family." Sara said that as a toddler she was forced to sit down in a hallway and was shown how to cut her wrists. This was one of the torturers' manipulative conditioning tactics to ensure Sara would die by suicide before ever telling on "the family."

Elizabeth, who has chosen to be identified by her first name, spoke of a similar ordeal. She described being NST "taught" to die by suicide if she ever spoke about the NST group (Sarson & MacDonald, 2018c):

> It took recovery and healing to know and understand what they did because for a long time I was in flashbacks, feeling/seeing releasing

the torture ordeals. I was seeing the men's hands around mine on the knife, holding it pressed into my stomach, hearing their words "die if you tell." I understood I had to kill my-Self if I told…When I began to tell or even thought about telling the knife torture flash-back would be right up front…If I killed my-Self with a knife they would be able to say "she was crazy…she did it to her-Self" because it would be my hands on the knife and my fingerprints…they told me this lots of times…men usually the Uncle…forced me to hold the knife to my stomach and told me to kill my-Self with the knife if I ever told.

Metaphoric imagery and storytelling were useful interventions that counter suicidal conditioning. One such metaphoric intervention was immediately effective for Elizabeth, who shared being taught to "use" a knife to die by suicide. We asked Elizabeth to envision that the torturers had placed her, as a toddler, on their MO suicidal train. They kept her on their "die if you tell" suicidal train for 50 years. Unknown to her, this was why she always felt suicidal whenever she tried to tell. We explained that as a child, she had no choice, she was "put on" the train. But now, as an adult, she had a decision-making choice to either stay on the torturers' suicidal train or get off. She immediately designed her ticket to get off the torturers' NST suicidal train. She got off, never to return. Metaphoric imagery and storytelling interventions need to fit uniquely for each woman. This one created a freedom solution for Elizabeth because her father frequently traf-ficked her by taking her to the train station where she was forced to wait until picked up by other criminals. Elizabeth could relate to train rides.

Self-Directed Suicide

Self-directed suicide is a way to escape NST family systems. Hope, who participated in our kitchen-table research, wanted to explain that toddlers can be suicidal:

I had two periods during my toddlerhood that I can remember not wanting to be present in my family. Once, sometime between the ages of 18 months and two and one-half years old, I walked out into the road in front of a semi-truck. My mother pulled me out of the truck's path. Then, when I was over the age of two, I tried to place a rifle to my head and pull the trigger but my arm was too little. I wanted to get rid of my head. Adults sat around, watched me, and laughed. As young as I was I knew if I could use the rifle it would mean I would be no more, the suffering would end. On my grandfather's farm, I used to imagine jumping out of the upstairs hall window. I can still see this window in my mind but I never did try to jump. Maybe I looked like a "depressed" child but by the age of three or four I knew, an intuitive sense is what I call it, that if I was to survive I would have to take care of myself. I did in whatever manner I could!

Triggering Self-directed suicidality was an emotional blackmail MO. Sara came to a meeting and explained that when she was alone at work a woman and man entered her work site and raped her. They had a camera. Sara said they told her they were filming raping her and would circulate the film to discredit and shame her. She believed them. This also triggered her sense of humiliation—her suicidality. To reduce her suicidality response Sara needed to be encouraged to think critically. She needed to question that if a video was really being made and these two perpetrators circulated it, this would criminally implicate them given their positional power in the community.

For Sara, having suicidal conversations was a minute-by-minute need in the early years. It would eventually decrease to become her coping response whenever she was overly stressed, or got into a Self-negative emotional cycle. Her coping responses involved unhealthy behaviours such as buying stuff she did not need. This cluttered her apartment, triggering negative Self-deprecating Self-talk. This created a cycle of more

Self-harming, more stress; Sara would then slip into her familiar coping of feeling she wanted to die by suicide. The norm of healing interventions meant that suicidal conversations could occur daily. Until that is, Sara let go of her "best buddy"—suicide. This did not happen until 2019. It took Sara 26 years to let go of her "best buddy." Letting go left her with an emotional feeling of emptiness, something like grief. Sara had developed and kept a relationship with suicide since she was a child. She did not want to let this relationship feeling go. It eventually occurred spontaneously. This was a surprise for Sara. As valued as daily suicidal prevention conversations were, it was an enormous relief for me, Jeanne. It had been extremely fatiguing to intervene with Sara's suicidal emotional responses for 26 years.

ON KILLING

Conditioned Suicidality. The MO of the family-based torturer-traffickers would be femicide if Sara did die because of being "trained" or conditioned to die by suicide. It is clear from women's disclosures that if they died their deaths would be considered suicidal versus identified as a consequence of suicidal-femicide conditioning. The torturers' MO was to make it appear that women had died by their own hands. These violent criminal NST families and groups will only be exposed when women have a truth-telling legal right to disclose the grievous destruction they have been subjected to. Conditioned suicidal-femicide must be identified as a MO of these torturer-traffickers, so women can gain informed support to undo their beliefs about the deadly risk such conditioning imposes. Conditioned suicidal-femicide is a form of killing. It is an act of human evil. As Sara described, she was "trained" to die by suicide if she ever told on "the family." Other women disclose the same form of victimization. This must be understood as a potential MO tactic of femicide.

Femicide. Another possibility is femicide could occur based on the types of physical tortures inflicted. Sara and Lynn, for example, were both subjected to water-torture. Lynn describes how her husband (Sarson & MacDonald, 2020c):

> Used to put me in the tub, face down, dunking me under water, yanking on my hair to pull me up, and then holding me down again. I'm hearing his voice echoing in my right ear mostly, counting, "One…two…three…four…five…six…seven…eight…nine…ten… bitch." He'd go on and on. "If you're still alive bitch I might plug in the radio and throw it into the water."

This is a form of asphyxiation torture that impairs oxygen intake and is described as non-fatal drowning in the torture literature (Beynon, 2012). Although Lynn did not die, death from such forms of NST can occur later. For example, Lynn could have developed pneumonia and died from inhaling the tub water she was submerged in.

Snuff Films. Sophie suffered NST perpetrated by an aunt and uncle. She was trafficked out of the US into Europe at approximately nine years old. Held captive, she described witnessing the horrific sexualized killing of a young girl for a snuff film (Sarson & MacDonald, 2019b). Other women told us snuff films were a tool used to terrify them when they were children. At one time, snuff victimization was considered not to exist. Police now have evidence that snuff killings do exist (Burke et al., 2000).

Serial Killing. Earlier in this book, we wondered if family-based non-State torturer-traffickers could also be serial killers. Women have disclosed witnessing killings of infants whose births were never documented. They responded to our reproductive questionnaire by describing infants who disappeared after their birth.

During our kitchen-table research project, Hope especially spoke about the killing and dismemberment of a young boy she said was brown-skinned.

She thought he was from another country. Another woman, as a child, spoke of the torturers' MO of picking up a street woman, then witnessed her being tortured to death. She understood the torturers knew the street woman would not be missed when she disappeared. In Canada, women who were exploited in prostitution do go missing (Lepard, 2010). The question remains: Are these family-based torturers also killers?

Dave Grossman (1996) examined the key processes involved in the human act of soldiers killing other humans. He wrote that killing was like experiencing a high, filled with a sense of having absolute power and control. Some soldiers, he said, compared this to a sexualized climatic high. This description fits what we understand from listening to the repeated testimonies of many women. They describe that torturers get sexualized pleasure in their acts of torturing, including bringing women and girls to near death.

We spent several hours with author Elliot Leyton discussing his understanding that serial killers gained a sense of fulfilment when killing (1986).[9] His analysis was similar to Grossman's.

Society must be prepared to listen and gain an understanding of torturers' MO. This is one reason for writing our book—it is about unsilencing women's testimonies about the NST they were subjected to within intimate family relationships. The destruction of intimate relationships is the torturers' pleasure. Such damage provides a sense of fulfilment as stated in the writings of Grossman and Leyton.

---

9   In 2008 we travelled to Saint John's Newfoundland on a brief vacation. We telephoned Elliot Leyton in the hope he would agree to talk with us about his research and his book *Hunting Humans*. He did. Inviting us to his home, we discussed that wilful intent to commit atrocities existed for the torturer-traffickers we were learning about and the serial killers he wrote about. As we described the actions of the torturer-traffickers Elliot wondered why he had not heard of their crimes. We explained that women and girls' attempts to tell were generally disbelieved or they were labelled mentally ill. We left appreciative of the insightful conversation and visit.

The following is Sara's recall of the ordeal that could have killed her. If Sara had died, her death would probably have been investigated and deemed accidental. This is her story.

Sara: In the Snow Bank

I'm in my bedroom in our house. Our house is surrounded by a high white picket fence with a gate which opens to the walkway. I had been alone in the darkness, feeling hot and cold, coughing, choking. At the time, I remember I felt weird, weak, dizzy with pains in my head, ears, vagina, chest, stomach and legs. I had pain everywhere. I was really hot. I felt as if I was floating so I wrapped my-Self into a ball.

My mom and dad came into my bedroom. They were…telling me there would be no doctor coming. Then, in the darkness, my father carried me outdoors. My father laid me in a big snow bank. My mom and dad looked at me and said: "I was a bad, bad girl." My mom and dad, they turn and walk back into our house and shut the door.

I heard somebody—crunch, crunch…I'm going to be still. Somebody's getting me…Mr. and Mrs. Dicks…they're coming to get me. Mrs. Dicks screams, "Oh my god! Sara, Oh my god." I'm floating…I hear her screaming, "What's she doing here?" Mr. Dicks picks me up. "How in the darn did this kid get out here in the dark? She's going to freeze to death." They knocked on the doors a whole bunch of times before my father answers. Mr. Dicks says to my father, "What are you trying to do to her? For Christ sake get a blanket. Poor little Sara."

Mr. Dicks is telling my dad to take me to the hospital. "Turn the heat up; turn the heat up for god sake!" Mr. Dicks yells at my dad.

I'm not dead, Mr. Dicks, I say to me…I just can't talk to you because I'm floating…I'm going up to the sky…I'm going with my friends in the sky…My dad's saying…I was sleepwalking. He's saying…

he thought the door was locked…but…I don't leave footprints in the snow.

"We're losing her! We're losing her!" The doctor is too sad. It's okay Dr. Jim. . . I don't want to come back…I don't want to go home…I don't want them…don't want my mom…I want to go to the sky.

I'm just going away where I don't hurt no more…I'm going to be okay…don't be sad Mr. Dicks…I'm not hurting. Mr. Dicks is saying he could have gone for a walk earlier instead of watching TV.

"She's coughing! She's coming back." I'm coming back, Mr. Dicks… it's not your fault.

I don't want to come back…coming back to the table…sore throat again…my throat is hurting me on the table…I'm hurting…why won't you let me go…I'm angry…I'm angry…I'm too angry…I didn't want to come back.

Dr. Jim gave me a needle. I sleepy…I don't want to go to sleep…bad things will happen…don't go to sleep Santana [this was an "insider name" they gave to Sara].

I'm not in the woods. I have to wake up my hands and feet. I'm an angry little girl because I didn't go away. Throwing up blood. I'm choking on the blood. Sorry, I made a mess, Dr. Jim. The blood is coming.

"Have to watch her carefully, poor little girl. She's too cold, cover her with blankets."

Stupid needle…my back is hurting…I have pains…I'm cold… my hands aren't working…stupid needle…my toes are hurting… my ears are hurting…I don't want to be here…poor little girl…I'm scared of the blood…the blood is choking my throat…I'm scared like the sacrifice.

Sara's description was of her near-death ordeal. Had it been investigated, not as sleepwalking as her father lied to explain, would it have been identified as a possible intentional girl child femicide? Were there questions as to why Sara, who was critically ill, was not taken to the hospital? It is now known the family can be the most dangerous place for children, where they face the highest risk of being killed by parents or someone known to them (Stöckl et al., 2017).

STORYTELLING

Storytelling as a therapeutic intervention can help individuals cope with a disease such as cancer (Chelf et al., 2000), or offer help to a person in understanding their emotions (Hazelton, 1991). We used the healing power of storytelling to help Sara and other women as frequently as possible, and as often as women requested.

Storytelling invites another way of thinking about an issue, to shift a belief, or to have women consider their own moral spirituality. Women often wondered where their spirituality went, given that they were exposed to massive actions of human evil. This is why initiating a discussion of their evilism anxieties, fears, and terror is an essential intervention. They need healing space to shape their own spiritual goodness. For Sara, her goodness and spirituality were built by her efforts to try and save other children from being harmed. She explained she would say to the torturer, *"Take me, take me."* Despite being surrounded by torturers, highlighting her actions meant she could connect with her sense of goodness and her own spirituality. As she healed, Sara asked for our inventive storytelling not to always have a moral ending—enough was enough. She was starting to seek humour.

Being read to from children's books also helped Sara heal the child-hood growth and developmental gaps she suffered when, for instance, she only remembers:

> When little and maybe two or three my mom and dad put me in the dresser drawer and slammed the drawer shut. I be in the dresser drawer for a long time, squeezed in…I hated it in the drawer, hated that I had no clothes on…I remember smells of poop and pee in the drawer…if I had diapers the pins got stuck into me…The dresser was high…it felt like a cage…don't ask nobody to pick you up you get hurt…they'd do bad stuff to you…touch you in bad places… choke you.

When a woman is re-feeling her NST captivity, there is no escape for her. We do not leave the processing of her emerging memory until she says she is ready to exit the NST memory. Then, we frame an escape from the captivity using imagery and storytelling, mixed with a little get-even justice. We also make this storytelling fit the woman's age she was when, as a child, she was trapped and NST victimized. There is always an escape ending so the woman can reframe that she is not left in the ordeal with the torturers. To share what a storytelling escape could be like, we created the following example:

> Imagine a magic pink and green butterfly that becomes invis-ible except to the innocent and beautiful little girl you were. It can fly into the NST room and wrap you in its warm cozy wings to cover your nakedness and coldness. On your way out of the room the magic butterfly has a glue gun spout. It shoots glue at the torturers, sticking them to the ceiling. They will never be able to get off. As the glue dries it covers the torturers with grey globs that grow prickly thorns. If they move they will feel the thorns. Serves them right, they were very bad adults.

(This adds a sense of justice.) Away you and the beautiful but-
terfly escape to a safe and warm Cocoon land where you can
climb into cozy warm pj's and snuggle until you feel better.

For us, storytelling escapes have been an essential, transformational
intervention. Escaping was never possible in real life for women when they
were children, so doing the opposite of what the torturers did promotes
healing. When flashbacks hit, sending the woman back into the NST childhood captivity ordeal, the captivity needs to be transformed and reframed
into an escape.

Elizabeth Gordon: Escaping via Rescue Storytelling

Elizabeth Gordon explained 'Rescue Storytelling' was critical to her
healing (Sarson et al., 2019):

> If in the process of telling I didn't have the opportunity to leave the
> original torture environment of the child I was, I would stay stuck in
> the torture memory. So feeling like the child I was in the adult I am
> today might be overcome by the "die if you tell" programming and
> be triggered into a suicidal response.

> In a rescue I feel my little child body is protected, soothed, and
> wrapped in a blanket which replaces forced nakedness and the
> voices of the men shouting "no one" and their objectification, rape,
> and destruction of me as a human being...A released memory
> ordeal without a rescue or a different ending to the original torture
> story is abandoning, re-victimizing, and re-traumatizing. It would
> be repeating the torture without a resolution. Feelings of craziness,
> lostness, shame, captivity, and dissociation would continue, and the
> torturers would win.

> The rescue is real and concrete to the child I was in the memory
> and to the adult woman I am. It is important care in the present
> where there was none before. The dissociative barriers that had once

compartmentalized my childhood ordeals begin melting one by one. Anger replaces helplessness. Compassion for my-Self replaces the brutality of the perpetrators without humanity, warmth replaces numbness and coldness, and the kindness of my supporters replaces the cruelty of the perpetrators who wanted to destroy me. Where there were wounds, there are fresh scars. Now I feel hopefulness and awe, I see beauty and colour, and each rescue allows a little more pastness to begin to happen. Escape is about justice, justice for me and for the child I was.

I believe rescues are a social, moral, and ethical responsibility both for the person so harmed who is reliving the torture and for persons who are supporting. Each rescue is an exit opportunity toward freedom. A rescue helps me learn I am important enough to be cared about. It is always a surprise to me to receive gentle care.

This is almost unbelievable…I create new memories…of being cherished and soothed and memories of kindness and laughter; I can feel joy. I can make statements which I couldn't before like, "When I was five I was taken to a house with a basement where several men tortured me. I was subjected to forced nakedness, caging, and was raped while hung up on some bars on the wall." I can say this because what the perpetrators did and my responses are named and recognized as torture and because I was rescued which makes a different ending to the story.

NST victimizations hurt every growth and development process of a child who is born into NST human trafficking family systems. This creates gaps that need to be filled with knowledgeable caring. This is made easier when, for instance, it can be explained to women that if their victimizations began in infancy they can re-experience growth and development gaps when processing infant memories. An intense sucking need may arise, because for them as an infant or toddler sucking often meant being harmed, for example, they may have been kept hungry then sucking meant oral rape. Using a water bottle with a drinking spout that is similar to sucking heals this developmental victimization and it generally resolves. Another re-experience is a woman may have episodes of urinary or bowel incontinence so easy access to a bathroom is needed. Women are to be respected and not infantilized. Our experience is these growth and development gaps heal. If torturers can use destructive MO creativity, we must do the opposite and be creative in offering safe, kind, compassionate, respectful, dignity-inducing healing, and caring interventions.

SARA'S QUESTION: "WHAT DID EXITING MEAN FOR ME?"

To understand the challenges Sara faced, or any woman may face, when exiting NST human trafficking family systems they were born into, we drew on our transcultural nursing theories and experiences and the writings about cultural shock by Jean-Marc Hachey (1998). Cultural shock or acculturation adaptation causes stress. It challenges one's familiar way of living, one's relational connections, and everyday routine practices. In her own way, Sara had survived by devising two ways of cultural living—the "insider" co-cultural way which exerted the most impact and the "outsider" way in which she memorized how to behave in her outsider role. Letting go of the familiar "insider" and adapt fully to the "outsider" way was a serious, stressful adaptation.

As Sara increased her connection with the "outsider" world, the responses common to cultural shock became apparent. These cultural shock emotional responses included confusion, disorientation, frustration, anxiety, anger, and fear. This created further challenges to Sara's frail esteem and confidence. The cultural shock leaves a person feeling like an alien. This resonated strongly with Sara because, hundreds of times, she expressed feeling like *"an alien."* The task of adjusting felt almost impossible and was exhausting for Sara.

There are four stages to transcultural adjustment: the honeymoon stage; the anxiety stage; the reject and regression stage; and the adjustment stage. Learning these stages helped us to understand the dimensions of the struggles Sara faced. The dimensions had names—cultural shock, acculturation adaptation, and fatigue.

The Honeymoon Stage

As Sara succeeded in freeing her-Self from "the family" and other like-minded torturers—men and women—she did experience the honeymoon stage. She felt free. But this was short-lived. The work of integrating the NST reality she had lived became increasingly painful. It was demanding work for all of us.

The Anxiety Stage

Certainly, the anxiety stage added to Sara's already challenging responses. This stage involves feeling "homesick" and the need to return to their familiar. A fact we needed to understand. Sara wavered for a long time about whether or not she would go back to "the family." In later years, she did go back on several occasions. Each time she was seriously harmed. She was missing the relational tension and the relational NST violence because being "*torture touched*" she said was all she knew. This physiological conditioning of tension and NST violence had been engrained as her relational familiar for almost three decades. The loss created more anxiety. She struggled over the need to revert to her familiar ways of coping, including Self-harming with increasing feelings of Self-directed suicidality.

The Rejection and Regression Stage

For Sara and us, this stage meant being constantly confronted with new problems. For Sara these outsider problems were often difficult to understand. Nothing seemed to work out. She could not stop buying stuff she did not need. This sent her into negativity and Self-harming responses. She would feel increasingly alone, angry, and stomp out of our office banging the door shut, telling us she was not returning. Feeling more and more alien when trying to adjust, Sara was feeling emotionally hopeless about succeeding, so why even try.

The Adjustment Stage

This would take years. Even after 28 years of work, there are still social, structural, and relational realities Sara does not fully comprehend. This was also true for other women. They all needed the freedom to ask clarifying questions without being judged negatively. The hard and painful work of recovery from the NST victimizations perpetrated against Sara, and the consequential traumas she suffered, could only advance at a pace she could safely and psychologically cope with. Sara faced challenges that took years of support. On August 5, 2019, Sara said to Jeanne, "*I am almost through the layer cake. Not quite all there but very close.*"

This reference to the layer cake was a metaphor Sara related to. We used this metaphor to explain that developing a relationship with/to/for Self was like going through the many levels of a layer cake. Sometimes it was only inching up through one layer and falling backward, then picking up and trying again. It was a monumental day in 2019 when Sara said to Jeanne, and to her-Self, that she just realized she had a relationship with suicide and she had just let this go. She explained her realization that suicide had been "*my best buddy*" over her lifetime. Sara was emotionally feeling this "best buddy" as a relational loss. As she moves through another layer of the cake, Sara will work at healing this emotional hollow she feels, knowing she is okay.

The following statements were examples of Sara's challenges, related to her cultural shock or acculturation adaptations. These were her questions and her need for supportive caring as she stumbled into a world she had never integrated. Although she lived in it, she did not understand it. She wondered about being *"almost through the layer cake. Not quite all there but very close."* This means she keeps finding her way to answering her questions.

Where in the World do I Fit? How do I Continue to Cope with Exiting and Cultural Re-Integration?

Letting go of NST co-culture and re-entering the outsider society differently as a woman and not in an actor role and establishing new Self-caring patterns—how will I achieve all of this?

Creating meaningfulness for and in my own life versus being in a state of functional captivity for "the family," to keep my pay cheque, to learn to buy my own food, to learn how to cook my food—how will I manage all of this?

Will I be able to create a new sense of having my own home and community? How will I see and understand this world when people look at me and think my questions are stupid because I am an adult and should know stuff? I can't explain to them I never learned or don't even understand a lot of the outsider language—how will I cope?

Gathering new information, being curious, taking healthy risks to develop my own interests when I was never allowed to do so—how will I succeed?

Practicing new ways of being, learning new skills, like how to write a bank cheque, what will the bank think of me? How will I do all of this?

Learning how to read people, learning about people, developing safe relationships which I never had before—how will I know when the people are dangerous or not?

Realizing it takes time to settle, understanding mainstream language, relationships, culture—just so, so much to learn. Will I be able to learn all of this?

Taking time outs; learning to cope with mistakes, with failures, learning, learning, learning—so much learning. Can I do this?

Finding humour you tell me helps, but what is there to find humour in? Will this ever happen to me to laugh, to even smile—will this happen?

Building resilience takes practicing at living life, but I've never had my own life so how do I learn to live my life? How do I learn how to feel being genuinely and authentically caring in my relationship with/to/for my Self?

The process of learning to be a person is frightening, confusing, overwhelming, painful, emotionally contradictory, time-consuming, filled with trials and errors, feelings of going crazy, mind-boggling with responsibilities for making my own decisions—just for being ME.

Although for many years it had been a hellish and painful journey, Sara has declared she is almost there. She has been amazing to watch as she has needed to tackle so much. She keeps finding her way, is thankful to have a best friend, and is working at making her-Self a home. She is succeeding at managing her finances more wisely and withdrawing from buying "stuff" as a response to decades of deprivation. Sara has had to meet health challenges that complicate her wellness and cause pain, limitations, and stressful demands. Her life can sometimes be disrupted with nightmares and herstorical body talk. She now knows some of her anger is social anger because society wants to ignore her NST victimization, and not develop

NST victimization-traumatization informed care. Not having a law to specifically name NST as torture is distressful; it devalues her victimization and her as a person. She has quietly stepped into social advocacy. She awaits the outcome, as she manages her final journey through her layer cake of years of victimizations. But with the letting go of her "best buddy," laughter is becoming spontaneous. This is so wonderful to hear!

In 1993, we started this journey because we held a personal and professional stance that women's and girls' responses to violent victimizations must not be pathologized as a mental illness. Sara was not mentally ill; she was overwhelmed; she had been placed into a struggle for her life since she was born. She was surrounded by people whose pleasures were inflicting acts of human evil. Being tortured and trafficked was all she relationally knew. Not only was she born into a family that aimed to destroy her for their pleasure and benefit, but she was also born into a patriarchal society that supports pandemic violence, misogyny, and misopedia.

It is global knowledge that torture is a human rights crime of such severity that it stands alone and apart from other crimes. It must not be that powerless infants are abandoned to be tortured by those entrusted to care for and about them. It must not be that children are told they are lying when they struggle to tell, and it must not be that a woman is told she is crazy when she too tries to be heard. It must be that each and every society, including our own in Canada, stands firm on the legal elimination of torture, regardless of who the torturers are. The non-State torture of women and girls is a crime against humanity.

CHAPTER 13
TO THE FUTURE: NST VOICES OF WOMEN AND GIRLS EVERYWHERE

When a person—a woman or girl—has survived NST victimization, she must be given the opportunity to tell her story. To do so, she needs the freedom and support to be heard, to be believed, to be understood, and she needs to speak the language of the NST victimization she has survived. Telling her NST story is generally the first action she may take; this is what Sara meant when she kept saying she needed to "get it out." Although Sara initially could not name what she was telling, she was doing so with her flipchart sheet writings. She was learning to be a woman unsilencing her years of NST human trafficking victimizations.

We intentionally use the terminology of NST victimization-traumatization informed care in order to be accurate, respectful, and acknowledge that the woman has suffered a victimizing crime. This naming validates her personhood; it respects her dignity. NST is a human rights crime that causes her to have traumatizing consequences. We refuse, and the women we support refuse, to accept being told or labelled with a mental illness disorder, hence our reason for revising the victim-blaming term PTSD to the more accurate term post-traumatic stress response (PTSR) to identify the responses to NST victimization.

From our perspective, NST is a form of violence against women and girls that is socially invisible. Consequently, women's victimization and traumatization responses are not recognized or understood. Girl children born into, or women married into a NST family system developed survival responses—they had to. They suffered repeated acts of human evil. They witnessed how the torturers, the very people society says were to care about them, took pleasure in attempting to destroy them. Women's negative thoughts about them-Selves did not arise from within, their perception of being an "it," a "nothing," or non-human were responses to the torturers' endless actions of human evil that can leave them struggling with the emotional feelings of worthlessness—so worthless that suicide feels like their only way out. To prevent such desperation, an intervention Sara and other women repeatedly call for are safe houses or a safe gathering space to be made available. These safe spaces should offer NST victimization-traumatization informed care and knowledgeable protection.

Women must work incredibly hard to exit or escape NST ordeals perpetrated against them. Not to be embraced by caring and social inclusion is deeply hurtful; NST is a reprehensible human rights violation and a crime against their humanity. They and we have spoken out in this book. This book is the unsilencing of women's voices. In this chapter we share models that helped us support women's recovery. We hope these will be successful in supporting others.

GLOBAL CATEGORIES OF NST

As our knowledge grew, we began to see the larger global reality of many forms of NST inflicted against women and girls. In our efforts to make women's and girls' NST victimizations visible, we valued the science of Capra's model-making, and developed a global model that identified three categories of NST victimizations perpetrated against women and girls.

Our model includes global subjective observations advancing as the world recognizes evolving forms of violence that amount to torture perpetrated against girls and women, such as child marriage.

Global Categories of NST Model

This model is illustrated in figure 45. The three categories in the model are named "classic" NST, commercial-based NST, and socio-cultural, traditional, or religious-based acts (Sarson & MacDonald, 2016b, 2018b).

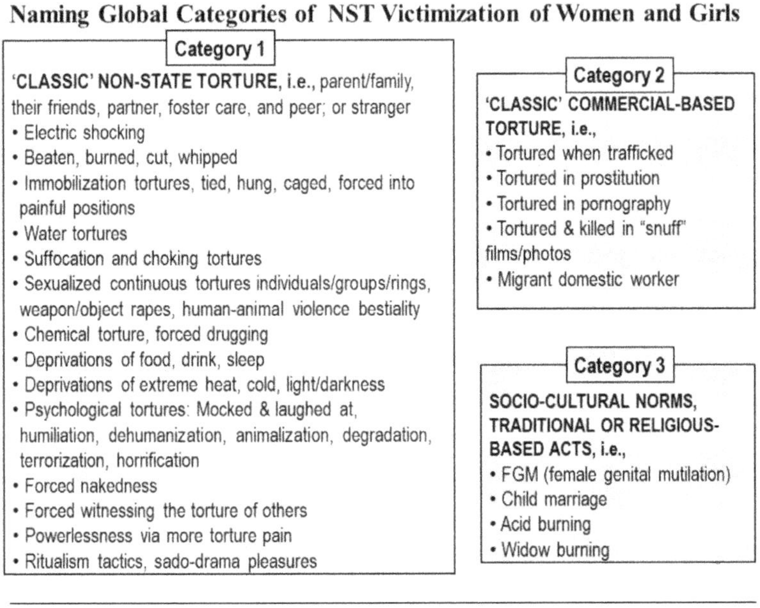

Naming Global Categories of NST Victimization of Women and Girls

Category 1

'CLASSIC' NON-STATE TORTURE, i.e., parent/family, their friends, partner, foster care, and peer; or stranger
• Electric shocking
• Beaten, burned, cut, whipped
• Immobilization tortures, tied, hung, caged, forced into painful positions
• Water tortures
• Suffocation and choking tortures
• Sexualized continuous tortures individuals/groups/rings, weapon/object rapes, human-animal violence bestiality
• Chemical torture, forced drugging
• Deprivations of food, drink, sleep
• Deprivations of extreme heat, cold, light/darkness
• Psychological tortures: Mocked & laughed at, humiliation, dehumanization, animalization, degradation, terrorization, horrification
• Forced nakedness
• Forced witnessing the torture of others
• Powerlessness via more torture pain
• Ritualism tactics, sado-drama pleasures

Category 2

'CLASSIC' COMMERCIAL-BASED TORTURE, i.e.,
• Tortured when trafficked
• Tortured in prostitution
• Tortured in pornography
• Tortured & killed in "snuff" films/photos
• Migrant domestic worker

Category 3

SOCIO-CULTURAL NORMS, TRADITIONAL OR RELIGIOUS-BASED ACTS, i.e.,
• FGM (female genital mutilation)
• Child marriage
• Acid burning
• Widow burning

Fig. 45: Global Categories of NST Model

Category 1

Non-State torture uses the word "classic," a term from State torture literature. State torturers, regardless of their country, inflict what is considered universal acts of torture. Classic acts of torture such as electric shock, water torture, sexualized torture, and deprivation tortures are the most well-known. However, Category 1 classic non-State torture includes the same acts of torture that State actors commit; thus, we use the word "classic." Category 1 clearly defines the many acts of NST that Sara and other women speaking in this book survived.

Category 2

We titled this commercial-based torture because there are torturers who are not NST family-based, although many are. We include in this category human traffickers, pimps, johns or buyers, and pornographers. They all participate in the supply and demand of the global, sexualized, exploitative, victimization of women and girls, for financial profit, or other Self-gratifying actions of human evil interests, including their pleasure of inflicting NST. Human traffickers may, and do, inflict acts of NST to maintain power and control over the women and girls they traffic (Human Trafficking National Coordination Centre, 2013), but they may also perpetrate NST for pleasure. Pornographers also inflict sexualized torture and killing in "snuff" video crime scene pornography.

Non-State torturers who fit into category 1 can also fit into category 2. Lynn, for instance, explained the pleasure her husband had when he tortured her. As shared earlier, she said he would say to her, "I enjoy seeing the terror in your eyes, bitch." But he also participated in the organized crime of supply and demand when trafficking, "selling," or "prostituting" Lynn.

Although we have not worked with women who were hired as domestic workers, who were then enslaved and tortured by their employers, their NST victimization has been documented (OSCE et al., 2013).

Category 3

Socio-cultural, traditional, or religious-based acts provide insights into forms of violence against women and girls that UN experts have designated as acts of torture. These are FGM (Méndez, 2011), acid burning, widow burning (Nowak, 2010, 2008), and child marriage (Méndez, 2016). These acts are inflicted by non-State as well as State actors. We have not worked with women in this category, but the voices of women and girls who suffer acts of torture must be heard and acknowledged as a human rights violation everywhere on this planet.

NST QUESTIONNAIRE

Categories of classic methods of torture are generally physical, psychological, and sexualized as listed in figure 46 (Shrestha & Sharma, 1995). Our questionnaire on harms inflicted in non-State torture

	QUESTIONNAIRE: Harms inflicted in NST			
1.	food/drink withheld ___	26.	raped with a weapon (gun or knife) or other objects ___
2.	chained or handcuffed to a stationary object ___	27.	raped with animals ___
3.	savagely and repeatedly beaten	28.	prevented from using toilet ___
4.	savagely and repeatedly kicked ___	29.	smeared with urine, feces, or blood ___
5.	hung by your limbs ___	30.	forced under cold or burning hot water ___
6.	burnt ___	31.	placed in a freezer ___
7.	cut ___	32.	near drowned when held under water in the tub, toilet, bucket, stream ___
8.	whipped ___	33.	drugged with alcohol ___
9.	soles of feel beaten (falanga) ___	34.	drugged with pills ___
10.	fingers, toes, and limbs twisted ___	35.	drugged with injections ___
11.	fingers, toes, and limbs broken ___	36.	drugged with mask ___
12.	fingers, toes, and limbs dislocated ___	37.	choked ___
13.	tied down naked for prolonged periods of time ___	38.	suffocated by object placed over one's face ___
14.	sat on making breathing difficult ___	39.	pornography pictures taken ___
15.	forced to lie naked on the floor/ground without bedding/warmth	40.	pornography or snuff films made/used ___
16.	confined to a dark enclosed space ___	41.	forced to harm others ___
17.	placed in a crate/box ___	42.	forced to watch others being harmed ___
18.	caged ___	43.	forced to watch pets being harmed or killed ___
19.	electric shocked ___	44.	forced to harm or kill pets or animals ___
20.	forcibly impregnated ___	45.	threatened to be killed ___
21.	forcedly aborted ___	46.	called derogatory names ___
22.	forced to eat one's vomitus (throw-up) ___	47.	put down ___
23.	forced to eat one's bowel movements ___	48.	treated as non-human ___
24.	raped by one person ___	49.	Comments
25.	raped by a family/group ___		

Fig. 46: Universal list of many acts of "classic" NST

victimization provides examples of these. Physical tortures, for example, include being savagely and repeatedly beaten, kicked, hung by one's limbs, burned, cut, whipped, electric shock, and more, as this figure shows. Psychological torture involves being treated as non-human. It includes deprivation tactics, such as withholding of food and drinks, being confined to a dark enclosed space, placed in a crate or box, and prevented from using toileting facilities, which leads to degradation and humiliation. Tactics inflicted under the category of sexualized torture include torture-rapes committed by one person or by a family and/or group, raped with a weapon and/or objects, by animals; forced impregnations and abortions; and pornographic victimizations. Although separation into categories helps to offer educational insights, all tactics in each category can and do occur at one time. When, for instance, a non-State torturer urinates on a woman or girl, rapes her with a gun while calling her "good for nothing," she suffers many forms of NST ordeals at once. This list provides examples of the brutal tactics of non-State torturers. Women who responded to the questionnaire added NST tactics they suffered that are not on this list.

One woman from the US wrote this statement following her completion of the questionnaire:

> I was not abused, I was tortured! Torture is <u>SO TOUGH</u>. I am recovering, but it is crucial to call it by its real name. I am even more encouraged to do so after filling out this survey. Thank you!

Sara described the NST she suffered when trafficked by her parents to a man with high-ranking political positional power. In her ordeal she, as other women have, illustrates the extensive combination of NST acts inflicted during one horrifying trafficking ordeal. She described that (Sarson & MacDonald, 2019c):

> At 14 made to go with "G," my dad's friend…He took me many times. He terrorized you in the car. He hits you on the side of the

head…almost knocks you right out the side door…He would get mad if you cried…choke you until you would almost pass out… punch you…say he would kill you. He would laugh a scary laugh, looks scary in his eyes.

On the boat he would get the shock things out [MO: Electric shock], throw you down…hit you, make all kinds of bruises with tools like whips, chains, knives, and guns [MO: Physical tortures]. He blind-folds you so you don't know what he's doing [MO: Psychological torture]. He sticks a broken bottle in your ribs and sucks the blood. He says "smile." He had a big black dog [MO: Sexualized torture of bestiality]. He gets food…does not give it to you, no water either [MO: Deprivation torture]. He puts you in a cage, throws you over-board…drags the cage in the water with the boat. He drowns you [MO: Water torture]. He pulls you up, throws you on the deck, rapes you…you were supposed to say you wanted more [MO: Sexualized torture of Sara as a child].

THE NON-STATE TORTURE (NST) WHEEL: A FACT SHEET

To further elaborate and share our knowledge gained since 1993, we developed "The Non-State Torture (NST) Wheel: A Fact Sheet" in col-laboration with the London Abused Women's Centre (LAWC), of London, Ontario (Sarson & MacDonald, 2018d, 2019d). The Centre provides services to women and girls from the age of 12 years onwards. To our, and their knowledge, LAWC is the only Centre in Canada acknowledg-ing and respecting the voices of women and girls to Self-report NST victimizations. Approximately 60 women a year report that they suffered NST victimization.

The NST wheel reflects our systematic observations of women's telling of their subjective experiences which Capra stated are elements for model-making that broaden the framework of scientific knowledge. Our wheel is an educational tool to assist women name and understand the violent NST actions committed against them, as illustrated in figure 47.

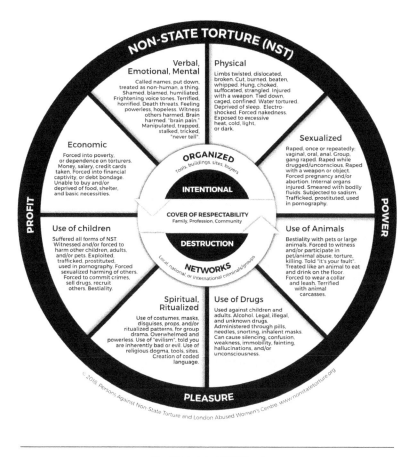

Fig. 47: Model of NST Wheel

The private individuals, families, and like-minded groups that commit acts of NST are listed and the model suggests how some families can be organized and can have connections to like-minded others.[10] Beginning with the outer ring, our learning model identifies the power

10 A wheel image framework was developed by Duluth to explain different forms of domestic abuse. https://www.theduluthmodel.org/wheels/

derived through exerting totalitarian control and pleasure, when inflicting acts of NST. If the non-State torturers are involved in human trafficking, specifically sexualized human trafficking, they can profit financially or in other ways. For example, Lynn's husband and his three friends, who held Lynn captive, tortured, trafficked, and prostituted her, gained safety and protection from the corrupt policemen who tortured Lynn. Women born into a NST family system that trafficked them as children said they were uncertain if their parent(s) gained financially.

The NST wheel is divided into eight major segments. Each segment is named with headings. Under each of the eight major sections, we list examples of the tactics non-State torturers inflict.

The inner center of the wheel identifies the intentional destruction inflicted by non-State torturers. Acts of torture are not accidental; they are always deliberate and purposeful, for the reasons of pleasure, totalitarian power and control, and for acquiring benefits or financial gain when profit-making applies. Non-State torturers blend in with mainstream society and are cloaked in respectability. They can have connections to networks of like-minded torturers who reside in their community, or have associations regionally, nationally, and internationally. If family-based torturers have connections with networks, they organize their torture group gatherings or "parties." They arrange transportation by land, water, or air; provide and administer their drugs of choice whether by mouth, injections, or inhalants. Torturers may satisfy their fantasies for drama by dressing in costumes and using tools such as whips, ropes, chains, needles, markers, knives, guns, and caustic substances. The list of their destructive tactics is endless. It depends on the degree of their brutality, their acts of human evil, and the locations. For instance, if there is water available then water torture happens; if electric shocking tools are present, electric shock is inflicted (Sarson & MacDonald, 2005). There are no limits. Every woman's

NST story is the worst crime committed against her humanity, her dignity, and her personhood.

Because of global patriarchal socialization, the herstorical truths about pandemic forms of violence inflicted against women and girls have existed and continue to exist on a continuum—from being disbelieved and ignored to being justified and supported. For instance, because Canada does not legally acknowledge NST as a crime of torture in its *Criminal Code,* it could be said that Canada intentionally ignores NST crimes. Thus, as a country, Canada fails to uphold the human rights equality of women and girls not to be subjected to the torture inflicted by non-State actors. Consequently, women who have suffered NST crimes are silenced, socially and legally.

For countries that are members of the UN, such as Canada, there are legally binding UN treaties that Canada has ratified. This means Canada has agreed and is legally bound to act according to the meaning of the treaty. However, there is no UN legally binding human rights treaty addressing the global pandemic of violence against women and girls. Therefore, women are also globally silenced, as they cannot legally hold Canada or any UN member country to account for failing to specifically confront NST crimes.

To remedy this global human rights and legal inequality, Rashida Manjoo, the previous UN Special Rapporteur and expert on violence against women, its causes and consequences, presented her 2014 report to the UN General Assembly. In it, she concluded that in order for women to gain access to legal human rights justice, the UN needed a universal legally binding instrument on violence against women (Manjoo & Jones,

2018). Rashida's identification of this gap at the UN level has become a global campaign.

The campaign is entitled "Every Woman Treaty" (Nwadinobi et al., n.d.). It focuses on developing a global legally binding treaty on violence against women and girls so they could have a place to seek justice when there are no other justice options available to them in their own country—when the crimes against their humanity are disregarded. On September 22, 2020, President Cyril Ramaphosa, president of the Republic of South Africa and African Union (AU) Chair, announced at the 75th UN General Assembly Debate that, "At a continental level, we are working to finalise and adopt, an AU [African Union] Convention on Violence against Women during the course of this year" (South African Government, 2020).

We have travelled to the UN Commission on the Status of Women (CSW) in New York City almost yearly since 2004. Each year we have spoken about NST victimizations; each year we see increased grassroots awareness. However, achieving global UN support for women and girls not to be subjected to torture by non-State actors has not yet become an acknowledged and routinely named human right violation inflicted against women and girls globally.

In *A Short History of the Commission on the Status of Women,* Carolyn Hannan and co-authors explain that on June 21, 1946, the Commission on the Status of Women became a reality (2019). The aim was to ensure and promote women's equality and human rights. Since 1946, women have struggled to realize this achievement. Our connection to this aim is that every year since 2004 when attending the CSW, we have worked towards achieving the feminization of NST, for it to be defined as a specific human right violation of women and girls, as stated in Article 5 of the *Universal Declaration of Human Rights.* Women who have survived NST have joined by presenting with us on panels. They have unsilenced their invisibility; they have unsilenced the human rights discrimination they endure.

This struggle—their—our struggle—is for non-State torture (NST) to be recognized and named as a form of violence against women and girls, given that the UN has a goal of working towards reaching the Sustainable Development Goal of the elimination of discrimination and all forms of violence against women and girls by 2030 (UN Women, n.d.). However, the truth is we as women and girls of all ages are still standing on the outside of the human rights window. We are still watching patriarchal misopedic and misogynistic attitudes and practices that maintain human inequality, subordination, and oppression of women and girls as "Other" even though we are of the same species as men and boys. This struggle for human equality, dignity, freedom, and human rights—the human right not to be subjected to non-State torture—will begin to end globally when the UN declares that the non-State torture of women and girls is a distinct human rights violation as declared in Article 5 of the *Universal Declaration of Human Rights*. Non-State torture is a part of the global pandemic of violence against women and girls and is a crime against humanity. We and the women in this book are unsilenced.

EPILOGUES

Fig. 48: Persistence

We have been persistent. We have welcomed every opportunity to speak with the press, as displayed in figure 48. We are unsilenced about non-State torture victimizations perpetrated against women and girls by private individuals or groups, such as family members, spouses, human traffickers, pimps, buyers, and pornographers. Today, radio hosts and journalists state that we are "Persons Against Non-State Torture," so casually that it seems the term has become increasingly familiar. We are persistently gaining social awareness!

LINDA'S CLOSING THOUGHTS

Not long after I started to witness Sara's story I realized she would not be the only baby girl born into a non-State torture family. From that moment on, I began thinking and caring about these babies. Twenty-eight years later, I shudder to think how many more wee ones have been born into such human cruelty. Many are young adult women now. I truly hope that *Women Unsilenced* will find its way into their hands and help clarify their lives of suffering, the human right violations and crimes they have endured, and offer some ways to heal.

And I care about the young women who become captive in marriage to non-State torturers, the clutches of torturing pimps and buyers in human trafficking and prostitution, and the horrors of torture by pornographers. Perhaps our book will enter into women's lives to give wing to their flight into freedom.

I dream of young students reading our book as part of their studies in universities. And perhaps frontline staff at women's centres and transition houses, as well as paramedics, nurses, doctors, dentists, police, teachers, counsellors, social workers, clergy, lawyers, judges, politicians, and others who will learn from our words and the words of women who have survived non-State torture. When professionals come in contact with little girls or women who are enduring or have survived non-State torture, I hope they will see them as persons responding to grave injustices in their lives and not as disordered or mentally ill women and girls.

I also hope *Women Unsilenced* helps the everyday person to think about these little girls growing up to be women and gives them information and understanding to view families differently—with a new knowing that some parents torture their children for pleasure, profit, and power. Such a reality is hard to accept but is crucial for humanity to move forward.

As a survivor of family violence my-Self, I know how brutal my life was as a little girl, and as a young person trying to make sense of my father's violent actions, my mother's selfish responses, and the trauma I was left to heal from (MacDonald, 2010). I refused to believe that I was mentally ill and I was never silent about the violence I witnessed and endured. Most around me were silent. I learned very intimately that talking about the violence in my life, my emotions, and my suffering was my lifeline. This is how I healed. And this is how Jeanne and I help women who have endured non-State torture to heal as well. Silence is a tool of the perpetrators to keep people isolated in their gruelling ordeals of getting by each day. I refuse to be silent.

This book is part of my caring commitment to never silence the atrocities of non-State torture that girls and women are enduring all over the world. I hope the words of Jeanne and I inspire girls and women to raise their voices and demand dignity and respect, knowing they are persons with human rights. And that the people around them will care and stand with them in pride, supporting their fight for their equality, justice, and freedom. Maybe in time the little baby girls born into such families who torture them will be recognized very early and will not have to spend years healing because the torture ordeals stopped when they were tiny. My ultimate dream is that we will evolve enough as humankind that we will prevent non-State torture altogether. I believe that day will come…maybe not in my lifetime, but it will come.

"How do you cope?" This is a question Jeanne and I are asked all the time, and so, it is most likely people will have the same question after reading our book.

A lifelong way of coping has always been talking, and once I started working with Jeanne on non-State torture, it became even more vital. I talked to Jeanne about my feelings of confusion, anxiety, fear, anger, rage, shock, hurt, caring, determination, pride...and much more. All these feelings arose as I grappled with the reality of non-State torture and my human rights work against this horrid crime. My main coping was and is that I am not alone on this journey—I share it with Jeanne.

People would constantly say, "You must distance your-Self. Do you?" I never distanced or disconnected my-Self from the reality of non-State torture. I picture my-Self standing right in the midst of the horrors with the women who have survived, telling others about the crimes and their suffering. I am a woman who survived relational violence and so are they. Thus, we are connected. I learned about the holocaust as a seven-year-old and explained to my-Self that I must expand my knowing about human

evil behaviour by non-State torturers who walk among us every day. I cope by loving my-Self, my family, and friends, and by valuing my beliefs in human rights, feminism, the power of caring, my Self-awareness work, activism, and networking. I also appreciate meeting other feminists. I stopped the unhealthy coping that kept slipping in, like a cigarette at night, or too much alcohol and sugar. I continue to keep laughing, cooking, eating delicious food, listening to music, admiring art, enjoying

Fig. 49: Linda's daisies

flowers, travelling, walking, watching movies and documentaries, finding the beauty in life, learning, challenging my-Self to try new things, staying positive, and finally by always having hope.

When I was seven years old, I felt totally bereft, consumed, and trapped in the loneliness of knowing I was surrounded by family violence and silence. No one was willing to talk to me or to help me escape my agonizing pain. I remember walking to a field of daisies and lying down on the grass, surrounded by the beauty of these everyday blossoms, shown in figure 49. I looked up to the sky for an answer. Suddenly, I saw an image of my-Self as a very old woman talking to many people in a large room. A sense of peace and hope came over me. This told me I would live and survive my ordeal. I thank Cathryn Young, who took this present-day photo of daisies. It is a fond reminder of my transformative day when hope became a conscious friend of mine.

Before I started work with Jeanne on non-State torture I understood that some women could be cruel. Little did I know how hurtful such a reality would become over these 28 years. There have been some caring women who have supported our work. But I must say the hurt inflicted by many women and women's organizations—other feminists, nursing groups, women lawyers, members of non-governmental organizations, and women politicians who tried to stop our work or who withdrew support—was an extremely painful process for me. Learning that women will be cruel and take great effort to hold back girls and women enduring non-State torture atrocities, indeed condemning them to remain silenced, was one of my greatest shocks. Oppression from one's own kind is brutal. I have developed a much tougher skin and resilience but not without gut-wrenching awareness work.

When Jeanne and I started the work, my three children, my son and two daughters were eleven, nine, and seven. I kept thinking of them growing up in a world where non-State torture was invisible and insisted to my-Self this was just not going to happen. Now I have two little grandgirls and am even more determined for them and all children. I keep a long view of evolution with an ever-present belief that as humans we will grapple with the reality of non-State torture and it will become a part of everyday conversation. It is my conviction that non-State torture is one of the worst crimes of humanity, as little children are intentionally tortured by those who are supposed to care about and for them. I live in hope of transformation.

JEANNE'S CLOSING THOUGHTS

Shortly after Linda and I began supporting Sara in 1993, etched in my mind is the moment I said to Linda, that we might die with this story. Obviously, what I thought back then has not deterred us from persistently breaking the silence about NST victimizations. Probably because growing up I was determined never to be shut up about relational violence.

Coming face-to-face with Sara, who was disclosing grievous atrocities, and knowing this had been her whole life, deeply disturbed me. That this is all she knew is a disturbing reality that has never left me. This was happening in Canada, and it seemed as if no one had cared or dared to care, or maybe were too frightened to care about her. This was discomforting. It still is. The depth of injustice was and remains disturbing. Over the years my sense of feeling disturbed has become a struggle against letting a stream of social anger run freely over the hurdles placed in the path of truth-telling. Many of these hurdles were enforced by women. I knew if I reacted I'd be seen as the crazy one; obviously, this was not a good idea.

Twenty-five years ago, Linda and I were labelled by a nursing peer as toxically over-involved in our supportive care of Sara. I am not sure what label she would apply today: maybe still over-involved or crazy for speaking up.

I was and remain haunted by the question of how it can be that NST is happening in our communities, within families, to babies, children, youth, and adults? It makes no justifiable sense to me. Sara and other women lived as babies, children, youths, and adults in relational-terrorism. They lived every day, including the extra day of a leap year, in fear and horror of being tortured, maybe killed. How can it be that our political climate is discriminatorily silencing NST by naming it assault? We must rescue the art of caring. And we must—we must—hear all the stories in this book, not as victim stories, but as women's unsilenced truth-telling herstories.

Sara never had a chance to survive in any other way except through survival adaptation into the NST family and co-culture into which she was born. I gained privilege by making it through my childhood without being silenced. It felt to me that I owed something back—and this was to give Sara a fair chance of survival and a fair chance of experiencing her-Self by discovering what life without torture-trafficking was like.

Did I know what the journey of supporting Sara would mean? Absolutely not! I innocently thought that a few years would see us all through the worst, but there was a never-ending worst. Worst and more worst. It changed the direction of my life. It changed my family life. It changed Sara's life. Could I do the same journey again? I think not. It was like maintaining Sara on never-ending life-support for years. To do this work undercover, at the same time as fighting off enemies, never free to scream out for help, made exposing our caring about Sara professionally dangerous, even a lethal threat. This book does not tell all. It does not tell of our battles of confronting oppression and corruption that intentionally aimed lethal threats at Linda and me. But now, our undercover caring is unsilenced, and of this, I am deeply proud.

Survive we all did. Survival brought its gifts of developing the ability to persist and support others. To have earned the trust of many women who survived, to share their voices, and together celebrate each taste of ever-increasing success—this is our gracious and cherished award. To whom we are born or adopted is but a roll of the dice. Any one of us could have been born into, adopted into, or married into a community of human evil relationship connections. I could have been Sara.

My world has expanded to a life I might never have imagined. I have travelled to places I never thought of going because Linda and I continue to be unsilenced. I do hope that for the women Linda and I have supported and continue to support, that our caring and our lives have touched them as deeply as they have touched ours.

On the frequently asked question of how I cope, I believe I developed a strong resilience at a very young age. This has sheltered me. I grew up learning not to get stuck in a problem. There are always solutions. I spent the first nine years of my life with a misogynistic, cruel, and violent father, then in the latter part of my childhood, when my mother left my father for good, I realized my mother could not cope with all the issues of working and raising my brother, Raymond, and me alone. With this realization came accepting I had to function on my own, whether I liked it or not. I learned acceptance. It was okay. Not that acceptance meant that I agreed with an event before me, but acceptance was acknowledging whatever was before me, just was. The next step was how to handle situations about which I disagreed that I could do something about.

My sense of acceptance and resilience began at age three. My father's mother came to look after me when my mother was in hospital delivering my brother. She locked me in a room. I am not sure for how long, but it still feels as if it was for a prolonged period. I experienced being surrounded by white light, and a knowing I had to look after my-Self if I was to survive. This sense of Self-responsibility—of what to do with the event before me—remains with me. I took the opportunity to express the injustice I felt towards my father's mother. When my mother arrived home from the hospital, I stood behind her left leg and called my father's mother "*a bitch*" (Sarson, 2010). Obviously, a word I picked up from my father's misogynistic ranting and knew how to use it to obtain my justice.

Not accepting injustices is a core principle for me. This has meant I usually was considered argumentative, and opinionated. A nursing director said to me many times that if I did not agree with some of the issues I found unjust, maybe I should leave nursing. That was never a solution for me. Resilience served me well. I did not take such negatives personally. I accepted that this was her issue, not mine. She saw me as a problem; I saw injustice—very different concepts.

When Sara entered my life, how did I cope? I had to accept that non-State torturers existed—this was the reality before me. It just was. There was no other option. Accepting there are those of our species who enjoy torturing was and remains a fact. Acceptance and resilience came naturally. I decided to tackle this horrendous injustice head-on. It was and still is not one-person work—this was work Linda and I had to share.

I am hoping *Women Unsilenced* will make the future easier for other women and girls who are tortured and trafficked, and easier for others to safely care about them. Writing is unsilencing for me too. Sharing through writing what Linda and I, and the women who connect with us, have learned from each other helps me cope—profoundly. I will not die with my story untold. By my writing, Linda and I continue to push for a law to hold non-State torturers criminally responsible for their acts of torture. Law that covers NST is essential for prevention. Based on this 28-year journey, these torturers appear not to stop until they drop—dead.

I also have everyday activities that bring quality to my life, and my family relationships. I am fortunate to live where I do. Gardening feels essential. I pick the berries I grow. I like transforming these into homemade juices and jams and sticking the berries into muffins I bake. I get to watch the tomatoes ripen on the plants I grow. I eat the beans and peas that manage to survive the little critters that also thrive in my backyard garden.

The beautiful blossoms of the zucchini plant are exciting to watch, as shown in figure 50. Opening big and bright during the day, then squeezing closed at night, to then transforming into green or yellow zucchini—is amazing. They contribute deliciously to the chocolate cake I negotiate with my-Self to make. The recipe calls for over two cups of grated zucchini. I

Fig. 50: Jeanne's zucchini blossom

justify eating a chocolate cake full of such a vegetable. How marvellous this is if chocolate is a craving! Every day I appreciate my wellness, and accept that I have an unhealthy habit which I am reluctant to totally give up—my drink of regular Coca-Cola that I do enjoy! It helps me cope with isolation, struggling alone into the wee night hours to write.

I have never resented being initiated into the reality of my and Linda's decision to deal with NST victimizations. It has changed my life. It has also changed the lives of other women—and this is priceless. To answer Sara's frequently asked question: Do I regret my decision to offer her support? My answer is *"No."* One day I dream the acronym of NST will be self-explanatory. NST must end.

I continue to be frustrated that abuses of power and otherization make it possible to shape the "we" by disconnecting from the "them." Why must there be a discriminatory "we" and "them"? Linda and I, and the women this book represents, are all at the same time the "we" and the "them."

Sometimes I write poems, long or short, to cope and to express my-Self. One day out of frustration, I wrote this little poem entitled "In connection." I believe we must all consider being the "we" and the "them."

In connection

I am always in connection

for

I am

"the we"

and,

I as "the we"

am—"the them."

I as "the we"

and

"the them"

am

the community

so

I am always in connection.

... Jeanne'97

REFERENCES

Amnesty International. (2000). *Respect, protect, fulfil women's human rights State responsibility for abuses by 'non-state actors'*. https://www.amnesty.org/download/Documents/140000/ior500012000en.pdf

Amnesty International. (2001). *Children's booklet: Stop torture*. https://www.amnesty.org/en/documents/ACT76/001/2001/en/

Associated Press. (2006). Nurse who killed 29 sentenced to 11 life terms. http://www.nbcnews.com/id/11636992/ns/us_news-crime_and_courts/t/nurse-who-killed-sentenced-life-terms/#.X3ZIz2hKiM8

Banks, A., & Jordan, J. (2007). The human brain: Hardwired for connections. *Research & Action Report, 28*(2), 8-11. https://www.wcwonline.org/Research-Action-Report-Spring/Summer-2007/the-human-brain-hardwired-for-connections594

Begley, S. (2007, January 19). The brain: How the brain rewires itself. *Time*, pp.1–5. http://content.time.com/time/magazine/article/0,9171,1580438-1,00.html

Benner, P. (1984). *From novice to expert excellence and power in clinical nursing practice*. Addison-Wesley.

Beynon, J. (2012). "Not waving, drowning". Asphyxia and torture: The myth of simulated drowning and other forms of torture. *Journal on Rehabilitation of Torture Victims and Prevention of Torture, 22* (Supplementum 1), 25–9.

Bobak, I. M., Jensen, M. D., & Zalar, M. K. (1989). *Maternity and gynecologic care: The nurse and the family.* The C.V. Mosby.

Bonnet, L., Comte, A., Tatu, L., Millot, J-L., Moulin, T., & Medeiros de Bustos, E. (2015). The role of the amygdala in the perception of positive emotions: An "intensity detector." *Frontiers in Behavioral Neuroscience, 9* (article 178). https://doi.org/10.3389/fnbeh.2015.00178

Boudet, A. M. M., Petesch, P., Turk, C., & Thumala, A. (2012). *On norms and agency Conversations about gender equality with women and men in 20 countries.* The World Bank. https://openknowledge.worldbank.org/bit-stream/handle/10986/13818/768180PUB0EPI00IC00PUB0DATE04012013.pdf?sequence=1&isAllowed=y

Bunch, C. (2018). Feminism and human rights the legacy of Vienna. *Canadian Woman Studies les cahiers de la femme, 33*(1–2), 21–25. https://cws.journals.yorku.ca/index.php/cws/article/view/37753/34301

Bunch, C., & Reilly, N. (1999). *Demanding accountability the global campaign and Vienna tribunal for women's human rights.* Center for Women's Global Leadership Rutgers University and United Nations.

Bunzeluk, K. (2009). *Child sexual abuse images: Summary report. An analysis of websites by cybertip.ca.* Canadian Centre for Child Protection. https://www.cybertip.ca/pdfs/CTIP_ChildSexualAbuse_Summary_en.pdf

Burke, J., Gentleman, A., & Willan, P. (2000, October 1). British link to 'snuff' videos. *The Observer.* https://www.theguardian.com/uk/2000/oct/01/amelia-gentleman.philipwillan

Canadian Femicide Observatory for Justice and Accountability. (n.d.). *Types of femicide.* https://www.femicideincanada.ca/about/types

Capra, F. (1988). *The turning point Science, society and the rising culture.* Bantam Books.

Chelf, J. H., Deshler, A. M., Hillman, S., & Durazo-Arvizu, R. (2000). Storytelling A strategy for living and coping with cancer. *Cancer Nursing, 23*(1), 1–5. DOI: 10.1097/00002820-200002000-00001

Coomaraswamy, R. (1996, February 5). *Report of the special rapporteur on violence against women, its causes and consequences, submitted in accordance with Commission on Human Rights resolution 1995/85* (E/CN.4/1996/53). UN. http://hrlibrary.umn.edu/commission/thematic52/53-wom.htm

Copelon, R. (2000). Gender crimes as war crimes: Integrating crimes against women into international criminal law. *McGill Law Journal, 46*, 217–240.

Cribb, R. (2015, April 26). Underground child porn trade moving toward youngest victims. *The Star.* https://www.thestar.com/news/world/2015/04/26/underground-child-porn-trade-moving-toward-youngest-victims.html

Dale, L. (n.d.). *Children of the wind Les enfants du vent. An international exhibit of children's art about their lives.* A Canadian International Development Agency (CIDA) project.

Denny, N. (2012, June 3). Zero degrees of empathy by Simon Baron-Cohen – Review. *The Observer.* https://www.theguardian.com/books/2012/jun/03/zero-degrees-empathy-baron-cohen

Department of Economic and Social Affairs. (2016). *Leaving no one behind: The imperative of inclusive development Report on the world social situation 2016.* UN. https://www.un.org/esa/socdev/rwss/2016/full-report.pdf

Draft, R., L. (1995). *Organization theory & design* (5th ed.). West Publishing.

Eisenberger, N. I., Lieberman, M. D. & Williams, K. D. (2003). Does rejection hurt? An fMRI study of social exclusion. *Science, 302*, 290–292.

Firsten, T. (1991). Violence in the lives of women on psych wards. *Canadian Woman Studies les cahiers de la femme, 11*(4), 45–48. https://cws.journals.yorku.ca/index.php/cws/article/view/10655/9744

Fohring, S. (2018). What's in a word? Victims on 'victim'. *International Review of Victimology, 24*(2), 151-164. https://doi.org/10.1177/0269758018755154

Frieire, P. (1993). *Pedagogy of the oppressed,* rev. (M. Bergman Ramos, Trans.). Continuum.

Gaer, F. D. (2012). Rape as a form of torture: The experience of the committee against torture. *Cuny Law Review, 15*, 293–308.

Gintis, H., & Bowles, S. (1981). Contradiction and reproduction in education theory. In L. Barton, R. Meighan, & S. Walker (Eds.), *Schooling, ideology and the curriculum* (pp. 45–49). Falmer Press.

Government of Canada. (2012). *National action plan to combat human trafficking.* https://www.publicsafety.gc.ca/cnt/rsrcs/pblctns/ntnl-ctn-pln-cmbt/ntnl-ctn-pln-cmbt-eng.pdf

Government of Canada. (2020, October 19). *Torture.* https://laws-lois.justice.gc.ca/eng/acts/C-46/section-269.1.html#:~:text=269.1%20(1)%20Every%20official%2C,term%20not%20exceeding%20fourteen%20years

Grant, M. (2019, February 1). Doctor who raped daughter hundreds of times sentenced to 8 years in prison. *CBC News.* https://www.cbc.ca/news/canada/calgary/doctor-rape-daughter-calgary-guilty-sentencing-1.5002998?fbclid=IwAR2z5AFDrc7yYXS5_YFEwtK2OfoZfyy0eN7KhrAtZGZQfG8f0FthhomyFo4

Grossman, D. (1996). *On killing the psychological cost of learning to kill in war and society.* Little, Brown.

Hachey, J. M. (1998). *The Canadian guide to working and living overseas* (3rd ed., pp. 31–36, 125). Intercultural Systems.

Hanle, D. J. (1989). *Terrorism T.H.E. newest face of warfare* (p. 104). Pergamon-Brassey's.

Hannan, C., Iiyambo, A., & Brautigam, C. (2019). *A short history of the Commission on the Status of Women.* UN Women. https://www.unwomen.org/-/media/headquarters/attachments/sections/library/publications/2019/a-short-history-of-the-csw-en.pdf?la=en&vs=1153

Hazelton, D. M. (1991). Storytelling as a therapeutic tool. *Focus*, 36–37.

Herman, J. L. (1992). *Trauma and recovery. The aftermath of violence—From domestic abuse to political terror.* Basic Books.

Human Rights Watch. (2005). *Smallest witnesses: The crisis in Darfur through children's eyes.* https://www.hrw.org/legacy/features/darfur/smallwitnesses/img/pdf/Smallest%20Witnesses%202007.pdf

Human Trafficking National Coordination Centre. (2013). *Domestic human trafficking for sexual exploitation in Canada.* Royal Canadian Mounted Police. http://www.cathii.org/sites/www.cathii.org/files/Project-SAFEKEEPING-EN-Unclassified-FINAL.pdf

Jones, G. M. M. (1995). Validation therapy: A companion to reality orientation. *Canadian Nurse,* 20–23.

Jones, J., Sarson, J., & MacDonald, L. (2018). How non-state torture is gendered and invisibilized: Canada's non-compliance with the committee against torture' recommendations. In Center for Human Rights & Humanitarian Law Anti-Torture Initiative (Ed.), *Gender Perspectives on Torture: Law and Practice* (pp. 33–56). https://www.wcl.american.edu/impact/initiatives-programs/center/documents/gender-perspectives-on-torture/

Lane, A., & Holodak, R.G. (2016). Brief to: The House of Commons Standing Committee on Justice and Human Rights in view of its study of bill c-242 an act to amend the Criminal Code (inflicting torture). https://www.ourcommons.ca/Content/Committee/421/JUST/Brief/BR8406577/br-external/LaneAlexandra-e.pdf

Larsen, M. M. W., Appel, A. M., Aon, M., Modvig, J., Brasholt, M., Van Den Bergh, B., Cakal, E., & Catovic, A. (2018). *Falanga.* Danish Institute against Torture. https://www.dignity.dk/en/dignitys-work/health-team/torture-methods/falanga/

Leach, M., & Fried, J. (1984). *Funk & Wagnalls standard dictionary of folklore, mythology, and legend.* Harper & Row Publishers.

Lepard, D. (2010). *Missing women investigation review. Vancouver police Department.* BC. https://www.bwss.org/wp-content/uploads/2010/08/36185748-VPD-Missing-Women-Report.pdf

Leyton, E. (1986). *Hunting humans: The rise of the modern multiple murderer.* McClelland & Stewart.

MacDonald, L. (2010). My feminist walk. In M. Andersen (Ed.), *Feminist journeys Voies feminists* (pp. 228–231). Feminist History Society. https://feministhistories.ca/books/feminist-journeys/.

Manjoo, R. (2014, September 1). *Violence against women, its causes and conse-quences Note by the Secretary-General* (A/69/368). United Nations General Assembly. https://www.refworld.org/pdfid/543673ae4.pdf

Manjoo, R., & Jones, J. (Eds.). (2018). *The legal protection of women from violence Normative gaps in international law.* Routledge Taylor & Francis Group.

Mantooth, M. D. (2012). *Reconstructing disrupted lives: The Canadian exhibition of children's art from refugee camps.* The University of British Columbia. https://open.library.ubc.ca/cIRcle/collections/ubctheses/24/items/1.0105180

McCurdy, D. B. (1990). Respecting autonomy by respecting persons: Taking the patient's story seriously. *Human Medicine, 6*(2), 107–112.

Méndez, J. E. (2011). *Female genital mutilation: Progress-realities-challenges.* [Statement presented] Side Event sponsored by Women's UN Report Network, Worldwide Organization for Women and NGO Committee on the Status of Women-Geneva 1 June 2011. http://preventgbvafrica.org/wp-content/uploads/2013/10/SR_Torture_Statement_for_FGM.pdf

Méndez, J. E. (2016). *Report of the special rapporteur on torture and other cruel, inhuman or degrading treatment or punishment.* [A/HRC/31/57]. UN General Assembly. http://www.reproductiverights.org/sites/crr.civicactions.net/files/documents/SR%20on%20Torture%20Report.pdf

Méndez, J. E. (2018). *Introduction.* In Center for Human Rights & Humanitarian Law Anti-Torture Initiative (Ed.), *Gender perspective on torture: Law and practice* (pp. xi-xiv). https://www.wcl.american.edu/impact/initiatives-programs/center/documents/gender-perspectives-on-torture/

Narrow, B. W. (1979). *Patient teaching in nursing practice A patient and family-centered approach.* John Wiley & Sons.

Nowak, M. (2008). *Report of the Special Rapporteur on torture and other cruel, inhuman or degrading treatment or punishment* [A/HRC/7/3]. UN General Assembly. https://undocs.org/A/HRC/7/3

Nowak, M. (2010). *"Strengthening the protection of women from torture and ill-treatment"* [Statement presented] Side event, "Acid burning attacks – Victimization, survivors, support." Sponsored by Women's UN Report Network, Worldwide Organization for Women, and NGO Committee on the Status of Women, Geneva 15 September 2010, Geneva. https://womenen-abled.org/pdfs/Nowak-torture-2010.pdf

Nwadinobi, E. A., Juaristi, F. R., Pisklákova-Parker, M., Aldosari, H., Khana, M., & Aeberhard-Hodges, J. (n.d.). *Safer sooner report.* Every Woman Treaty. https://mk0everywomanbbue31y.kinstacdn.com/wp-content/uploads/2020/03/Safer-Sooner-Final.pdf

Ochberg, F. M. (1997). Introduction: Twenty years after defining PTSD. *Mind & Human Interaction, 8*(4), 201–203.

OSCE Office of the Special Representative and Co-ordinator for Combating Trafficking in Human Beings in partnership with the Ludwig Boltzmann Institute of Human Rights and the Helen Bamber Foundation. (2013). *Trafficking in human beings amounting to torture and other forms of ill-treatment.* https://www.osce.org/files/f/documents/d/b/103085.pdf

Parker, B. (2002, March 29). Cambridge arts council funds art show Nepal exhibit focuses in sex trade. *Cambridge TAB*, p. 4.

Paterson, B. (2003). The nature of evidence. *Canadian Nurse, 99*(3), 16–17.

Penfold, P. S. (1998). *Sexual abuse by health professionals a personal search for meaning and healing.* University of Toronto Press.

Persons Against Non-State Torture. (n.d.a). *Questionnaire 1 abuse/assault vs. non-state* torture. https://www.nonstatetorture.org/research/participate/questionnaire-1

Persons Against Non-State Torture. (n.d.b). *Questionnaire 5 sexualized harms inflicted by "others."* https://www.nonstatetorture.org/research/participate/questionnaire-5

Persons Against Non-State Torture. (n.d.c). *Questionnaire 6 discrimination and stigmatization.* https://www.nonstatetorture.org/research/participate/questionnaire-6

Persons Against Non-State Torture. (n.d.d). *Questionnaire 7 suicidal-femicide criminal* victimization. https://www.nonstatetorture.org/research/participate/questionnaire-7

Persons Against Non-State Torture. (2015*). Non-state torture & violence against women & girls.* https://www.nonstatetorture.org/~nonstate/application/files/5516/0348/1217/CSWFLYERNAWO.pdf

Pietilä, H. (2002). *Engendering the global agenda: The story of women and the United Nations.* UN Non-Governmental Liaison Service (NGLS).

Rashid, F., Edmondson, A. C., & Leonard, H. B. (2013). Leadership lessons from the Chilean mine rescue. *Harvard Business Review.* https://hbr.org/2013/07/leadership-lessons-from-the-chilean-mine-rescue

Registered Nurses' Association of Nova Scotia. (1995). *Multicultural health education for nurses: A community perspective.* Retrieved 1995.

Richards, D., & Haglund, J. (2018). Exploring the consequences of the normative gap in legal protections addressing violence against women. In R. Manjoo & J. Jones (Eds.), *The legal protection of women from violence Normative gaps in international law* (pp. 40-72). Routledge.

Roussy, K. (2016, November 20). Indigenous children, stoic about their pain, are drawn out with art. *CBC News.* https://www.cbc.ca/news/health/aboriginal-youth-art-pain-hurt-healing-1.3852646

Salem, R. A. (Ed.). (2000). *Witness to genocide The children of Rwanda drawings by child survivors of the Rwandan genocide of 1994.* Friendship Press.

Sarson, J. (2010). 76 | Misogyny seeping from his pores. In M. Andersen (Ed.), *Feminist journeys Voies feminists* (pp. 297-299). Feminist History Society. https://feministhistories.ca/books/feminist-journeys/

Sarson, J., & MacDonald, L. (2005). Ritual abuse/torture. *Gazette, 67*(1), 32–33.

Sarson, J., & MacDonald, L. (2008). Ritual abuse-torture within families/groups. *Journal of Aggression, Maltreatment & Trauma, 16*(4), 419–438.

Sarson, J., & MacDonald, L. (2009a). Defining torture by non-state actors in the Canadian private sphere. *First Light*, 29-33. http://ccvt.org/assets/ccvt-first-light-2009.pdf

Sarson, J., & MacDonald, L. (2009b). Torturing by non-state actors invisibilized, a patriarchal divide and spillover violence from the military sphere into the domestic sphere. *Peace Studies Journal (PSJ), 2*(2), 16–38. http://citeseerx.ist.psu.edu/viewdoc/download?doi=10.1.1.553.2583&rep=rep1&type=pdf

Sarson, J., & MacDonald, L. (2011, September 8). *Sexualized torture in the domestic/private sphere and 'body talk': A human rights and relational feminist paradigm* [Paper presentation]. Sexual Violence Conference, Middlesex University, London, UK. https://www.mdx.ac.uk/__data/assets/pdf_file/0022/49504/Jeanne-Sarson-and-Linda-MacDonald.pdf

Sarson, J., & MacDonald, L. (2012). Torture victimization—Child to adult: Flashbacks and connection with first responders, part II. *Sexual Assault Report*, 15(6), 83, 84, 86, 94.

Sarson, J., & MacDonald, L. (2014). Torture victimization—Child to adult: Flashbacks and connection with first responders. *Family & Intimate Partner Violence Quarterly, 6*(3):47–56.

Sarson, J., & MacDonald, L. (2016a). *Truth-telling best practices for engaging men and boys in addressing and preventing violence against young women and girls.* [Paper presented]. House of Commons, Canada. https://www.ourcommons.ca/Content/Committee/421/FEWO/Brief/BR8391525/br-external/PersonsAgainstNon-StateTorture-e.pdf

Sarson, J., & MacDonald, L. (2016b). Seeking equality—Justice and women's and girls' human right not to be subjected to non-state torture. In J. A. Scutt. (Ed.), *Women, law and culture Conformity, contradiction and conflict* (pp. 263-281). Springer. https://link.springer.com/chapter/10.1007/978-3-319-44938-8_15

Sarson, J., & MacDonald, L. (2018a). Having non-state torture recognized by the UN and member states as an infringement of woman's human rights is imperative. *Canadian Woman Studies/Les Cahiers de la Femme, 33*(1. 2):143–155. https://cws.journals.yorku.ca/index.php/cws/article/view/37766/34313

Sarson, J., & MacDonald, L. (2018b). No longer invisible: Families that torture, traffic, and exploit their girl child. *Oñati Socio-legal Series, 8*(1), 85–105. http://opo.iisj.net/index.php/osls/article/viewFile/908/1078

Sarson, J., & MacDonald, L. (2018c). Suicidal-femicide conditioning: A tactic of family-based non-state torturers and traffickers of a daughter. *Femicide Volume X Contemporary Forms of Enslavement of Women & Girls*, 85-87. https://acuns.org/wp-content/uploads/2018/10/Femicide-Volume-X.pdf

Sarson, J., & MacDonald, L. (2018d). The Non-state Torture (NST) Wheel: A fact sheet. https://www.nonstatetorture.org/application/files/7415/3694/3648/NSTwheelFACTSHEETkeepv2.pdf

Sarson, J., & MacDonald, L. (2019a). *We make no apologies for explaining non-state torture (NST) inflicted in sexualized exploitation, in prostitution & in pornography.* Fondation Scelles. https://www.fondationscelles.org/en/news/274-we-make-no-apologies-for-explaining-non-state-torture-nst-inflicted-in-sexualized-exploitation-in-prostitution-in-pornography

Sarson, J., & MacDonald, L. (2019b). Herstorical forerunners to present day cyber crimes: Non-state torturers, traffickers, pornographers, and buyers. *Femicide Volume XI Cyber Crimes Against Women & Girls*, 18-23. http://femicide-watch.org/sites/default/files/FemicideVolXI.pdf

Sarson, J., & MacDonald, L. (2019c). Non-state torture human trafficking family systems: Coming out alive—normalizing women's survival responses. *Justice Report, 34*(3), 11–15.

Sarson, J., & MacDonald, L. (2019d). "A difficult client": Lynn's story of captivity, non-state torture, and human trafficking by her husband. *International Journal of Advanced Nursing Education and Research*, 4(3), 107-124. https://gvpress.com/journals/IJANER/vol4_no3/13.pdf

Sarson, J., & MacDonald, L. (2020a). Pandemics: Misogynistic violence against women and girls and COVID-19. *The Nova Scotia Advocate*. https://nsadvocate.org/2020/05/08/pandemics-misogynistic-violence-against-women-and-girls-and-covid-19/

Sarson, J., & MacDonald, L. (2020b). Actions of human evil – On the Nova Scotia mass shooter and others like him. *The Nova Scotia Advocate*. https://nsadvocate.org/2020/06/18/actions-of-human-evil-on-the-nova-scotia-mass-shooter-and-others-like-him/

Sarson, J., & MacDonald, L. (2020c). Developing a normative standard: Acknowledging non-state torturers' act inflict femicidal risks. *Femicide Volume XIII Data collection*, 95–102. https://www.unsavienna.org/sites/default/files/2020-11/20201124-Femicide%20XIII_0.pdf

Sarson, J., Gordon, E., & MacDonald, L. (2019). Family-based non-state torturers who traffic their daughters: Praxis principles and healing epiphanies. In J. Winterdyk & J. Jones, (Eds.), *The Palgrave International Handbook of Human Trafficking* (Vol. 1, pp. 839–864). Palgrave MacMillan.

Schmemann, S. (2000, April 23). To Vietnam and back. And back. And back. *The New York Times*, section 4, p. 1.

Shatan, C. (1997). Living in a split time zone: Trauma and therapy of Vietnam combat survivors. *Mind & Human Interaction, 8*(4), 204–222.

Shrestha, N. M., & Sharma, B. (1995). *Torture and torture victims a manual for medical professionals*. Centre for Victims of Torture, Nepal (CVICT) in collaboration with Nepal Medical Association and RCT/IRCT, Denmark.

Smith, C. P., & Freyd, J. J. (2014). Institutional betrayal. *American Psychologist, 69*(6), 575–587. https://doi.org/10.1037/a0037564

South African Government. (2020, September 22). *President Cyril Ramaphosa: 75th United Nations General Assembly debate.* https://www.gov.za/speeches/president-cyril-ramaphosa-75th-united-nations-general-assembly-debate-22-sep-2020-0000

Staub, E. (1993). *The roots of evil: The origins of genocide and other group violence.* Cambridge University Press.

Stöckl, H., Dekel, B., Morris-Gehring, A., Watts, C., & Abrahams, N. (2017). Child homicide perpetrators worldwide: a systematic review. *BMJ Paediatrics Open, 1*(1). https://bmjpaedsopen.bmj.com/content/bmjpo/1/1/e000112.full.pdf

Tappen, R. M. (1983). *Nursing leadership: Concepts and practice.* F.S. Davis Company.

Tavares, P., & Wodon, Q. (2018). *Ending violence against women and girls Global and regional trends in women's legal protection against domestic violence and sexual harassment.* Children's Investment Fund Foundation, Global Partnership for Education, & The World Bank. http://pubdocs.worldbank.org/en/679221517425064052/EndingViolenceAgainstWomenandGirls-GBVLaws-Feb2018.pdf

The Chronicle Herald. (2004). Authorities seize child porn, bestiality DVDs. p. A7.

Tomlinson, S. (2002, April 28). Postcards of their horror. *Boston Sunday Globe,* p. 12.

UN Commission on the Status of Women. (2007). Agreed conclusions on the elimination of all forms of discrimination and violence against the girl child. https://www.un.org/womenwatch/daw/csw/Agreedconclusions/Agreed%20conclusions%2051st%20session.pdf

UN Committee against Torture. (2008, January 24). *General comment no. 2: Implementation of article 2 by states Parties* (CAT/C/GC/2). http://docstore.ohchr.org/SelfServices/FilesHandler.ashx?enc=6QkG1d%2FPPRiCAqhKb7yhskvE%2BTuw1mw%2FKU18dCyrYrZhDDP8yaSRi%2Fv43pYTgmQ5n7dAGFdDalfzYTJnWNYOXxeLRAIVgbwcSm2ZXH%2BcD%2B%2F6IT0pc7BkgqlATQUZPVhi

UN General Assembly. (1993, December 20). *Declaration on the elimination of violence against women* (A/RES/48/104). https://www.un.org/en/genocideprevention/documents/atrocity-crimes/Doc.21_declaration%20elimination%20vaw.pdf

UNICEF. (2012, May 26). *'After the big wave': Exhibition of children's art and photos from the Maldives shows the impact of the tsunami.* https://www.unicef.org/infobycountry/index_25613.html

Universal Declaration of Human Rights (UDHR). (1948). (resolution 217 A), adopted 10 December 1948.

UN Women. (n.d.). *Sustainable development goals goal 5: Achieve gender equality and empower all women and girls.* https://www.un.org/sustainabledevelopment/gender-equality/

UN Women. (2018). *Turning promises into action: Gender equality in the 2030 agenda for sustainable development.* https://www.unwomen.org/-/media/headquarters/attachments/sections/library/publications/2018/sdg-report-chapter-3-why-gender-equality-matters-across-all-sdgs-2018-en.pdf?la=en&vs=5447

UN Women, IDLO, The World Bank, & Task Force on Justice. (2019). *Justice for women high-level group report Executive summary and key messages.* https://www.unwomen.org/-/media/headquarters/attachments/sections/library/publications/2020/justice-for-women-high-level-group-report-en.pdf?la=en&vs=4044

Vorbrüggen, M., & Baer, H. U. (2007). Humiliation: The lasting effect of torture. *Military Medicine, 172,* S29–S33. http://dx.doi.org/10.7205/MILMED.173.Supplement_2.29

Weinberg, C. A. (1997). Torture: victims, perpetrators, sequelae, and treatment. *Mind & Human Interaction, 8*(4), 232–244.

Welner, M., O'Malley, K. Y., Gonidakis, J., Saxena, A., & Stewart-Willis, J. (2018). The depravity standard III: Validating an evidence-based guide. *Journal of Criminal Justice, 55,* 12–24. https://doi.org/10.1016/j.jcrimjus.2017.12.010

WHO. (2017, November 29). *Violence against women.* https://www.who.int/news-room/fact-sheets/detail/violence-against-women

Wilson, D., & Ratekin, C. (1990). An introduction to using children's drawings as an assessment tool. *Nurse Practitioner, 23–35.*

Wood, B. (1995). *Childhood stolen: Grave human rights violations against children.* Amnesty International.

GLOSSARY

Brain-pain: When the women we support are working to heal their mental harms and are transforming their beliefs and attitudes, they frequently tell us that they are experiencing "brain-pain" which is different than having a headache. They physically feel that their brain is changing.

Co-culture: The families and individuals in this book that we identify as torturer-traffickers are people who live, work, play, and volunteer in their communities. They are highly skilled at hiding that their interest and pleasure is committing acts of torture, especially sexualized torture, and that they frequently have connections to like-minded others. Because they exist so easily among us, we had to learn how they functioned so we named our understanding as learning about their criminal co-culture.

Depressiveness: Based on our experience, is an emotional response women express as an emotional outcome of suffering NST victimizations. For us the meaning of this term is to differentiate between naming that a woman is 'depressed' versus acknowledging depressiveness is her emotional response to being victimized. As she heals her depressiveness can also heal.

Evilism: We use this term because women told us they had fears that they could only describe as being evilism-based, because they perceived that the men and women who tortured them committed acts of human evil.

Femicide: Is a term used to describe the killing of women and girls by countless forms of violence inflicted against them, most often by men within their most intimate of relationships.

Herstorical: We use this term to separate women's and girl's herstorical reality from the history of men and boys.

Hopelessness: Is the term we use to respectfully identify a woman's emotional response as a consequence of the torturers infliction of NST victimizations she survived, compounded by a belief she may never escape. We observe how she regains hope as her healing progresses.

Modus operandi: Is a Latin phrase which is often shortened to MO. We have used MO repeatedly to explain the torturer-traffickers' criminal and violent torture tactics.

Necrophilic: This refers to a morbid sexualized attraction to a dead body. When we refer to pseudo-necrophilic we mean that women as children are poly-drugged into a state of being unable to move their bodies. Lifeless they appear dead to the torturers who achieve sexualized pleasure by torture-raping them.

Non-State actors: This phrase was developed by Amnesty International as a way to identify private individuals, families, groups, or corporations—actors—who commit human rights violations. This differentiates them from individuals or departments who commit human rights violations as representatives—as State actors—of a country commonly referred to as a State.

Non-State torture: We shortened the term non-State actors and applied it to the torturers' actions by saying they commit non-State torture. We also created the acronym NST. Because the acts of non-State torture are the same or similar to the torture inflicted by representatives of a State, such as police or military, sometimes we use the term "classic" non-State torture which is the term often used to define acts of State torture.

Post-traumatic stress response: We developed this term to promote the understanding that when a girl or woman is subjected to non-State torture, to survive she develops survival responses; her responses need to be recognized as such. We shorten this phrase using the acronym PTSR.

Relational: We use this word to show that a relationship connection exists and needs to be understood.

Re-remembering: We created this term to honour that women will re-remember the torture ordeals they survived if they are cared about and it is safe for them to let them-Self re-remember. Safe meaning not only physical safety but also mental safety, that they have informed support that will understand how their memories will surface.

Ritual abuse-torture: This is the first term we used and created a model for as it represents how the first woman described her victimizations. We eventually realized that it was one form of non-State torture. We also use the acronym RAT.

State torture: This phrase refers to acts of torture committed by those who are employed and who are representatives of their country. Examples include embassy staff, and police or military officials. The acts or patterns of torture committed by State torturers are sometimes referred to as "classic" acts of torture.

Suicidal-femicide: We created this term to explain that non-State torturers can and do try to condition their daughters that they torture to never tell what was being done to them. But if the girls did try to tell, the torturers forced them to believe that they must act to die by suicide. This ensured that the non-State torturers would never be suspected of having caused the girl's or woman's death. The non-State torturers would escape being charged with femicide.

Torturer-traffickers: We linked these two terms because our evidence is that most often family-based torturers have connections with other like-minded individuals or groups to whom they traffic their daughters. We realized this reality needed to be exposed using this term.

INDEX

D

death(s), 5-6, 41, 55, 77, 83, 87, 120, 144,
153-154, 183, 203, 231, 269-272, 274

decision(s), 17, 19, 21, 23, 35, 64, 77, 123,
129, 135, 174, 176, 182-183, 196, 221,
228, 251, 267, 282

deconstructing, 95, 108, 131

degradation(s), 81-82, 113, 147, 289

depravity standard, 123-124, 127, 138,
146-147, 153

depressiveness, 233-234, 258-259

deprivation(s), 81, 145, 282, 286, 289-290

dignity, 9, 119, 207, 278, 284, 293, 295

discrimination, 11, 58, 72, 189, 207-208,
214-217, 223, 227, 295

dissociative, 21, 29, 44, 60-61, 69, 85, 111,
117, 136, 141, 162, 166, 197, 231, 236,
239-241, 243, 245, 247-248, 258, 276

distancing, 36, 44, 231, 251

drawing(s), 25-26, 28, 30, 34, 63, 100,
102-105, 112, 114, 133, 150, 164-165,
185-186, 188, 191-192, 231-233,
238, 246

drugging, 81, 144, 149, 157, 205, 260-262

E

electric shock, 139, 238, 286, 289, 290, 292

emotion(s), 6, 25, 28, 39-40, 91, 114, 138,
151, 168, 174, 177, 181, 229-230, 239,
251, 259, 274

equality, 11, 13, 22, 207, 220-223,
256, 293-295

Ertürk, Yakin, 190

escape, 16, 21, 23, 26, 32, 39, 40, 53, 72, 78,
88, 100, 120, 125, 130, 154, 160, 197,
199, 203, 206, 232, 236, 247, 252, 267,
275-277, 284

evil, 45, 49, 55-56, 64-65, 68, 82, 87, 89-90,
92, 94-102, 105-110, 112-114, 117-124,
130, 132, 140, 142-143, 145-146, 152,
158, 160-161, 163, 169, 173, 185, 201,

204, 218, 227, 241, 246, 264-266, 269,
274, 283, 285, 287, 292

*evilism, 68, 95-100, 102, 105, 108-112,
114, 116, 122-123, 126, 137, 142,
146, 150, 153, 274*

exit, 40, 129, 241, 243, 260, 275, 277, 285

S

W

Y

ABOUT THE AUTHORS

Jeanne Sarson and Linda MacDonald spent twenty-eight years developing ways of offering care and healing to women who, as children and or as adults, survived being tortured, trafficked, and who suffered other forms of sexualized exploitation inflicted by their parent(s), a guardian, or a spouse. And they welcomed hearing from other women who suffered torture when exploited in prostitution or pornographic violence. They have stood persistent to defy social willingness to ignore that such violence existed by calling for non-State torture to be criminalized and they utilize their website www.nonstatetorture.org to promote global awareness.

Their ground-breaking work began in 1993, fifteen years before the United Nations Committee against Torture ventured to write, in 2008, that acts of torture committed by private individuals or groups are specific human rights violations. Since 2004, they have been promoting its recognition in side event panels at United Nations sessions in New York, Geneva, and Vienna. With a co-authored chapter included in the book, *Gendered Perspective on Torture: Law and Practice*, launched at the United Nations by Ambassadors from Denmark and Norway, in response to former United Nations Special Rapporteur on Torture Juan E. Méndez's innovative work on gender perspectives on torture. They celebrate this publication because back in 1993 they could find no literature on how to offer recovery care to women who survived such torture; they made it a goal to break this silence. They have done so with dozens of publications. Now they detail the intimacies of their journey in *Women Unsilenced*.

They value their friendship that has flourished as they travelled through offering care, hope, and belief to women during their work of recovery. They are often asked how two women—two nurses—who live in a little Canadian Nova Scotia town managed to achieve what they have. Their answer is simple: "We cared!"

CPSIA information can be obtained
at www.ICGtesting.com
Printed in the USA
BVHW041332181121
621899BV00008B/122

9 781525 593222